INSIDE THE COCAINE CARTEL

Max Mermelstein

with

Robin Moore &
Richard Smitten

A division of Shapolsky Publishers, Inc.

Inside The Cocaine Cartel

S.P.I. BOOKS
A division of Shapolsky Publishers, Inc.

Previously published in hardcover
by SIMON AND SCHUSTER
as *The Man Who Made It Snow*

ISBN 1-56171-254-X

For any additional information, contact:

S.P.I. BOOKS/Shapolsky Publishers, Inc.
136 West 22nd Street
New York, NY 10011
212/633-2022 / FAX 212/633-2123

Manufactured in Canada

10 9 8 7 6 5 4 3 2 1

To Steve, Al, Dick, and Bob—
thank you

Contents

Contents

INSIDE THE
COCAINE
CARTEL

Author's Note

As recently as 1975, only a few thousand pounds—less than $10 million worth—of cocaine was making it into the big cities of the United States. There were no drug lords. No one had heard of Pablo Escobar. The Ochoas, whose dynasty today rules over Colombia's vast cocaine empire, were a middle-class family from Medellín with a harmless passion for breeding horses. The Colombian connection was nothing more than a few disorganized gangs of petty thieves and murderers. Within a decade all that changed. Juan David, the eldest of the Ochoa brothers, founded his family's coke enterprise and a full hierarchy of drug barons emerged. When I first met the smooth-cheeked Fabio Ochoa in 1978 in Miami, I had no idea that he and his clan would end up on *Fortune*'s list of the richest men in the world. By 1985, the Medellín cartel controlled a massive, highly disciplined organization that trafficked tons of cocaine into this country and netted billions of dollars annually. The figures have burgeoned since then. Today it is estimated that 900 tons—$16 billion worth—of cocaine reach our shores every year.

It was a combination of unlikely circumstances that landed me squarely in the middle of the cartel's drug-smuggling empire and led me to become one of their major operators. I had grown up as the middle son in a working-class Jewish family in Brooklyn. My parents had labored industriously for the welfare of their children. I pursued a career in engineering and, after vocational college, earned a fair living as an engineer. But fate eventually swept me inside the intimate circle of the powerful death merchants from Colombia. I came to walk their palaces, sit at their tables, know their children, share their dreams, serve their collective will—and become the only American to live to tell the tale.

In my service to the cartel, I was personally responsible for sending them over $300 million in cash and bringing fifty-six tons of the white powder into America. I made it snow in Florida. And I am paying the price.

As I wrote to Judge Ideman prior to my sentencing, "I am trying to retrieve my soul from the devil, I am trying to right some of the wrongs I brought about." That is my purpose in telling this story: to shed light on the little-known group of people I helped to become the scourge of this land.

The book was written after many sessions with writers Robin Moore and

Richard Smitten. All of our meetings were conducted in "submarines," safe houses provided by the U.S. Marshals Service, which administers the government's Witness Protection Program. There is a reason for such precautions: the Medellín and Cali cartels have put a $3 million bounty on my head. I know the cartel's wrath all too well, and so I have changed the names of three people who might otherwise pay for my openness with their lives.

Here, then, is my story. I am not proud of it. May it teach others.

—M.M.

Part One

* * *

BAPTISM IN BLOOD

CHAPTER ONE

*

Christmas Massacre

It was two in the morning, Christmas day 1978, and I was driving through the streets of Dade County in a rented van. Rafa sat next to me, staring out the window in silence, his black eyes glazed from freebasing. There was a dead man sprawled in the back seat of the van.

The night had begun with a Christmas party at my house, a family affair with the kids and the wives gathered by the pool. Alicia Delgado, the young niece of my Colombian wife, Cristina, and Alicia's husband, Willy, were our houseguests and had helped with the preparation of the food.

The food was presented buffet style: a forty-pound whole pig was the centerpiece, and coleslaw, potato salad, morcia (blood sausage), chorizos (more Colombian sausage), arepas (corn bread), aguardiente (Colombian anisette liquor), Colombian sodas, Ron Caldos (Colombian rum). It had been a grand spread Colombian-style, organized by Cristina for her friends.

That night a cluster of Colombians passed through my house, or maybe I should say a "coven" of Colombians, because many of our guests were the witches and warlocks of the tropical snow trade, as cocaine trafficking was often called in Miami. These were the vampires. To be with them, as Cristina and I constantly were, was to become one of these undead who lived by sucking on the addictions and weaknesses of others. Presents were piled under the tree for everyone and handed out. The party at my house, totally devoid of drugs on my orders, ended at eleven. Cristina was about to add a third child to our family and she needed her rest. She and I went to bed.

But Rafael Cardona Salazar, a man I hardly knew at the time, a man who would within hours dictate my life, moved on to the house of Livia Cardona with the rest of the Colombians. Livia, a beautiful cocaine queen, was called Biscocha, "Cream Puff"; she was no relation to Rafa

Cardona. She came from Medellín and reigned over the independent Miami cocaine market; she sold everywhere the Ochoa brothers—the drug kings of Medellín—did not. She was a powerful woman with a will of iron.

Years later, she told me what had happened at her house that night.

A two- or three-day freebasing party for the men was planned at Livia's house, where they would indulge in the three Colombian D's: drugs, drinking, and dancing. Sex was out because the men would get too blitzed on the coke. Livia was married to Fideo, or "Spaghetti," called that because he was tall and lean. Fideo stayed permanently drunk or high; I never saw him straight. He was a kept man and he enjoyed it. Livia was extra gorgeous on Christmas Eve in a skintight red silk evening gown that accentuated her slim figure, full breasts, and new blond hair that contrasted in a trashy-sexy way with her black eyes.

Twelve men settled down around the coffee table, sitting in a circle on the floor like Indians around a campfire while Livia brought out the essentials, cartons of Marlboro cigarettes and a pile of high-quality cream-colored cocaine base. After she set this up, she retired to the kitchen with the rest of the women to drink strong coffee and talk of Christmas, the men, and the children. The women left the men alone when they were basing.

Rafa started by stripping the tobacco out of three cigarettes and piling it in the center of the table; the other men followed his lead until there was a four-inch-high pyramid. The cocaine base was sprinkled into the tobacco until it was mixed about half and half. Gently, the men fed the cocaine-laced tobacco back into the empty cylinders of paper until the cigarettes were half packed, then they twisted the unfiltered end, leaving a fuse like a tail, locking it closed.

Rafa was small, five foot three, and slim. He looked even smaller in his safari suit and size 6 ostrich-skin shoes. His eyes always scared me, two black, lifeless pools framed by a full Afro and a black bushy moustache. His dainty hands trembled in anticipation as he held a match under the cigarette to heat it. He toasted it before he lit it, until the oil from the base stained dark through the white paper, just enough so it wouldn't burn. Once the oil showed, Rafa quickly lit the cigarette. He examined the tips of his fingers; they were burned black from the many times he had freebased. He grinned at the others, waving his fingertips at them in an almost effeminate manner. The others ignored him. They were too preoccupied with what they were doing.

Rafa grunted to himself and started arming the next cigarette while he puffed on the first. He squeezed the carton of Marlboros in front of him for reassurance, and took the time to read the small print "200 cigarettes" stamped on the end of the carton. If things went well, he would do the entire carton; he would personally smoke two hundred base cigarettes by the next night.

Rafa was an experienced smoker and the first few puffs hit his bloodstream almost immediately. Soon, his eyes glazed over, he stopped blinking and just stared ahead, not focusing. The men around him started talking faster and faster as the smoke filled the room and the high-powered alkaline powder was ingested into their bloodstreams.

But Rafa remained silent. He was welcoming the paranoia-devil. He was letting it creep in and permeate him. He liked the feeling. He could imagine it entering at the tips of his toes; like dark smoke it started climbing up inside his legs to his thighs, stopping for a soothing few minutes inside his groin, then drifting through his chest and filtering up his neck until it entered his brain, filling it like an evil cloud.

Cesar, a college student, entered through the front door and slipped into the kitchen to say hello to Livia and wish her a merry Christmas. Cesar had come looking for Flaco, his brother. Flaco was a dealer and Rafa's roommate, but Flaco, the "skinny one" as his nickname proclaimed, was not there.

Rafa saw Cesar out of the corner of his eyes and immediately snapped out of his trance. "Is that Flaco's brother?" he asked the men around the table.

"Who knows?" Fideo answered. "Who cares? Put away your grudge, Rafa. He's only a boy, a student."

"*Un hijodeputa*, who thinks he is too good for a peasant like me! *La coca* is for peasants and fools, he thinks."

"Rafa, please, this is my house. Be kind, it's Christmas," Fideo begged.

Rafa curled upward like an uncoiling snake, off the floor, and out of the circle. He sat on the edge of the couch, watching the women in the kitchen. He watched with black, unblinking eyes as he quietly opened the buttons of his safari suit and felt the cold steel handle of his .38.

Cesar poked his head around the kitchen doorway and shouted, "Merry Christmas! Anyone seen my broth—"

He never finished the question. Rafa stood and in a blur he whipped the pistol out of his waistband. The first shot rang out in the living room, snapping the men out of their freebase trance. They sat dumbfounded with glazed eyes, their mouths open.

The first bullet caught Cesar full in the face, driving him out of the doorway, back into the nest of women, blood spurting everywhere.

The slanted eyes of Chino, "The Chink," popped open and he sprang across the couch, pulling the gun out of Rafa's hand after the second shot split the wooden door molding.

Rafa snatched his gun back and jammed it into his waistband, grimacing slightly as the hot barrel touched his groin.

"Out!" Livia shouted. She didn't have to say it twice. The men and women disbanded quickly, cars sped out of the driveway, tires burning the tarmac. "I will take care of this," Livia said quietly to no one in particular as she watched her maid squatting on the kitchen floor, covering Cesar's bleeding face with a towel.

Chino shoved and pulled Rafa into the driveway and opened the passenger door of their rented van. He helped Rafa in and drove away.

"You're too fucked up to drive," Rafa later remembered screaming at Chino, fingering the pistol in his waistband.

"I'm too fucked up? Do you know what *you* just did?"

"Max lives only six blocks away . . . take me to Max's house," Rafa ordered sullenly.

Chino did as he was told and stopped the van in front of my house. It was two in the morning. Rafa jumped out and leaned on my front doorbell until I answered.

"Max, we need a driver. We're fucked up; we been at Livia's party. You drive us for a while, OK?"

I was surprised to see him standing there; Rafa and I were not exactly close friends. But if you're married to a Colombian girl, the other vampires try to make you like themselves; they think they own you.

One look at those deadly dark eyes was enough. "Sure. I'll drop you guys off and bring the van back here. Who's in the car?"

"Chino. He's a little pissed. We had a little trouble at Livia's. Don't pay no attention. He's fucked up real bad on the stuff tonight."

He's not the only one, I mumbled to myself. As I got dressed I told my wife I would be right back. "Don't get lost!" I could hear Cristina yell from inside the house as I slipped behind the wheel of the van.

Chino moved into the back seat so Rafa could stay sitting in the passenger's seat. You could feel it in the fetid air of the van—the real anger, deadly anger, between these men—it was the feeling of death. Chills went through me as I put the van into gear.

"Where we going?"

"Drive nice and slow, Max, no rocking and rolling. Drive around for a little while till we come down from this high, then let's go to my house," Rafa said.

"So why did you do it? Why'd you have to shoot the little fucker for?" Chino whined from the back seat.

"He bugged me, that's why. He made some remarks I didn't like. He was playing with me!"

"So you shot him? A stupid little college kid."

"He wasn't just a college kid, he was a smart-ass little college kid. I hated the little bastard."

"Rafa, you shot him in the face. You killed him. What are you going to tell Flaco when we get home?" Flaco, Chino, and Rafa shared a house together in Miami.

I pushed harder on the accelerator, afraid to turn my head and look at either of them. I glanced at the gun in Rafa's waistband, a cold, gray .38 revolver.

"It was stupid to shoot him. How could you do something so stupid? *Estupido!* He was nobody." In the mirror I noticed Chino's normally slanty eyes were thin slits of anger. "*Hijodeputa!*"

"What difference is it to you, Chino?"

"You should have said something before, told me. I take the heat now from Flaco just like you. Mother of God, we all live together! Everyone who was there will have to take the heat and lie for you. If Flaco finds out he will kill you."

"So what the hell is it to you? You still got those three missing kilos to answer for." Before Chino could respond, Rafa screamed at the top of his lungs, "Fuck you! *Puta!* You motherfucker, you stole from me. I got proof you sold three of my keys to Saporro!"

Rafa reached down for the revolver in his waistband. He spun in his seat . . . five blinding flashes . . . five sharp cracks like two bricks smashing against each other. Rafa was kneeling in the seat, his eyes blazing. The pungent smell of cordite filled the van. My foot was frozen to the gas pedal, everything was locked, my arms, my hands, my legs, my eyes were staring straight ahead. Maybe if I didn't acknowledge it, it wasn't happening.

Rafa spun back around and hunched down in the seat. He emptied the spent cartridges and held them in his open palm.

"Stop! Stop here at this canal, Max."

I hit the brakes. Rafa jumped out and threw the empty cartridges into the canal and jumped back into the passenger's seat.

"Keep driving, Max. Don't say a fucking word . . . not one fucking word." Rafa reached into the glove compartment and pulled out a second gun, sticking it into his waistband. He looked straight ahead, still holding the murder weapon, spinning the empty cylinder.

I don't know how long we drove, but I remember the smell of blood and excrement slowly wafting forward from the back seat, permeating the van. I knew Rafa was thinking about what to do with the only witness to the murder. His eyes bored into me; I could feel them. But I wasn't turning to look at him. I stared straight ahead. He didn't say a word as I drove.

"Stop here!"

I stopped by a canal and watched as Rafa slid out of the van once more. He stood by a high cyclone fence and threw the empty gun with all his might. It splashed dead center in the canal. He returned, and we drove on in silence for another ten minutes.

"Stop. Stop the fucking car!" Rafa yelled suddenly.

I stopped in front of 10800 SW 84th Street. I remember numbers. I'll always remember that one. "Help me," was all he said as he opened the doors of the van. We each tucked a hand into one of Chino's armpits and pulled. Chino wasn't bleeding anymore; dead bodies don't bleed.

Chino's crumpled corpse collapsed out onto the strip of lawn between the sidewalk and the road. I got his feet, Rafa grabbed him under the arms, and we carried him into the bushes off the road.

"Further, further, deeper into the bushes," Rafa grunted. His chest heaved and perspiration formed on his brow. Finally, we dumped the body and strode back to the van. I started it up and looked at him.

"Let's go," was all he said, staring straight ahead.

I pulled out from the curb and we rode in silence for a few minutes.

"Chino boosted three keys from me and sold them. The shipment last week from the Ochoas was short three fucking keys. Maybe he thought I can't count, or a hundred thousand dollars doesn't mean shit to me anymore. I don't like it when people steal my shit, Max."

I didn't answer.

"Max, let's go to my house."

I looked at him and nodded. I knew my life was in the balance.

I parked in the driveway of the house that Rafa shared with Chino and

Flaco. When we walked into the house he turned on the lights in the living room. I saw that he was covered with blood, Chino's blood.

"Stay with me," he said, ripping off his tan safari suit. "I'm taking a shower."

"All right," I answered, flopping down on the couch. "I'll wait here."

"No, you come with me." Rafa motioned me into his bedroom. He stuffed his bloodstained suit into a pillowcase and tossed it in a corner. He held the .38 dangling at his side, and didn't let go of it even as he pulled down his shorts. Was the gun for me, or Flaco when he walked in, or for both of us? He slid the glass door open and turned on the shower, placing the gun on a shelf where I could see it.

"Sit on the can there, Max, where I can see you," he yelled above the noise of the steaming water.

I did as I was told and watched Rafa's thin tan-olive body. In his nakedness he was so small and slight. He looked like a young boy through the translucent glass, no more than fifteen, but he was twenty-seven, and a killer.

I sat in fear that Flaco might burst in and want vengeance for his brother. Then I would be in the middle of a real gun battle, and we'd have an even bigger massacre out of the evening.

It was a long shower, very hot. The sliding glass door stuck a little in the track, making a noise as he climbed out. The sound roused me out of my reverie. He was standing there, one foot still in the steam, naked, the steel-gray gun in his hand hanging limply at his side. He was looking at me, his deadly black eyes not blinking, and I knew what he was thinking . . . should he kill me or not?

He lifted the barrel of the gun and pointed to a closet. "Pass me a towel, will ya, Max?" he mumbled. Dazed, I did as he said. He dried himself slowly; I was too scared to say a word.

He slipped into jeans and a bright blue silk shirt. "You saw what just happened?" Rafa waved the gun slightly in the air.

"I saw what just happened."

"You with me now?"

My throat constricted as I said, "Compadre, I am with you now . . . you name it, I do it!" I was still anticipating the shock of a searing bullet through the chest.

"Good, now you know I do what I have to do. Let's go to your house. I'm not sleeping here tonight." I didn't blame him. Flaco would be after him soon.

The instant we walked through my front door, Rafa disappeared into the guest room, mumbling good-night and closing the door behind him.

I checked my watch: 4:00 A.M. Cristina woke up as I came out of the bathroom. I spent the next half hour telling her what had happened.

"What? What are we going to do?" Her eyes were full of tears. "This trouble is because of me . . . these people, all of these people you have met because of me."

I pushed her down on the bed gently and softly rubbed her stomach before taking her in my arms. She was eight months pregnant. I had legally adopted Cristina's two children, Luis, then ten, and his younger sister, Consuelo. She wrapped her arms around me, cradling her head in my shoulder and waiting for me to speak. "There is nothing, nothing we can do now," I murmured. "Shall I call the police?" I whispered in desperation.

She pressed her finger against my lips. "You know we cannot do that— the family, here and at home, they will all be in danger." She sighed deeply. She is Colombian; she knows what drug people are capable of.

After a while Cristina's breathing calmed down and became even as she pretended to sleep. But neither of us could sleep, so we just lay there waiting for the dawn to come.

That morning Rafa and I had to clean out the van. I had never seen brains and bone before—blood, yeah, but not brains or bone. Rafa never used regular bullets; he stagger-loaded the cartridges in his gun, as I would often hear him brag in the years to come. To do more damage he used dum-dums, armor-piercing bullets, and shot shell. They were designed to make a mess, and they did.

He kept watching me as we washed the van out with the garden hose, sizing me up.

Rafa had known from the beginning he would kill Chino. It was a carefully calculated plan. He got me out of bed on Christmas morning so I could see him do it with my own eyes. He wanted to do it in front of me so I would know what kind of a world he lived in.

"I'm going to get Arturo to help clean this shit out," Rafa said. "He lives only four blocks away."

Arturo was Cristina's brother. "Leave Arturo out of it," I said. "He doesn't know anything."

"He's coming! I'm also going to call Nicolado. This is too much work for us."

"Rafa, are you nuts? Nicolado is Chino's brother. You can't call him, you just whacked his fucking brother."

"Bullshit, I'll call him and tell him to come over here."

Twenty minutes later Nicolado was standing in the driveway next to the van listening to Rafa.

"I got very bad news for you," Rafa said, "Chino is dead. We were hit last night by Tostado, *el hijodeputa*, who hates your brother. He saw us at a light and two guys jumped out of his car and popped the door open on this van and shot Chino. They jumped back in their car and took off." Rafa stopped speaking to let the news sink in. Nicolado just stood there shocked and disbelieving.

"That's how it happened, isn't it, Max? Tell him. Tell Nicolado," Rafa blurted, glaring at me.

"Yeah, that's so," I agreed, still half expecting to take one of Rafa's bullets. "That's the way it happened."

Nicolado curled up his lip, snarling and holding back his tears; he did not believe me or Rafa but there was nothing he could do—not then. He just looked away and shook his head.

Rafa put on a reassuring air. "I'll take care of everything. I'll claim the body and ship it back to Colombia. Don't worry."

Nicolado said nothing. He just stood there and stared at Rafa with a grim expression on his face. I was nervous and let the cleaning bucket at my feet overflow, the water running down the driveway in a thick, dark, treelike pattern.

Arturo, Cristina's older brother, in his mid-forties, an artistic welder when he worked, walked into the driveway, a sort of permanently dazed look on his face.

"Ah, here's Arturo. Let's clean this shit up." Rafa pushed a stiff-bristled brush forward. Nicolado and Rafa locked eyes in an unspoken challenge. Nicolado snatched the brush from Rafa's hand and went to work scrubbing Chino's blood from the carpet.

But I knew Nicolado would not rest until he found out who it was that really killed his brother.

So together Rafa, Arturo, Nicolado and I cleaned out the van for over three hours; we finally turned the garden hose on full blast and soaked the upholstery. It was the only way to get the stink of death out. The blood had turned the deep red velvet interior of the van to dark brown. Blood doesn't come out; you can never really scrub it out . . . it is as permanent as certain memories.

I saw Rafa commit murder and he let me live, so in a weird, sick way, he had saved my life by not killing me. He owned me from then on.

But it was only much later that I figured things out and realized that he owned me because I let him own me.

Rafa left for Colombia a few days later to let things cool down.

Flaco's brother Cesar survived the bullet in the face.

Livia never went back to the house after the shooting. She left it, lock, stock, and barrel: furniture, everything. She just never returned.

And Rafa never claimed Chino's body, as he had promised Nicolado he would.

CHAPTER TWO

*

Escape to New York

The day after the Christmas murder I hustled Cristina and the two kids out of Miami. We left the house with everything in it, including my second car, drove up to Orlando with Cristina's niece and her husband, Alicia and Willy Delgado, and stayed overnight in a motel.

The next morning I bought a *Miami Herald* but there was no news about Chino's murder. I had about $5,000 on me. After putting Cristina, Luis, and Consuelo on the car train to New York with Willy and Alicia, I checked the Chevy Monte Carlo onto the freight car and boarded last.

I was terrified. Christmas had been the worst day of my entire life.

I didn't know which thought scared me more: that Rafa would suddenly get high again and decide to take me out so there would be no witness to the murder, or that the police might take me in for complicity in the killing. At thirty-six years old, I'd done a lot in my life but I'd never been in trouble with the cops.

I tried to let the clicking of the train wheels numb my brain as they sped us away from Rafa and the Miami cops. I tried not to think of the brain- and bone-splattered back seat of the van, but the grisly sight wouldn't fade from my mind's eye.

I could still see Rafa and those dark deadly eyes. I'm a Jewish street kid from Brooklyn and I know trouble when I stare it in the face. I only knew Rafa slightly. Three times he had helped me make an extra $1,500 by selling a kilo of coke to a member of the Aventura Country Club and Hotel, where, only three days earlier, I had been the chief engineer. Now here I was running from Rafa and the cops, Cristina was eight months pregnant, and I had only five grand to support my family. I couldn't even get a job in New York. Miami would surely have a bulletin out everywhere for Max Mermelstein.

I looked at Cristina and put my hand on hers. She just smiled back trustingly. Three days before, I had had a good job, a nice home, and a happy family about to be expanded by one. Now I was a fugitive fleeing a murder rap and the grasp of a wild Colombian drug dealer whose vicious nature I had seen firsthand.

How could such a thing happen to me? I looked at my wife's gorgeous face and the long wavy brown hair I loved to bury my face in. Much as I tried to hide from the fact, I couldn't; this beautiful girl only wanted to live a peaceful life with me. But when you are married to a Colombian, you will meet other Colombians, and the other Colombians I met were all in the dope business.

I looked at her silhouette reflected in the train window as the world flashed by outside, and I remembered how we had met and how far we had come so fast.

I was a well-paid engineer at the Sheraton Hotel in San Juan, Puerto Rico, when the problems first began.

My Puerto Rican wife at the time, Gladys, whom I had met and married in New York City, was a different person once I took her back to her own country. Like all Latin women, she seemed to have an inexhaustible supply of relatives. Finally she left me to go across the island and live with her feuding parents, who needed her as a buffer.

I was out one evening at the private club in the Sheraton, when I saw a stunning woman walk in with two other girls and sit down at a table. She was wearing a skintight black satin jumpsuit that accentuated every curve in her body and she was the most gorgeous thing I had ever seen in my life.

I sent over a round of drinks to the three Latin beauties. When the drinks arrived at their table, the waiter leaned over to tell them they were compliments of Mr. Mermelstein. The girls looked up at me and smiled invitingly. Next thing I knew I was sitting with them, and I spent the rest of the evening in the company of Cristina Jaramillo from Cali, Colombia.

She spoke no English, but I had a good command of street Spanish, and we quickly established a simpatico relationship. In less than three weeks I had fallen hopelessly in love with her. I moved into Cristina's place and out of the apartment Gladys and I used to share before her parents had repossessed her.

Cristina had a four-year-old daughter, Consuelo, and an older son, Luis, living with her.

Cristina had fled her hometown of Cali, just as we were running now from Miami, after divorcing her husband, the father of the little girl. It was only after they had been married three years that she learned this

Cali caballero, Alvaro Roa, a smuggler and brother of Efraim Roa, the biggest money launderer in Cali, had an extremely violent temper and was capable of doing her great bodily harm. Cristina rushed her two children to the Cali airport and flew to Puerto Rico, where she supported herself by modeling and dancing in nightclub revues.

I was getting bored in San Juan, and I had been bilked out of my interest in the hotel nightclub by my Puerto Rican partners, whom I had brought into the deal when I heard the management wanted to lease out the club. As an employee, I wasn't allowed to have an interest in a club or shop leased from the hotel. My partners were supposed to keep me on in a silent capacity; it was silent, all right. There were no signed papers, so I had no legal case when they decided to cut me out of the profits.

When the chance to spend a profitable year as chief engineer at the Princess Hotel in Freeport, the Bahamas, came along, I grabbed it.

I immediately ran into one big problem. Cristina couldn't get the proper immigration papers to accompany me to the Bahamas. I wanted to go, but not without her. There was only one answer: marriage. Since there were no records in Puerto Rico of my New York marriage to Gladys, it was easy enough; I got in touch with a well-connected Puerto Rican labor leader and friend. Within a few hours he found a doctor who gave us a phony blood test certificate, and from the court clerk he got us a marriage license. Then all we needed was a judge. It was late afternoon and it happened that a judge was still sitting on a murder trial. My friend borrowed the judge out of the courtroom and within a few minutes we were pronounced husband and wife.

With the marriage, the immigration paperwork became much easier, and a week after our courthouse ceremony I took off for Freeport. It didn't take long to establish myself in a neat little air-conditioned bungalow and Cristina and the two children were soon with me.

Months later, I flew to Florida and got an uncontested divorce from Gladys. Cristina and I were married for a second time, and I was no longer a bigamist.

Freeport was a disaster for Cristina. She had not learned much English and there was nobody she could talk to, no Latin friends to be made among the Canadians, Americans, and English who composed the management personnel of the Freeport hotels and casino.

The population of Freeport was predominantly black. I had been hired to train Bahamians to handle the engineering duties in the hotel. I liked the natives and approached my job with enthusiasm, becoming something of a hero and role model to the Bahamians. I'm naturally an aggressive character and inevitably I had conflicts with management over what I considered poor working conditions and salary scales imposed upon the natives. When I was fired by the manager before my contract was up, the entire Bahamian work force of the Princess Hotel in Freeport went on strike, effecting a hasty withdrawal of my termination notice.

Cristina fell into depression from loneliness and isolation; she spoke constantly of her sisters back in Cali. Cristina had two sisters, Berta and Melba, who kept in touch with her by telephone, and it was Melba who asked Cristina if she could work out a way for some of the family to get into the United States. All legal methods had been frustrated by American immigration authorities. Cristina begged me to find a way to gain entry for her family and friends.

At the Freeport air terminal I had noticed that a British Airways flight arrived every Monday from Panama and no papers were required for entry. Panamanians were welcomed since they freely spent American dollars, their national currency, at the gambling tables. It was easy for Colombians to get into Panama without documents. So the only leg of the trip from Colombia to the United States that required special planning was the relatively short hop from Freeport to Florida, less than a hundred miles.

A swashbuckling American pilot named Ed Savage used to hang around the Freeport hotels and casinos and I got to know him quite well. He had been an ace in the Korean War, and was now flying gamblers on charter flights from Miami to Freeport. For a price, he would be glad to set a few Colombians down at a clandestine airstrip somewhere in the vicinity of Miami. I arranged it with him.

When I went to the airport to pick up three members of the Jaramillo family, no less than eleven Colombians came off the plane, all broke. The eleven Cali immigrants slept on the floor of the bungalow, some as long as three weeks, before I could arrange for Ed Savage or his young apprentice in the smuggling trade, Russell Hodges, to deposit the last of them somewhere in Miami's Colombian enclave.

Although I was making a good salary and had no expenses for food or housing, shipping illegal immigrants into the United States was a drain on my resources. I ended up having to personally pay Ed Savage to make the illegal flights. But the influx of friends and relatives kept Cristina happy and chattering in Spanish, so I handled the financial burden without too much complaint. If she was happy, I was happy.

Finally, my contract with the hotel was terminated and Cristina, I, and the two children moved to Miami, where I landed a well-paying job as an engineer with the Aventura Country Club and Hotel.

I had sent over sixty illegal Colombians from Freeport to Miami before I was finished. By the time we arrived, many were happily pushing coke from Key West to Palm Beach.

In Miami, Cristina quickly and contentedly settled into the comfortable house we had bought close to the Westchester community. It was Melba who was indirectly responsible for bringing Rafael Cardona Salazar into my life. I had not the slightest inkling of things to come when Cristina opened our door to the dapper, moustachioed, friendly Rafa. The thing I remember best about this first meeting was his tiny feet and ostrich-skin shoes. I judged Rafa to be in his mid-twenties. He had come to collect three hundred dollars that he was owed for staking Julio, a friend of Cristina's family.

I paid him, and a relationship began which would eventually result in huge sums of money to and from the Colombian cartel passing through my hands. It was tainted money that would plunge me into a world of violence and death.

It started innocently enough, Cristina and I paying Rafa the money Julio owed him. Rafa and Cristina enjoyed a long conversation about the people they both knew in Miami and back in Colombia. Rafa chuckled at the street Spanish I spoke, unusual to hear from a gringo: real barrio Spanish.

A friendship blossomed and soon Rafa mentioned to me that if I had any friends who would like to make a purchase of cocaine he would be delighted to oblige. He mentioned a commission of $1,500 per kilo if I could find a buyer.

As it turned out, there was a real sport who played golf regularly at the country club where I was working, named Roger Tribaux. Originally from Boston, Tribaux, a man in his early forties, was wealthy and had once asked me if I had any coke connections.

And so came about my first, hesitating steps across the threshold of the dope business. I brought Tribaux and Rafa together. A kilogram of highest-grade cocaine was delivered to me, in a Ziploc bag, by a hippie-looking Colombian. A student, I thought; at least he had books under one arm. He introduced himself as Fabio, a friend of Rafa's, and we chatted at my home for a few minutes in Spanish. I couldn't imagine a more innocent-looking drug trafficker than this long-haired youth. Roger came by and picked up the coke, later paying Rafa $45,000 for the buy, and I pocketed $1,500, just like that. I didn't really consider this an excursion into the murky realm of the drug dealers; I hadn't personally touched a single gram of coke.

Twice again I acted as middleman between Rafa and Roger Tribaux, adding $1,500 to my savings each time. At one point I went to a luxuriously appointed town house in the Kendall section of Miami to pick up my $1,500. There I again met the student, Fabio, who for such a young fellow seemed to receive a lot of respect from everyone. Fabio and I chatted amiably, although I didn't ask him any pointed questions like "Where are you studying?"

Rafa chuckled as I left the town house with him, $1,500 richer. "Hey, compadre, you know who that boy is?"

I shook my head. He laughed again. "That's Fabito Ochoa, little Fabio. His father is Don Fabio. Fabito is one of the three brothers who are the biggest operators in Medellín along with Pablo Escobar."

None of those names meant anything to me at the time and I promptly forgot them. Then, out of the blue, had come that terrifying Christmas morning, and now we were rushing to New York, fleeing both Rafa and the police.

The train whistle screamed as we approached Washington, D.C., tearing me out of my reverie. Instead of becoming more cheerful as we came closer to my native New York, I was increasingly depressed. I knew the location of Willy and Alicia Delgado's house in the Brownsville section of Brooklyn. "It's an out-and-out war zone," I warned Cristina. "My folks left there fifteen years ago because the crime was so bad, and it's been getting worse ever since."

She said nothing, she just held her distended belly as we watched the Washington skyline loom into view.

I claimed my automobile when the car train stopped just outside of Washington, D.C., and we spent the night in a motel. The next day we drove to New York, to the house in Brownsville where Alicia and Willy lived. Willy led us up to the one-room attic and magnanimously told us we could live there until we found our own place. I stared at him unbelievingly. "What are we supposed to do, sleep on the floor?" I protested, remembering the extravagant hospitality we had just extended to Willy and Alicia in Miami.

"We'll find some extra mattresses," Willy replied.

But there were no mattresses available and we had one old mattress between us; the kids had to sleep on the floor. The first move I made was to find a doctor and a hospital where Cristina could have her baby. I paid the doctor and the hospital in advance and was left with $3,000 to exist on in the attic. I paid our way, bought food for Willy and Alicia as well as for my own family. I was afraid to look for a job or give my name out, convinced that the Miami police by this time would have a dragnet out to scoop up Max Mermelstein.

Before I could flee Miami for New York, Rafa had given me the name and phone number of an associate, Armando Melo. "You look him up and tell him where you are. I don't want to lose you, you know. I don't want you to disappear," Rafa warned. "And I will keep Arturo, Cristina's brother, with me," Rafa added. Arturo wanted no part of the coke business. Rafa was just keeping him as a hostage, and we both knew it.

Once I was settled in the attic I called Armando, who acted as some sort of parole officer on behalf of Rafa. His nickname was Carasucio, "Dirty Face." He sometimes worked as a mechanic. He came to see us every few days or at least telephoned us. However, Dirty Face, the watchdog, made us no offer of financial assistance on behalf of Rafa.

It was a time of quiet, deadly desperation. I held out financially as long as I could. Willy made a big thing out of feeding us any of the food he bought, and as my money ran low he became increasingly surly, an attitude that rubbed off on Alicia.

The baby was born and there were problems with the birth, which added to the medical and hospital fees. After more than a week in the hospital, Cristina brought our baby daughter, Ana, back to the attic to sleep in a cardboard box. When I was down to under three hundred dollars, Cristina and I decided to call Maria Monzano. Maria was a wealthy cocaine exporter in Cali and a girlhood friend of Cristina's. We asked Maria if she knew anyone in New York who might help us.

Several days later she called us back and advised me to look up Fernando Sanchez. She had spoken to him and guaranteed any money he might advance to us. We finally had a line of credit, a survival lifeline. Maria referred to Fernando by his nickname Carro Choquado, which literally meant "Crashed Car." Sanchez had cracked up four cars in one day when he first started as a taxi driver in New York. He had long ago parked his taxi forever and become one of Cali's most important cocaine dealers in New York.

In desperation I called Sanchez. He unhesitatingly lent me $1,000. Since Maria was good for it, he said, anything I wanted was mine for the asking. The money went fast: the baby needed extra medical care. Soon I was borrowing another $1,000 from the "Car Crasher." I had to find some way to make a living for myself and my family.

Then I remembered Roger Tribaux. By now, I figured, my friend from the Aventura Club would be wanting another key of Colombian coke. I talked to Sanchez about supplying it to me, but he was on his way back to Cali for a visit. He suggested I contact Carlos Rios, who had just come back from Colombia and was dealing in New Jersey.

I knew Rios; he had been at the fateful party in Miami on Christmas Eve. Carlos had the nickname El Bicho de Oro, "The Golden Cock," because he kept four or five wives and mistresses all at the same time in various parts of Queens and Colombia. Every time Carlos came up from Colombia he brought a new teenage bride with him. He was happy to service either a new wife or a new customer, so Tribaux flew up to New Jersey from Miami. I arranged the sale of a key from El Bicho de Oro every four weeks, netting me a monthly income of $2,000. Now I had a line of credit and an income.

So, I set about trying to find a job in earnest. After a month in the attic I felt that any heat generated by the murder of Chino was off me, and even my trauma about Rafa diminished as time went on and he stayed in Colombia out of my sight. I sent out résumés to a number of hotel companies. Cushman and Wakefield, agents for the new Bally Hotel and Casino being built in Atlantic City, asked me to come into their Manhattan offices for an interview. By now I had rented an apartment on Parsons Boulevard in Flushing, Queens.

Dirty Face, Rafa's watchdog, was still checking on us once a week, a living, not-so-subtle reminder that Cristina's brother Arturo was firmly in Rafa's custody. Someday, I knew, Rafa would once again call on me to render services. Even before the killing, Rafa had tried to get me deeper into cocaine trafficking, but except for the monthly key sold to Roger Tribaux, I had kept myself out of the drug business.

An inner awareness constantly worked on my head, telling me that one day it would get down to either Rafa or me, a final test of wills, and only one of us would walk away. I was not a triggerman, but I realized that a man pushed to the edge could become as capable of killing as a hardened murderer. Often, in deep sleep, the nightmare of Chino dead in the back seat of the van came to haunt me.

Finally, the Mermelsteins got a break. The Bally job in Atlantic City came through; I was deeply relieved to be able to take Cristina and the children out of the Queens Colombian environment. "We're not going to be making a lot of money," I told my wife. "At least we'll be away from all those drug traffickers, living clean."

But not for long.

CHAPTER THREE

*

The Cali Connection

Before going to Atlantic City there were two things I had to take care of.

First was the christening of my daughter, Ana. The ceremony had to be performed in New York, not Atlantic City, so that the largest number of friends and family could attend.

The second thing was Rafael Cardona Salazar. I felt a tightening pain in my gut when Rafa phoned me while on one of his frequent trips from Medellín to Miami. It was like someone was balling my stomach up into a knot with his fist. He called to say that even down in Colombia he had heard of Ana's impending christening. Then Rafa announced that he was going to stand godfather to my baby girl. I could feel my heart sink. "No!" I wanted to yell, but instead I heard myself saying, "Cristina and I will be delighted."

With that decided, Rafa went on to say that first he needed me to do him a favor. I felt that strange sense of being possessed by Rafa rise within me, his will overpowering mine. What the hell kind of favor?

Rafa was having trouble getting all the coke he needed out of Medellín. The Ochoa family and the other cocaine processors in Medellín were just beginning to move from small-time independent "Mom and Pop" cocaine cookers, like bathtub-gin distillers during Prohibition, to the big laboratories that would soon characterize the cartel's operations. Meantime, demand in the United States was in a crazy spiral. It far exceeded the available supply in Medellín.

Rafa's distribution organization couldn't get enough coke to take care of the expanding American market, and his carefully nurtured little army of Colombian pushers was complaining. Rafa decided to turn to rival Cali for his supply. Since Cristina was from Cali and close to Maria Monzano, Rafa knew she could help him. He asked me to make a few calls to Cali and then join him down there.

I wanted nothing more than to refuse. I wanted no truck with cocaine in general and Rafael Cardona in particular. Rafa talked in soft tones, too soft for the barrio boy I knew him to be. There was an intimidating quality to his voice as it purred over the phone to me. I felt the steely message in the soft tones in which he spoke as vividly as a blade against the throat.

To my practiced ear his Spanish words, though ordinary if literally translated into English, were menacing. Just hearing Rafa on the long-distance phone conjured up the recurring nightmare. I was back driving the van; Chino's head was splattered over the back seat. I knew the cold gray handgun was covering me. I was expecting the next shot to burn through me as Rafa tried to make up his coke-singed mind what to do about the only witness to Chino's murder.

Maybe, if I helped him, he would continue to let me live.

The christening was set for April 8, 1979. I talked to Maria Monzano in Cali and meetings to inspect the cocaine processing laboratories were arranged for Rafa and his party for the first few days of April.

I took the Avianca flight from New York to Cali on April 2, and was met at the shabby little air terminal by Rafa, who had just flown in from Medellín.

Maria Monzano volunteered to be Ana's godmother and had already flown up to New York to be with Cristina and help her with the baptismal preparations. Before she left she set us up with Nelson Urrego, the drug queen's chief Cali connection. He was on hand at the airport to escort Rafa and his people to the coke labs. Once Rafa had been guaranteed by Maria Monzano and identified by me, his credit was established.

At the terminal, Rafa introduced us to his entourage from Medellín, which included two bodyguards and a tall, cadaverous old man, Don Roberto, the cartel's chief chemist. Don Roberto had brought with him his young son Jose and a nephew, apprentices learning the trade. Rafa and Nelson Urrego shook hands and the connection was established. The business of purchasing the fifty kilos of cocaine Rafa needed to feed his Miami pipeline could proceed. Now that I had identified Rafa, my job was done and I should have been able to get on the next plane back to New York without leaving the airport. But Rafa had other plans for me.

"This is Loperra." Rafa pointed out a smiling cocaine cowboy standing behind him with a machine pistol hanging under his loose-fitting shirt. In rapid-fire Spanish Rafa told Loperra that if anything bad happened to me, he would be one dead bodyguard. With a wide grin Loperra nodded and stationed himself one foot to the rear and one foot to the right of me; he was now in charge of my life. And he stayed there for my entire time in Cali.

With the party now assembled, we all climbed into twenty-five-year-old American and foreign cars. (There is a 300 percent import tax on new automobiles in Colombia.) We drove off to the highest and most modern building in Cali, the glamorous InterContinental Hotel. Closely accompanied by Loperra, I was soon checked into my suite. Rafa and his bodyguard, Jaime, occupied the most spacious suite in the hotel.

The girls of Cali are among the most beautiful and accommodating in the world, I had always heard, but it didn't appear that I was going to test this promising maxim. Loperra, the swarthy, grinning bodyguard, was perpetually close at hand and he had never heard the word deodorant. He was well aware that he was guarding his own life as well as mine; I think that made him sweat even more than usual.

Furthermore, Cristina's sister Berta was on the lookout to ensure that no liaison took place between Cristina's husband and the ever-present and highly visible beauties of the city.

I went up to Rafa's suite, where he had wasted little time settling into a freebasing session; he had brought his own supply of base cocaine into Cali. The Marlboro cigarettes lying on the coffee table instantly turned my thoughts back to Christmas Eve. Rafa rose to greet me, his eyes locked open in a freebaser's stare, not blinking.

Don Roberto, Rafa explained, was one of the Medellín cartel's most skilled "cooks"; he would personally approve every kilogram of cocaine to be purchased. His long years of experience in the cocaine labs were evident by the color of his skin, a weird shade of gray, like a dead beached whale lying out in the hot tropical sun. The color was a badge of honor, verifying a lifetime spent absorbing the toxic vapors that rise when cocaine cooks. Don Roberto, master chemist, held the highest-paid job in Colombia. He could have been anywhere from forty to seventy years old by his appearance. The life of a cook is not a long one.

Nelson Urrego's mission was to escort Rafa and his people to the labs of Cali and guarantee them. All the purchases would be made on Nelson's credit. It was agreed that we would get an early start the next morning. Eight o'clock was the time set for departure.

With the plan set, Rafa immediately increased his freebasing in the hotel suite, then ordered up champagne, rum, and aguardiente, Colombia's favorite brand of firewater. I watched in suppressed disgust as

Rafa mixed the cream-colored cocaine base with the tobacco he had extracted from a Marlboro. Even as he freebased on one cigarette he was loading the next one.

That night I joined the Colombians, on Rafa's expense account, in spending money like there was no tomorrow, buying drinks for one and all in the bar. The spree was stupid, drawing unnecessary attention to us.

Loperra and I were waiting in the lobby promptly at eight the next morning. Don Roberto and his son and nephew straggled down about nine thirty with the news that Rafa was totally blown away on coke, but it wasn't necessary for him to visit the labs anyway; his job was to pay at the right moment. Don Roberto would select the product. Nelson Urrego, all smiles and cheers, arrived at ten thirty, equivalent to 8:00 A.M. Latino time, I surmised, and we were on our way to visit the local labs.

Nelson announced that he would take us to the labs in the city first and then later that afternoon and the next day we would visit the processing plants out in the country. Basically I had done my job bringing Nelson Urrego together with Rafa and presiding over the guarantee. I was not happy to be forced into going with them to the labs. But Rafa was like a fox; it was his wish, a command really, that I receive an education in the basics of the cocaine business. I was making the rounds of the labs with Nelson, Don Roberto, and the two boys for a specific reason: to learn the coke trade. As blitzed as Rafa got, he never completely lost his cunning.

And it *was* fascinating stuff. The first lab was surprisingly only a short distance from the hotel. I had imagined that the labs would be in the depths of Cali's slums on the other side of town from the international zone and the better residences.

The two venerable cars that Nelson had commandeered for the lab visits, an ancient Buick and a battered Renault, stopped in front of a brown stucco house set back from the sidewalk in Barrio Villa Nueva. It looked like a typical middle-class home. Cali being a friendly city, almost devoid of violence, there was neither a wall nor an iron fence around the place. Nelson walked up to the front door and before he could knock it was pulled open by an emaciated-looking old man with a dead-whale skin pallor like Don Roberto's. Obviously the house cook.

Nelson was greeted warmly and we were led into the laboratory. The house was hacienda style, built around a courtyard, in which, over a slow-burning charcoal fire, a fifty-gallon steel drum was simmering, giving off noxious fumes. My nose twitched and I almost threw up.

Nelson laughed. "This is very nice, outside cooking," he remarked. "The hydrochloric acid, ether, and acetone are mixed with the powder base, which comes up from the coca fields of Bolivia and Peru. It is when they do the processing inside without proper ventilation that the smell is really bad. You will see," he added cheerfully.

I stared at the softly bubbling mixture on the fire. Ether and acetone are both highly explosive. Combined, as they were here, along with hydrochloric acid and coca paste to form cocaine crystals, the brew had H-bomb potential.

The local cook led Don Roberto, Nelson, and me, followed by the two boys and Loperra, through the inner courtyard to a room in back. Spread out on large sheets of heavy paper, white powder and crystals were drying under a battery of sunlamps. Don Roberto had been taking in the surroundings and looked down suspiciously at the drying cocaine.

"It is true, this is not the nicest way to dry the powder," Nelson conceded. "The natural sun is the best."

Don Roberto said something to Nelson, who in turn consulted with the cook and then pointed across the room at a bench on which were laid out a row of Ziploc bags filled with white rocks. Don Roberto crossed the room and selected a bag at random which he opened. With a knife, he scraped a sample off the rock onto the tip of his forefinger. It looked like talcum powder from where I stood. He touched it to his tongue.

"An expert like Don Roberto can tell whether too much acid is still in the powder," Nelson commented. "Too bitter, too sweet, and it's not the best."

Again Don Roberto took his penknife and scraped the inside skin of the bag. He examined the minute residue the blade had scraped off.

"Pure cocaine will not stick to plastic," Nelson explained. "If it is cut with some substance to stretch it, then the material will stick to the bag." Nelson glanced down at Don Roberto's virtually clean knife blade. "Very good, so far," he said.

Next, Don Roberto pulled a tall, inch-wide test tube from his pocket and called for bleach. His host produced an unopened bottle of Clorox. Reaching into the bag, Don Roberto pulled out a small white crystallized rock and rapped it sharply on the table, breaking it. With the penknife he scraped some crystal powder from the inside of the rock. He filled the tube with four inches of Clorox and tapped the white powder from the blade into the tube. Everybody watched anxiously as the powder turned the bleach into a milky liquid as it dropped to the bottom of the tube and completely dissolved.

Don Roberto handed the tube to Nelson to hold for him as he cut off a small piece of the rock. He dropped the fragment into the Clorox and it slowly floated to the bottom and then back to the top, where it disappeared, leaving only a yellowish slick floating on the surface.

Nelson went on with my lesson. "Any impurities would fall back to the bottom of the tube," he said. "The little yellow oil slick proves this is pure stuff."

Don Roberto nodded his approval to Nelson. From the cocaine in another bag, he proceeded to make the skin test. He placed a small amount of powder in the fleshy triangle between the base of his thumb and his forefinger. Nelson explained that after a few minutes of vigorous rubbing, if the powder is pure cocaine it will disappear. Human skin absorbs cocaine but rejects any substance used to cut the powder's purity. Don Roberto's skin showed a dusting of white impurities. He rejected the bag.

In an hour the Medellín expert had chosen ten kilograms out of the first laboratory's stock, and Nelson marked and sealed each bag for future collection and payment. Forty more kilos were needed to fill Rafa's order. We left for the next laboratory.

"Where I am taking you now they make a very pure product but the lab is not so nice," Nelson confessed. "It is inside four walls, so the air doesn't ventilate it."

The lab was in a run-down wooden frame house located in the slums on the other side of Cali, a long way from the hotel.

"Not so *nice?*" I exclaimed to Nelson as we walked in. "It's a stinking hole!" I was almost sick to my stomach entering the decrepit structure. The vapor of the cocaine base cooking in ether, hydrochloric acid, and acetone was some of the worst gas I ever smelled.

"What about the neighbors? Don't they complain about the fumes?" I asked Nelson.

"They all work in the business. They make their money from the labs," Nelson answered.

"Can't the police smell this shit a mile away?"

Nelson smiled and shook his head. "They don't care, they are well paid."

Don Roberto and Nelson seemed impervious to the noxious fumes as they examined the powder offered them. Seeing my distress, Nelson suggested that I wait outside.

He accompanied me outside, his arm around my shoulder. "Max, this lab is really not so bad. Last week, just after I left a lab, it blew up right behind me and killed the cook and his family."

"Jesus Christ," I said, moving out toward the street. "Now you tell me. Do they blow up often?"

"Oh, *sí*, of course." Nelson shrugged. "But it is of little consequence. As fast as one blows up, another is started. Do not worry, we will get Senōr Cardona everything he needs."

"I'm not worried. But I'm sure the cook and his family might have a different view." I moved even farther out into the street. "I'll just wait here."

If ever I had been tempted to try cocaine, it was behind me now. After seeing and smelling the chemicals that went into the manufacture, forget it. I firmly resolved right there and then never to touch the drug or allow it in my home. What in God's name was I doing here in Cali anyway, I asked myself.

Rafa!

Somehow I would get free of the killer even if I had to become one myself. But I knew I was kidding myself. I didn't have it in me to kill anyone.

Don Roberto picked out a few kilos of the purest coke and we pushed on to the next lab, which Nelson said was not too far away in this Cali slum. Suddenly, as Nelson drove the Buick through the barrio, Loperra and I sitting in the back of the following Renault, a sharp explosion split the tropical midday air, a wave of concussion rocking both vehicles.

I looked questioningly at Loperra, who did not even shift his weapon as a spray of smoke and debris spewed into the air in front of us. "Another lab blows," he explained nonchalantly.

Nelson stopped his car. He jumped out and ran back to us. "That was going to be our next stop. They cooked a very pure product," he lamented. "I think maybe we will head out into the country now."

I nodded and slouched down, my eyes peering over the back of the front seat.

Nelson led the way through the twisting streets of the barrio and after half an hour we were outside of town, driving through a lush valley, the mountains rising on all sides of us. It was pretty scenery and I sat up straight to enjoy the view.

As Nelson had said, the laboratories out in the country were fairly free of the vile pollution that characterized the city labs. At the first lab we visited, the white powder and crystals were spread out in the sun on paper sheets. Don Roberto nodded approvingly. He went through his testing procedures and picked out ten kilos, which Nelson duly marked and put aside for later pickup.

The only problem with the country labs was that they were spread out miles apart and it would take a long time to accumulate the number of kilos that Rafa wanted. But by the time we returned to the Inter-Continental Hotel that evening, Don Roberto had selected the bulk of the order, some of the finest cocaine in Colombia, and we'd finish up the next day.

Rafa was a mess. He had been freebasing all day, probably done a hundred cigarettes. His eyelids drooped over widely dilated pupils, his complexion was gray, and he was sweating profusely, his jaw movements sporadic, his slurred words emitted from trembling lips. I could see a general paralysis setting in.

That night the Colombians and I spent more of Rafa's money. I found it difficult to take my own eyes off the smiling, enticing señoritas who made no secret of their desire to get the Americano away from his companions. But it was not to be.

Once again the following morning at ten thirty we got off to the projected "8:00 A.M. start." By late afternoon we were back at the hotel with the last of the kilos we needed. Mission accomplished.

The next morning Rafa roused himself and called my room to announce that he was going to the bank to arrange a money transfer from his bank account in Medellín to Nelson's account in Cali. And then he was going back to Medellín. He was paranoid as hell, but in the future I would often see his paranoia save him from destruction.

Loperra proved his worth the last morning of the trip.

"Something is wrong," he said as I was dressing. "I don't like it." He picked up the phone and called Rafa, telling him that he sensed bad vibrations.

There was a knock at the door. Loperra, his machine gun at the ready, opened it. Don Roberto's two young apprentices walked in to say they would all be leaving on the afternoon plane to Medellín.

I sensed Loperra's concern. Trusting his instincts, I grabbed my bag and, followed by the bodyguard, left the two boys in the suite and took an elevator to the lobby and headed directly for the front entrance of the hotel. Rafa also emerged from an elevator, carrying his own suitcase, his bodyguard behind him. They walked out of the hotel just as a contingent of Colombian police pushed their way inside.

I glanced over my shoulder and saw the police stride up to the front desk and then head toward the elevators. I knew our heavy spending at night would draw attention to us; of course one of the army of paid informants would have tipped off the police.

"I'm not taking the direct flight to New York, Rafa," I announced decisively. "Let's get to the airport and I'll take a local flight to somewhere inside the country so I don't have to show my passport."

It turned out I had made a wise decision. The police marched straight up to my suite and held the two boys there all day, waiting for me to come back.

At the Cali airport I caught a flight to Barranquilla and Rafa was on the next plane to Medellín. The local police, looking for an easy shakedown of a foreigner who had been spending a lot of money, had undoubtedly alerted the airport cops to look for a gringo trying to grab the next flight to the States.

Since there were no computers in Colombia, once I reached Barranquilla I was safe. I caught a flight to New York, thankful to have emerged alive from this lesson in drug trafficking. More than ever I resolved to keep clear of Rafa and all the rest of my Colombian friends, who seemed to share a single pursuit, selling tropical snow.

The first thing I did when I hit New York was to call Nelson Urrego back in Cali and ask him to rescue the two boys from the police. No problem, Nelson replied. Already his truck was transporting the fifty kilos from Cali to Medellín. Nelson was as good as his word. He bought the kids out of the local jail and even retrieved all the records of the case— among them the name and passport number of the big gringo spender, Max Mermelstein.

I returned to our apartment on Parsons Boulevard in Flushing just two days before the baptism of my baby daughter. Maria Monzano had been helping Cristina to make the arrangements for the ceremony and by the time I arrived back from Cali everything had been done. A preliminary rehearsal at St. Michael's in Flushing had taken place and it only remained for me to settle the details of the party that would be given at our apartment after the ceremony.

With Maria Monzano on the scene I telephoned Medellín to determine whether Rafa Cardona was still planning to be godfather. Rafa informed me that all the coke from Cali had been delivered by Nelson Urrego to Medellín and that he would indeed be on the next day's flight from Colombia to New York.

What a pair of godparents my daughter was getting, I mused, shaking my head. The snow queen of Cali and a drug lord of Medellín. I was already wondering how I would shield my little girl from the Colombian cocaine influence. It was everywhere around us. But I felt a profound sense of relief that we would soon be going to the Bally's project in Atlantic City. There at least we wouldn't be in the middle of the Colombian drug traffickers who had become our daily and nightly social companions.

The day before the baptism, I picked up Rafa at the airport and brought him to our apartment. I had made it clear that I wanted no cocaine used in my home. Cristina's two children, to whom I had legally given my name, were not, I was resolved, going to become coke users. The boy, Luis, might well have been susceptible.

Rafa respectfully abstained from any form of cocaine use while staying with us, although he and the other Colombians were constantly planning new coke routes into the most lucrative markets of America, particularly California, Texas, and Chicago. There was endless speculation on how best to open up the European market, and they talked about the good old days when they would fly to Iran with two or three kilos of coke strapped to their bodies and sell them for as much as $60,000 to the Shah's family and friends.

It was a festive crowd of Colombians that gathered at St. Michael's Church on April 8, 1979, for the baptismal ceremonies of Ana Mermelstein. A few Americans swelled the ranks, including the affable Roger Tribaux, my one and only customer. Roger took the occasion as an opportunity to come north and make his monthly purchase.

After the service at the church, the party went on all afternoon and evening at my home. While the guests respected our wishes that no cocaine be used on the premises, Fernando Sanchez spent some time in the bedroom weighing out the kilo for Roger Tribaux from a supply he had brought with him. Just as I was snapping a picture of Roger sitting in a chair with his girlfriend, Fernando appeared in the doorway behind them, a key of cocaine in each hand and a broad grin on his face.

Despite the apparent humor in the situation I felt an ominous moment of dread. The Colombian snowstorm was enveloping me and my family, swallowing us like an avalanche. I suppose I shouldn't have been surprised that Rafa and Maria Monzano immediately paired up and wasted little time in consummating their Medellín-Cali alliance. Indeed, it was Cristina and I who were responsible for the first friendly overtures between the two rival cities.

With the christening behind us, I prepared to make the move to Atlantic City. Cristina, although she would miss the company of her Colombian friends and relatives, happily accompanied me to the ocean resort and gambling center of the East Coast.

It was an uneventful though quietly fulfilling year I spent as facilities manager of the fast-building Bally Hotel and Casino. Totally separated from the Colombian drug scene, my two adopted children led normal American schoolchildren's lives. I would have been content to stay in Atlantic City permanently, but at the end of twelve months a facilities director was appointed from among the Bally family of executives and my job was terminated. Uneasily, I brought the family back to New York, wondering what I would do next. As always, I reported my change of station to Armando, Rafa's watchdog.

By now Alicia had divorced Willy and moved in with a young drug dealer from Cali, Alberto Bravo, who owned a run-down restaurant. Dirty Face Armando, always close at hand, immediately suggested that I take over the decrepit Colombian restaurant and open a new disco. The keys to the place were mine for the asking. Cristina and I went over to the closed-down restaurant, located in one of the oldest buildings in Jackson Heights. It was disgusting; a filthy place. In the kitchen we found a walk-in cooler that contained pots of food cooked and stored over a year before. But it was well located for the Colombian community, which I had hoped to keep away from—a vain hope since Cristina could barely exist without her family and friends in close proximity. The Atlantic City year, while at first a blessing to be away from the drug traffickers, had worn on her sorely, even when her Colombian friends came from New York to visit and gamble at the casinos.

I had by now sold the house in Miami and I used some of the money to renovate the restaurant; being a trained engineer also helped. I tore out the kitchen and created a bar and disco with a first-class sound system. The place was an immediate success, attracting the Colombian community despite my ban against the use of drugs on the premises. Unlike the other Colombian bars, there were not going to be any shootings at my place.

Even though we were making money, our hours of operation, from 8:00 P.M. until 4:00 A.M., took a toll on Cristina and me. During the time she ran the place with me we had to hire all-night baby-sitters. Once again we were constantly in the company of Colombians, both drug dealers and respectable working people, all of whom socialized together. From time to time I found myself doing favors, like picking up packages of cocaine sent by Maria Monzano that came into New Jersey on Colombian ships.

Maria's husband, Elmer, who liked New York better than Cali, asked to buy into the club. I was happy to recoup some of my investment and have a partner. Elmer, like most Colombian men, bedded every woman he could get his hands on. Maria responded in kind, sleeping with Rafa, Fernando Sanchez, Armando Melo, the Golden Cock, and anyone else who suited her fancy. Elmer had been given the nickname El Mudo, "The Mute," because he never said a word about his wife's many lovers.

It became obvious that there was no way for me to distance myself from the drug traffickers. When two of the most dangerous Colombian shooters, Paco Sepulveda and his nephew Toto, started snorting cocaine at the bar, my bouncer stopped them and threw them out. The two hoods waited until the disco closed and ambushed the bouncer outside. It was a real Wild West shootout; the bouncer was wounded in the arm and leg, but not killed.

The shooting convinced me that the disco club was no longer for me. As 1981 came in, I began to speculate on new ways to make a living.

CHAPTER FOUR

*

Point of No Return

"Get your ass down here, Compadre, and start making some big money!" Rafa laid the summons on me late in February of 1981. He was waiting for me in Fort Lauderdale and wanted me there—now!

Between the disco and moving a kilo here and a kilo there, I was keeping the family fed. But Rafa's call had come at the right moment. I wanted something more out of life than just making out in New York. And during this cold winter the urge to go south—permanently—gripped the whole family. I wanted to make money, real money, and still have plenty of time to fish and hunt and do the other things I enjoyed in life. By now the horror of Chino's murder had receded in my memory. The fear that the deadly little Colombian had once struck in my heart was outweighed by the prospect of establishing my family in a new environment and new lifestyle.

Two days after Rafa's call I hustled Cristina, the children, and Gigi, the family poodle, onto the afternoon flight to Fort Lauderdale for a little winter vacation.

"Compadre!" Rafa hugged me in a big embrace, using the word that would become my nickname from then on. "You have come to your new life." He kissed Cristina, patted the kids on the head, gave the dog a wary look, and turned back to me. "Good. You brought the whole family with you. That means you are staying. I have already been looking for your new home."

He dispatched a bodyguard to claim our luggage and put it in his Mercedes station wagon. Soon we were on our way, Rafa driving, followed by his shooter in a black sedan with black-tinted windows.

"Hey, don't worry about nothing." He gestured at the menacing-looking car behind us, and laughed. "I brought my best pistolocos up from Medellín to Miami."

I had forgotten what a crazy driver Rafa was and tried not to stiffen in the front seat beside him every time he threatened to peel a coat of paint off the cars he passed. It took an agonizing thirty minutes to reach the place where we would be staying, a comfortable garden apartment with four bedrooms in Fort Lauderdale. We found we were temporary guests at the home of two of Rafa's shooters—now our built-in bodyguards. Of the four bedrooms, two were assigned to us. After we were settled, Rafa told us to enjoy ourselves and get some rest, and he and the *pistolocos* drove away.

The next morning Rafa came by in his station wagon followed by the bodyguards, who had earlier left the apartment in their black sedan to convoy him around town.

"Compadre!" he boomed. "First we take Cristina and the children to the new Broward Mall. They can visit the stores and have something to eat in one of the restaurants while I show you some interesting sights around town."

Cristina and the children liked that plan and hopped out of the wagon at the mall entrance. "We will find you in a couple of hours," Rafa promised. We watched them enter the shopping center and I groaned at the thought of what Cristina would probably spend in those two hours.

For the next hour or so, followed by the shooters, Rafa gave me a sight-seeing tour of Miami Lakes, where he wanted to buy a home and where he felt I should settle. "We have much to do together, Compadre. We are going to make more money than even a beautiful Colombian woman like Cristina can find ways to spend," he laughed.

Then his beeper went off. He looked at the number displayed on the dial. "A call from George Bergin—*un hijodeputa*, but I need him until you join me."

He pulled up to the first pay phone we came to. I sat in the car a few minutes, then, seeing Rafa was working himself into a frenzy as he talked on the phone, I got out and walked over to him.

Rafa turned to me and in staccato Spanish rattled off, "Help me put a collect call through to Ochoa in Medellín. We lost a shipment of 235 keys. I haven't got the details." He gave me the number and code words in Spanish and I spoke to the long-distance operator in English. The call went through and I handed the receiver back to Rafa. I stepped away to give him privacy. He was nervous; his hands trembled as he passed the unwelcome news along to Fabio Ochoa.

Finally a shaken, ashen-faced Rafa hung up the telephone and started back to the car. I followed him, slipping back into the passenger seat.

"We're going to find George Bergin and hear what happened. Fabio is flying up from Colombia in the morning and has ordered me to call a meeting for tomorrow night."

The rough, slangy Spanish tumbled from the gash of his mouth. Rafa just assumed that I was his now, on his turf, ready to work. How a small rodent, a vicious Colombian barrio product, had come to manipulate me I wasn't sure. He had shown me how easily he could kill, he had stood as godfather to my daughter, he had promised me easy money, and he had succeeded in pulling me into his world. His power over me was near-hypnotic.

As Rafa and I drove to the destination he had in mind, there was no escaping the realization that he was firmly in control of my destiny, at least for the foreseeable future. I sat back in the front seat, resigned to letting Rafa take me where he would. Rafa was not one to explain his intentions in advance, so I had no idea where we were going until he pulled up in front of a dense thicket shielding a large plot of land off SW 104th Street, far to the south of Miami.

"Now we will find out what happened. You stay in the car, Max. I will call you when I want you." He reached for the handgun in the waistband under his loose-fitting sport shirt. The feel of the weapon and the sight of the sedan full of shooters behind us calmed him. He walked through the heavy shrubbery to the house beyond.

I sat in the car for some minutes and finally a disgusted Rafa returned. "George Bergin isn't home," he muttered, sliding behind the wheel. "We'll go find your family and take them home."

I couldn't help but feel sorry for him. Nothing could darken a trafficker's disposition more and leave him wondering how long he'd be alive than losing a planeload of cocaine, 235 kilos in this instance. Rafa had the ultimate responsibility, although George Bergin's life was also on the line. Bergin was responsible for the pilots.

Rafa was silent as we drove to the mall to find Cristina and the children. They had finished their shopping expedition and were waiting for us, their arms full of packages. Rafa drove us all back to the apartment.

"I have big problems, Compadre. It will be good when I can share them, *and* the money, with you." He laughed for the first time since hearing about the last shipment. "I will be back in a few hours and we will all go out for a good meal at my favorite restaurant."

That evening when Rafa returned to take us to dinner the dark mood still hung over him.

He took me aside while Cristina was getting dressed. "I still can't find out exactly what happened, Compadre," he admitted helplessly. "The pilot, Skip Coltin, is one of the best. He is a full-time Eastern pilot. He and his co-pilot picked up the 235 keys right on schedule. Six hours later, at dawn, they landed on an access road beside a canal halfway out to the Everglades, which they had staked out two weeks ago."

His moustache twitched nervously as he spoke. "Skip and his co-pilot together unloaded the plane and left the duffel bags full of coke hidden in the bushes between the road and the canal. Then they took off and Skip's people were supposed to pick up the 235 keys just before sunup."

After a string of choice Colombian obscenities he went on. "It seems that two of your American swamp people, how do you call those cops who watch out for the animals?"

"Game wardens?"

"Yes. These two game wardens were looking for people who kill alligators and sell their skin which is so valuable now that there is a law against hunting them." He glanced down at his own shiny alligator shoes. "And what do the motherfuckers do? They stumble across my 235 kilos just as Skip's boys come to get them."

"Bad luck." I shook my head. "Blind, dumb luck," I consoled him, thinking to myself, yeah, these cocaine cowboys really do have shit for brains.

Over dinner at the Rusty Pelican out on Key Biscayne, the best seafood restaurant in Miami, Rafa ordered oysters Rockefeller, his favorite appetizer, and continued to bitch about the bust.

My children, Luis and Consuelo, had no idea that we were discussing a cocaine shipment. We never used the word nor anything related to it when we talked business in front of others. Nobody could understand our free-form repartee.

After a terrific supper on Rafa, he drove us home. While Cristina and the kids went inside, Rafa talked to me. "You will go with me to the meeting between Fabio, myself, Bergin and the pilots tomorrow."

"What do you want me to do?" I asked.

"You can translate the excuses this *hijodeputa* Bergin and his pilots try to give us. You and Fabio know each other, so he will feel among friends when he sees you. It looks like you're getting into the middle of the operations even sooner that we thought. Our meeting with Fabio is for six o'clock."

"I'll be standing by for you, Rafa," I replied. Despite my fear of him, or perhaps because of it, and knowing that my brother-in-law, Arturo, and I were his hostages, I found myself developing warm feelings of comradeship toward Rafa. I was grateful for my good life, my financial well-being, and I felt a growing affection toward my captor.

The next morning I lazed in the warm February sun with Cristina and the kids. Everyone hated the cold New York winters. I assured my family that northern winters were a thing of the past. By now I knew my future lay in South Florida.

Perhaps Rafa would be useful to me in getting some start-up money together for a future legitimate business enterprise. I knew I did not want to become a full-time coke trafficker for the rest of my life. Cristina felt the same way.

Rafa arrived in his station wagon in the early afternoon, the ever-lurking black sedan behind him with the shooters. We spent several hours cruising northeast Miami, looking at locations for a new stash house to store the air shipments of cocaine that would be coming in. The Ochoa operations were centered in southwest Miami, the Kendall area, and he wanted to keep the stuff stashed as far as possible from where the people involved actually lived and maintained legitimate-appearing offices.

We also cruised through Miami Lakes again, looking for a house where I could live with Cristina and the children.

The meeting with Fabio Ochoa was set to take place at the King's Inn, across the street from the old entrance to Miami International Airport. Rafa and I arrived at 6:00 P.M. We were both dressed in designer jeans and moccasin-type shoes sans socks.

The King's Inn had seen better days, and was a strange place for any sort of business meeting. It was perfect for our purposes. As we headed for the bar I could see from Rafa's expression that this situation was as grim as one could get. If blame for the loss of the coke was pinned on Rafa, since he was the ultimate guarantor of the flight, he would pay, if he was lucky, out of future earnings. Lives might well be terminated as a result of the decision made by Fabio Ochoa when he had heard the full story.

Fabio Ochoa was sitting at a banquette against the wall in the far corner of the bar, the two bodyguards flanking him stood as we walked over. They took posts on either side of the table. Rafa sat beside Fabio and I sat next to Rafa. The others, when they showed, would sit across from us. Rafa's two shooters also placed themselves strategically and we were ready to talk.

I had met Fabio twice before in Miami. I gave him a large smile and a handshake. He didn't like being called Fabito, "Little Fabio," but the nickname stuck since his father was called "Big Fabio." He had another nickname he hated more, Niño, "Little Kid." But Fabio could pass the death sentence on anyone and everyone he deemed guilty in the matter of the lost coke. The meeting started on a tense note.

We had purposely arrived a few minutes before the time set for George Bergin and the two pilots to show up. It was hard to realize how powerful and rich Fabio Ochoa—this twenty-four-year-old doe-eyed youth, so slender and soft-spoken, with shoulder-length light brown hair—really was. He wielded life-and-death control over thousands of his people in Colombia, America, and elsewhere around the world.

Nervously, Rafa explained to Fabio what he knew about the failed mission. There had been no newspaper reports of the bust as yet and Rafa knew that this case would not be closed until Fabio had seen newspaper accounts of the 235 kilos. Without press confirmation of the find by lawmen, there would be more than passing suspicion that the load had been appropriated by either the pilots, the ground crew, or others, including Rafa. If these suspicions became too strong, the Colombian shooters would be given their orders to kill.

George Bergin, a rugged, gap-toothed heavyweight, wearing a dingy shirt, chino pants, and deck shoes—an unmade bed of a man—ambled into the lounge. Rafa had told me a bit about him. He had lived a colorful life as a white hunter in Africa, a soldier of fortune, and, for the last decade, as a smuggler of marijuana from Panama and Honduras. Now he had turned to the more lucrative cocaine traffic.

Bergin had made all the arrangements with the Ochoas and Rafa for the pilots to bring in regular air shipments of coke, and his cut of the transport fees paid to the pilots was $1,000 a key. He had also lost his ass on the game warden bust; at $235,000, it was a substantial loss, but small compared to the damage suffered by the pilots and the Ochoas.

George Bergin was followed by an athletic-looking, thirty-year-old man with brown hair and a genial expression on his face somewhat marred by a nervous twitch that flitted across his features as he spotted Fabio and Rafa.

I recognized Russell Hodges, who had been the co-pilot on the ill-fated mission. When I was sending my wife's Colombian relatives and friends illegally into Miami out of Grand Bahama Island with Ed Savage, Russell Hodges had been one of the pilots who flew with Ed. Russell had always performed well and I had grown to like and trust him.

Russell smiled in relief to see a friend at court. He was well aware that Fabio and Rafa were waiting to pronounce judgment on the pilots' story, their menacing bodyguards alert to follow any orders that might be given. Rafa's eyes narrowed as he watched Bergin and Russell walk across the room to us. Where was Skip, the pilot? He had not, as the Colombians put it, "shown face." That in itself was reason enough to put out a contract on Skip's life.

Rafa gestured to the seats across the table and brusquely shot out in Spanish, "Where's Skip?"

Bergin translated for Russell. "Tell them where Skip is."

Russell started to answer, but Fabio cut him off as a waiter approached. It was obvious Fabio was insulted, and if he hadn't been an Ochoa, upper-class instead of a street campesino like most of the cocaine cowboys, Russell would have been wiped out then and there and the shooters ordered to find and kill Skip that night.

"Everyone order something," Fabio said curtly. "This should not look like a conference."

George Bergin grinned broadly and ordered what I would soon learn was his steady drink, Myers's 151-proof dark rum and Coca-Cola.

After everybody ordered something, Russell began talking in English. Rafa asked me to translate for him and Fabio.

"Skip is making the arrangements so that we can keep in operation, keep flying," Russell began hurriedly. "We need new landing strips, an engine change, and a lot of other vehicle and personnel realignments if we're going to keep flying. I figured I could explain to everyone what happened, since I was sitting in the right-hand seat when we put down."

I translated for Rafa and Fabio and added that I knew Russell personally and briefly explained the flying he had done for me. Fabio was still visibly annoyed that Skip wasn't there, and I could see that Rafa was on the verge of blowing up. I knew if Rafa got much hotter he wouldn't hesitate to order his bodyguards to shoot Russell, even though there were other patrons in the lounge. George realized that with just one look from Fabio, he and Russell could be dead. Fortunately, Fabio realized that what Skip was doing at this moment would get the next load of coke transported from Colombia to Miami sooner; he nodded in understanding and gestured to Russell to continue.

"We landed where we were supposed to," Russell explained. "We had kept surveillance on the landing site for two weeks and never saw anyone come near it, not any kind of lawman, certainly not a game warden looking for alligator poachers. It was a perfect spot. What happened was a freak accident." His words came faster, a near-pleading note to them.

"We piled up the bags where we had practiced hiding them. The ground crew made its approach at the right time after we took off. Then these game wardens drove up out of nowhere in a four-wheel-drive Bronco, yellow lights flashing, and stopped, by complete accident, right on top of the duffel bags we'd stacked up in the bush."

The arrival of the waiter with the drinks shut Russell off. He shrugged an appeal to Rafa and Fabio, his judges and, if they so decreed, his executioners.

"It was a fluke," he continued when the waiter had left. Only George Bergin touched his drink. "It couldn't happen like that again in a hundred missions. A natural hazard of this business. You can't win them all, no matter how careful you are."

Fabio nodded judiciously. I translated his reply for an anxious Russell, who was well aware that he was on trial for his life at this back table in the decaying bar of a once-popular hotel, now little more than a hot-pillow motel.

"Yes," Fabio agreed, "such accidents can happen, the cost of doing business." He shrugged expressively and then fixed Russell with a suddenly piercing look. "Why isn't the story in the newspapers?"

As I translated, Bergin smiled, nodded, and reached into the back pocket of his rumpled slacks. He pulled out a folded news clipping. "I just bought the evening paper; the story is right here." He pushed the clipping from the late edition of the *Miami News* across the table to Fabio.

I translated the news story for Fabio and Rafa. The facts as reported in the paper corroborated the facts as Russell had presented them, with one exception, which drew a much-appreciated laugh from Fabio. The authorities just couldn't resist exaggerating the importance of their bust and reported that 250 kilograms had been recovered by the game wardens, fifteen more than we all knew had been shipped. I couldn't help but wonder what the effect on the Ochoas might have been if the lawmen had reported receiving less than the exact number of keys the cartel had shipped.

Now that I had committed at least a piece of my future to the Colombians, it immediately occurred to me that here was a powerful weapon against the American smugglers that the drug catchers had at their fingertips, if only they knew. They could spread terror among the pilots, ground crews, and even the importers like Rafa if they withheld all information on major drug busts from the press.

Fortunately for the traffickers, the cops couldn't wait to broadcast the news of their latest exploits. Such publicity had a direct effect on the size of their budgets. The more shit they grabbed and publicized, the more money was allocated to their operations.

Fabio, once he had assimilated the story and heard me read the press clipping, nodded his acceptance of the situation and declared the loss written off as a cost of doing business.

Fabio's eyes flickered from Bergin to Russell. "When will you be ready to make another flight?"

"Skip is working on that now," Russell answered eagerly. "He and the crew are working all night. The engine change will be finished by morning."

Fabio nodded. "We have a surplus of product right now and we want it shipped soon."

"Is a week soon enough?" Bergin asked.

"One week then," Fabio agreed. "Rafa will give you instructions."

Recognizing the dismissal, Bergin threw down the last of his 151-proof rum and Coke and stood up. A relieved Russell hastily made an exit behind Bergin. Fabio watched them leave the lounge. Then he turned to Rafa and me.

"And how does our friend fit into our operations?" Fabio asked Rafa.

"Max will be the most valuable American we have working with us," Rafa replied. "He is my compadre. All of his time and effort is ours."

Fabio held up his glass to me and took a sip of the scotch and water. A nice gesture, since I knew he was practically a nondrinker.

But my mind wasn't on the pleasantries. Rafa had startled me. He had just announced that I was to be the most valuable American serving the cartel's interests. In no way did I want to sanction such a commitment. But when Fabio looked at me for confirmation of Rafa's statement I gave him a weak nod.

They had me. A big grin lit up Rafa's face.

"Compadre," Fabio said, his salutation and warm smile making my status with the cartel official, "I would like you to visit us in Colombia. We are having a meeting at the ranch at Vera Cruz, and I would like the others to get to know you."

I bowed my head slightly. "Thank you, Fabio. I will be most happy to come."

"Good. We will do it soon."

Fabio took another sip of his drink and then, his mood lighter now, told some jokes. As I would soon learn, Fabio loved telling jokes. I noticed that never in our conversation that evening did Fabio use the word "cocaine" or any other term for the white powder. We could have been bankers, for all the reference he made to our line of business.

Fabio left for the Ochoa home in Kendall, and Rafa and I drove toward North Miami. Now that Fabio had accepted the loss of 235 keys, Rafa began talking about future operations.

"This George Bergin, he thinks he is king of the sky," Rafa began. "He is always complaining, and he is old, he is more than fifty. He wants to retire. I pay George to supply good pilots and be where I can find him any time, day or night. But yesterday when I needed him, I couldn't find him. He will never be part of the family. He is not one of us, yet he is important to us. Or he *was*, until you came along. Now we have you, like family, Compadre, to handle our flight operations."

Rafa was happy. The danger was over and things would be better than ever.

"Fabio has invited you to visit his family home in Colombia. That is a great honor. Your future with us, your new family, will be very rich." For an instant he turned away from the road in front of him and fixed me with his coal-black eyes. "Men like Bergin come and go, but when you become part of the family, Compadre, you never walk away. Never!"

I had just passed the point of no return.

That night after Rafa dropped me at the apartment, Cristina and I sat out on the lawn and discussed the future. Until now I had merely dabbled in the Colombian cocaine trade. I had no desire to become a full-fledged member of the family. I knew as well as Cristina that once you were in, there were only two ways to get out, prison or death.

We evaluated the situation. Cristina was as fearful as I of saying no to Rafa, especially after he had trapped me in front of Fabio Ochoa. Also, her brother, Arturo, was still a hostage of Rafa's, ensuring my cooperation. Much of Cristina's family was in Colombia, where, in one of his frequent irrational moments, Rafa could kill them.

We toyed with the idea of telling Rafa that I would help him for maybe a year, but we both knew better. I put my hand on hers. "Rafa says I'll make a lot of money. That would be nice. I haven't made much since that Christmas Eve two years ago."

Cristina shuddered and then smiled. "You've taken good care of us." After a long thoughtful silence she added, "It's up to you, Max. I'll be happy with whatever you decide."

"Let's sleep on it." But I knew there wasn't any choice. I stood up to go inside and she followed.

As though she knew what I was thinking, Cristina said, "I think we'll all like being back in Miami. It's so cold in New York in the winter." I dropped an arm around her shoulders and hugged her to me.

The following day Rafa came around to pick me up and, shepherded by his ever-present shooters, we drove around Miami and talked. By the time we returned to the apartment everything was decided. I would take the family back to New York for as long as it took to organize the move. Then we would come back and rent a house in Miami Lakes.

"What about our disco club?" I asked.

"You tell Dirty Face he is buying it, for $25,000," Rafa answered imperiously. "You know him, the car mechanic." Of course I knew Armando Melo. He had been Rafa's watchdog when we went to New York after the Christmas Eve murder. He was more than a mechanic; he operated a fast-moving coke trade, and was beholden to and afraid of Rafa. Selling the disco was done.

Although he didn't tell me how much money I would make working for him, Rafa did outline some of my tasks. I would be in charge of the system that transported the cocaine from the airfields in Colombia to our stash houses in Miami and then oversee the final delivery to the distributor. George Bergin and his pilots would report directly to me. Even Rafa realized that his transport operations needed an overhaul.

Four days after arriving in Miami, Cristina and I and the three children flew back to New York.

"I will be waiting here for you, Compadre!" Rafa called as he waved us off.

The family was happy at the prospect of a fast move to Florida, so the bitter winds that whipped around us as we looked for a taxi to take us to the $400-a-month apartment in Queens didn't faze us.

There was always some problem in Cristina's family to plague me, so naturally I walked right into one when we got home. Cristina hit the phone the second we walked in the door, calling her sister Melba, who was living in Flushing. Suddenly there was weeping and wailing and I shouted to Cristina to tell me what had happened. It seemed that Melba's daughter, Alicia, and her boyfriend, Alberto Bravo, had been arrested by New York City narcotics cops for selling coke to an undercover agent. The police had searched their home and found a collection of guns and almost a kilo of coke.

Alicia was not Cristina's favorite niece, after the way she and Willy had treated us when we were forced to live in their attic for a couple of months. It was only after much moaning between the sisters that I finally shut them up by promising to get the money to bail Alicia out and hire a lawyer.

"Just tell that stupid niece of yours I'm not getting her boyfriend out," I stormed. "With him, I hope they throw away the key."

So now, on top of everything else—the arrangements to move our household to Miami and to sell the disco to Armando—I had to get Alicia out of trouble.

The day after our return from Miami, I went looking for Dirty Face Armando and found him at his garage, his face thrust under a car on the hydraulic lift. When I told him that Rafa wanted him to buy the club for $25,000, he swallowed a couple of times.

"I just got two keys from Rafa," he said finally. "I'll start getting the money in a couple of days as soon as I put the coke on the street. I'll pay you then."

"As it comes in, take it to Alicia's family for bail and lawyer's fees," I instructed, "as I still owe them for the purchase of the restaurant."

Everyone in the Colombian community had heard about Alicia's bust and sympathized with her. Her friends had been telling her to lose Alberto since the day he moved in on her.

Armando was happy that not only was he carrying out Rafa's wishes, but helping Alicia as well. Just how thrilled he was to own a disco club, I couldn't say—but Rafa had spoken, and his word was law.

No sooner had the $25,000 purchase price been agreed upon than Armando had a favor to ask of me. I had just bought a new Mercury station wagon and he wanted to borrow it for a special date he had that night with a girl who had just come to New York from Colombia. It was quite a game they all played, trying to be the first guy to lay the new girl up from Cali or Medellín or wherever. I couldn't deny Armando my car; after all, he was taking the disco off my hands.

"But no shit in the car," I warned. That's all I needed, my car picked up with a stash of coke in it.

Armando took me home in the wagon. I shook my head as he drove off. Dirty Face was an unpredictable man, to say the least.

When Cristina heard I was close to raising the money for Alicia's bail and legal defense, she kissed me with joy and immediately called Melba, who was delirious at what appeared to be Alicia's salvation. I didn't remind them that Alicia still had to beat the rap.

Cristina's pleasure at the prospect of getting the bail money died down when I told her I had lent Armando our new station wagon. She loved it dearly as both a status symbol and a convenience with three children.

We were both relieved when Armando brought the wagon up in front of our apartment building the next afternoon, apparently none the worse for wear. I took him back to his garage and asked him how the date had gone.

He grinned broadly. "At first she did not want to go to the motel with me," he chuckled. "But I convinced her."

After leaving Armando at his garage, I drove through Queens and across the Queensboro Bridge to Manhattan to complete some business. A strange whistling noise came from under the floor of the front seat and I detected a slight draft. When I arrived home I examined the floor and saw several holes drilled right through the floor. Immediately, I climbed back in the wagon and drove over to Armando's garage, where, as usual, he was working on the engine of a car.

Angrily I questioned him about the holes. "Oh, I forgot to tell you," he said. "This señorita was becoming a problem about the motel. I pulled out my gun and fired a few shots around her feet. That was the end of the motel problem. I have another date with her tonight."

"Not in my car," I snapped.

"Oh, any car will do, now that I have tamed her," he answered airily. "If you bring your wagon in next week I will put in a new floor. I have already ordered the parts from Mercury."

It took over two weeks to make the move from New York to Miami. Armando had already paid part of the money for the club to Alicia's family and she was home on bail with her parents. Armando promised to have the rest of the money for the lawyer in a short time. Since Rafa was personally interested in the transaction, there was no doubt in any-one's mind that the rest of the money would be paid.

By mid-March we were back in the Fort Lauderdale garden apartment with Rafa's shooters, looking for a home to rent. Rafa immediately introduced me to the business that would be my life for the next four and a half years and earn me more money than I ever thought I would see in my entire lifetime.

It was a Monday. Skip and Russell had brought in another load over the weekend. This load, two hundred kilos, was to be transferred from the pilots and their ground crew to Rafa.

Rafa arrived at the apartment in a car with George Bergin and two other men. "Get in, we're going to pick up two hundred keys," he said simply. I climbed in back and we were on our way. I learned the two men in the back seat with me were drivers and the pickup was scheduled to take place early that afternoon in the parking lot of the Holiday Inn at 79th Street and I-95. When we reached the motel, they stepped out of Rafa's car and walked among the parked cars. Each driver picked out a sedan, opened it, slid behind the wheel and drove out of the lot. It was a smooth operation. But I was terrified during the entire transfer of the two hundred kilos of cocaine.

Rafa had given the drivers the keys to the cars and now we were following them up I-95 to North Miami. Rafa was in control of the load.

The two cars ahead of us continued to NW 125th Street, in a middle-class neighborhood. We drove to the corner of Second Avenue and turned into the driveway of a typical three-bedroom ranch-type house. As we watched, the double garage door, remotely operated, lifted open. The two cars drove directly into the garage. The doors dropped closed behind them. Rafa drove his car into the driveway and pulled it up against the garage door. With his front bumper pressing against it, the garage door could not be opened. A safety measure; in case a bust was attempted, we would have time to get out the back.

I followed Rafa and George Bergin out of the car and up to the front door, which was swung open by a gaunt woman in her fifties. She was a combination Hispanic, Negro, and Indian, with kinky graying hair. Since Miami was filling up with Latinos, she was not really out of place in this neighborhood.

Rafa introduced the woman as Chava. He had already explained to me how the stash house was maintained. An apparently normal middle-class couple lived in it. Every day from Monday to Friday the man left at eight thirty in the morning and returned at five thirty in the evening. Sometimes he came back for lunch and drove away again. On Saturdays he mowed the lawn and on Sundays he washed his car in the driveway. The consistent routine satisfied the neighbors that there was nothing sinister going on.

Since the house frequently contained millions of dollars' worth of cocaine, the stash-house couple was well known to Rafa, and the location of their relatives in Colombia was also known. I could spot weaknesses in the system, but not in regard to this part. The man of the house was supposed to be at work, so it was normal for him to be absent on this Monday morning, if anyone was watching.

Even as we were walking in the front door, the two drivers were unloading their cars in the garage. They piled up the duffel bags on the floor of the adjacent laundry room. Each was full of football-shaped duct-taped packages containing one kilo of coke inside one Ziploc bag inserted into a second Ziploc bag, reinforcing it. I followed Rafa through the dining room and kitchen to the laundry, where he began the process of unloading the duffel bags and counting and inspecting the packages one by one. Each individual one-kilo packet had a marking on the tape and the bags were stacked neatly, separated into piles according to their markings.

"My keys are marked RC, my initials," Rafa explained. He picked out a plastic bag marked CIA—Spanish for "company," like Co. in English—and another with CASA stenciled on it. "These are cartel-owned bags." He lifted another key with SONY marked on it. "This is Pablo Escobar's private stock."

I noticed a growing stack of packages marked 8A and pointed to one. "Ochoa?" I guessed, *ocho* being Spanish for "eight."

"The personal stock of Fabio, Juan David, and Jorge Ochoa," Rafa confirmed.

Rafa was carrying a spiral notebook and he noted the number and code of each package. Then George Bergin made his count. He represented the pilots. He confirmed Rafa's count. This was an on-the-job training exercise, and Rafa handed me his notebook. On a clean page he had me count and note the codes of the bags of coke. Finally, since Chava was responsible for the stash house, she too counted the bags and noted the number and codes. She signed for delivery of them. Rafa co-signed with her. When it was determined that all of us had arrived at the same count, we went on to the next phase of the operation.

After they had been sorted and counted, all of us pitched in and moved the bags from the laundry to the empty rear bedroom with its one small window. There we stacked them on the floor and in the closet according to their markings.

Despite the heavy plastic wrapping, you couldn't miss the hospital smell of ether and acetone. To combat the chemical stink generated by 440 pounds of pure cocaine, Chava placed several open bottles of vinegar in the corners of the room.

Now the stash was complete and ready for delivery. I noticed a bright gleam in Rafa's eye, a look of extreme satisfaction on his face, as he stood at the door to the bedroom and feasted his eyes on the two hundred kilos of coke. Even though stashing the load had been completed, Rafa seemed reluctant to leave the physical proximity of this hoard worth many times its weight in gold. Finally, when the drivers had left and George Bergin and I were impatient to leave, Rafa turned away and walked downstairs, an extra lift to his gait.

The drivers that had brought in the load left the two cars in the garage and drove off in another car which came to pick them up. "OK, let's go," Rafa said. "I've got things to do."

"What?" I asked.

"I've got to call Ochoa and find out who belongs to what." We drove off in Rafa's car and out of the housing development. Back on Biscayne Boulevard, Rafa stopped at a pay phone in a parking lot and asked me to put through a collect call to Ochoa's office for him. He still couldn't speak enough English to put the call through himself.

When Fabio came on the line, Rafa began scribbling down the delivery list, who was supposed to receive what, which code to use when calling the customer, and what that customer's responses must be.

With the beeper numbers and codes written down, Rafa drove to another pay phone, where he dialed the beeper of the first person to whom a delivery would be made. When the answering tone came over the line, he dialed in the number of the pay phone, hung up, and waited. Less than a minute passed before the phone rang.

"Did you just beep me?" the voice on the other end asked.

"Sí," Rafa replied. "I'm looking for Octavio."

"I'm Octavio."

"Are you expecting something?"

"Yes. A friend is sending me some records."

"How many records is he sending you?"

"Fifty LPs."

"I've got your records."

"When can I get them?"

"They'll cost eight dollars apiece. As soon as I get the four hundred dollars you can get your records."

"Let's talk."

"Will you have the money for the records with you?"

"Sí."

"Okay. I'll be at the Winn Dixie on Eighty-second and Biscayne in front of the pay phones in an hour."

Hearing this, I understood why Rafa, his two shooters, and a driver had spent so much time studying the traffic flow in and out of that shopping center on Saturday. They were looking for lots of movement and several exits out to the streets. Rafa had cased two other shopping malls and a Publix supermarket as well.

Rafa hung up and made another call, activating the delivery plan he had worked out. I was expected to watch, learn, and improve upon present operations. One hour later Rafa had a shooter pretending to be talking on the pay phone next to where Rafa was waiting for Octavio. Another of Rafa's bodyguards was nearby, and a driver was out in Rafa's car. I was on a pay phone close enough so I could listen to Rafa's conversation.

Octavio, or the man so code-named, was a cadaverous, middle-aged, gray-haired man wearing a white sports shirt and slacks. He walked up to the phone bank exactly an hour after he had returned Rafa's beeper message. "Are you Octavio?" Rafa asked.

"Yeah. So what do we do?"

In a vernacular virtually unintelligible to non-Colombians, Rafa and Octavio arranged for $400,000 to cover transportation costs at $8,000 a kilo to be paid at the same time the fifty kilos were delivered to Octavio.

Toward the end of the negotiations I began to understand their dialect. "The cash is in your car?" Rafa asked.

"Of course." Octavio shrugged elaborately. "You think I play games?"

"Nobody plays games." Rafa slapped his shirt over his piece. "Drive up Biscayne to Denny's," he directed. "We will have a cup of coffee."

Rafa's black moustache bristled over his toothy Latin grin. "Now you begin to learn how we work, Compadre."

Followed by his pistolocos in the car behind, Rafa drove up Biscayne and pulled into the parking lot at Denny's.

We sat in the car a few minutes until a big black four-door sedan, the kind that has a large trunk, drove up and parked next to him. Rafa got out, walked by the other car, and took the keys from his driver, who then followed us inside Denny's.

"Octavio's man will hand my man, Curri, the keys to a car. Curri will go out and drive away. He will go to the stash house and count the money. If it is right, then when he comes back I give Octavio the keys to the car with the fifty kilos in it and Octavio's man drives away, checks the product, stashes it, and brings the car back. Meantime Octavio and I talk about how we miss life in the old country."

I was even more scared than I'd been before. All this passing around of keys, car and coke keys, seemed incredibly dangerous. There had to be a better way.

We walked over to the table and sat down with Octavio, whose companion slipped a set of car keys to Curri. I watched Curri saunter out of Denny's. Through the window I could see him unlock a car, get in, and drive out of the parking lot. Meantime the rest of us sat and talked about nothing.

Every second I expected a squad of undercover cops to grab us. If anything could look more like a dope deal going down, I couldn't imagine what it was. Rafa and Octavio were right out of a Hollywood casting agent's office. I could see my work had been cut out for me.

Curri wasted no time getting to the stash house, counting the money in the garage, leaving it with Primo, the house-sitter, and getting back to us. Maybe twenty minutes at the most. He walked into Denny's and gave Rafa the nod. Now Rafa none too secretively handed the keys to the coke car to Octavio, whose man took them and walked out of the place.

"I hope your man works as fast as ours," I said to Octavio, swearing to myself that never, never again, would I permit such a sloppy exchange to go down. I suffered through every one of the next twenty-five minutes Rafa and Octavio held each other hostage until Octavio's man came back, nodding happily. Rafa took back the keys to what had been the coke car, and we all said adiós.

The entire exchange actually took less than one hour, while Rafa and Octavio sat impassively making conversation.

The actual purchase of the cocaine from the Ochoas had taken place in Colombia a week or more before the delivery. It only remained for the transportation costs to be taken care of. When Octavio and Rafa had both been assured by their people that the money and the product were correct they had stood up, bowed slightly, and gone their separate ways.

It had been a long, stressful day. From now on I would be expected to do everything I had seen with Rafa, and do it better. The many security flaws in the operation made me cringe. I would be transforming the entire method of operating in a short time. Also, I wanted to meet Skip, Russell's partner.

The next day I started getting ready for the first load to come in under my control, and I didn't want any problems. My first move was to beep Russell Hodges and set up an immediate meeting with him, without George Bergin, who worried me.

We picked an International House of Pancakes convenient to both of us, and in a corner booth, over pancakes and coffee, we reminisced awhile and then got down to business.

"You and George were really close to being the subject of a Colombian shooting spree," I began. "Well, I'm going to be in it up to my ass, right beside you, and I don't want any more fuckups. I can think of a lot of ways you could have avoided that stupid game warden bust."

Russell had the good sense to shut up and not make excuses. I hammered on. "I need to meet with Skip and have a talk with him. I want you to set it up. It was damned stupid of him not to come to the meeting with Fabio." I held up my hand as I saw Russell was going to give me the he-was-busy-on-maintenance-all-night bullshit.

"What is it with Skip?" I asked. "For the kind of money you guys get, there shouldn't be any problems at all."

"Yeah, Skip's careless, and getting worse," Russell conceded. "He's used to being first pilot on a big airline. The mechanics do all the flight checks. All he has to do is get in the cockpit and fly the bird. He gets lots of time off to rest up between commercial flights. That's when we do our thing."

"Just the kind of 'rest periods' the Eastern managers have in mind," I commented wryly.

"I do all the pre-flight checks, or there wouldn't be any, before our flights south." Russell shook his head. "Skip loves to fly around in his own Cessna 210. I flew with him just once and he wasn't going to give it a pre-flight. I wouldn't fly with him unless he let me do a check."

"Maybe we should get another pilot," I suggested. "You fly in the left seat and we get you a co-pilot."

Russell shook his head. "When it comes to the hairy stuff, there's no pilot better than Skip."

"I need to talk to him. Look, the shippers pay eight thousand dollars a kilo to get their load from some airstrips in Colombia into their hands in Florida. There are a lot of us splitting that money. You pilots walk with twenty-five thousand dollars a key and you never fly less than two hundred keys, usually more like three hundred. But at two hundred keys you come up with five hundred thousand dollars a flight. It seems like half a million bucks should be enough to keep you from getting careless."

"That's what I keep telling Skip," Russell agreed.

"Bergin gets a grand a key. Rafa gets two thousand a key and another twenty-five hundred goes back to the Ochoas on top of the selling price for their shit. That's eight grand total per key. That's a lot of responsibility. You and Skip better understand how many people get hurt when you fuck up. Now I want you to arrange a meet between Skip and me. Maybe he doesn't understand what .45 slugs out of a Colombian pistoloco's Mac-10 can do to a guy's health."

"Max, I don't need to hear any more of this stuff," Russell protested. "I am not a fuckup, to use your terminology."

I guess I was being a little hard on Russell. "I know that, Russell. But I need to talk to Skip."

"I'll see what I can do. Skip figures that the only guy he's got to answer to is George Bergin."

"You see? I gotta talk to him, get him straightened out."

"I'll be in touch, Max."

Russell stood up and walked out of the pancake house. Just by his walk I could see I had given him a lot to think about.

Later that morning Cristina and I drove around North Miami looking for a house to rent. We knew that what we wanted was the Miami Lakes development. Unfortunately the house we fell in love with rented for $1,500 a month and I was used to paying $400 for the large, comfortable, rambling apartment in Queens. I had no idea how much money I would be making with Rafa, as he had never mentioned a figure; he had just said I'd be well taken care of.

Rafa had brought his wife, Odila, up from Colombia and he was looking for a suitable home for her. That afternoon the two of us took a drive to Miami Lakes and I showed him the place Cristina and I liked. Four big bedrooms, a deck overlooking the lake, and plenty of living and recreational space.

"But I can't pay fifteen hundred a month," I lamented.

"Is that the one you like?" he asked.

"That's the one my wife likes," I replied.

"So rent it!" Rafa said decisively. "If we can't make enough to pay fifteen hundred a month, we don't deserve to be in this business."

Once again that fear-affection relationship with Rafa hit me. I remembered reading about the hostages that were kept in a bank vault with their captor-thieves for a week in Sweden. The captives began to have genuinely warm feelings toward their captors. Perhaps I didn't appreciate it at the time, but I was becoming a clear example of the "Stockholm syndrome."

I didn't know how much money I would be making, but I accepted $4,500 from Rafa, and the next day I paid the first and last months' rent plus another month's rent for security. We sent our furniture, which had just arrived from New York, over to 6720 White Oak Drive, and happily said adiós to Rafa's shooters, our housemates.

We were home sweet home.

Part Two

* * *

THE CARTEL

CHAPTER FIVE

*

Rancho Ochoa

It was April of 1981 and I was sitting in my living room watching the local Miami news, looking for murders, seeing if anyone I knew was going to be featured. The cocaine wars were raging in South Florida; Colombians were busy killing one another.

Rafa walked in without knocking and said, "Max, we are going to Colombia."

"Why?"

"Jorge wants to meet my compadre, and he wants to introduce you to some other people inside the organization."

"When do we go?" I asked.

"Tomorrow, you go. I am leaving this afternoon; I will meet you down there."

"Sí, señor."

That night I told Cristina that Jorge Ochoa wanted to meet me. "You are an honored man," she said, and told me of the legendary Ochoa clan. She knew the family and had ridden the famous show horses, the Paso Finos, that the family bred. She had ridden for Don Fabio, the father of the three famous Ochoa brothers: Jorge, Juan David, and Fabio junior.

She giggled as she spoke of the old man. The "human football," she called him, over four hundred pounds on a five-foot-five frame. "A football with a hat," she said, smiling, her graceful hands arching out and making a sweeping movement as she described the swayed back of the poor horse that had to carry Don Fabio.

I packed for about a week's stay; when Rafa said a few days, it always turned out to be at least a week. Too many times I had taken only an overnight bag and returned with a full suitcase because I had had to buy clothes on the trip.

I flew by commercial airline to Barranquilla, a stinking open sewer on the edge of the ocean. It was a convenient jumping-off point. The Ochoa ranch was close to the coast between Barranquilla and Cartagena. Rafa had told me that Jorge maintained a yacht in Cartagena, a forty-eight-foot Hatteras. He also told me that he had just ordered a fifty-five-foot Hatteras for himself.

Rafa and his entourage met me at the airport. I renewed my acquaintance with Fernando Loperra and Jaime, whose last name I now learned was Pecas—men I had met on my first trip to Cali. They were to be my bodyguards. Then Rafa introduced me to Jorge Perez and his son Junior, both pilots.

"This is Max, my compadre," Rafa said, putting his arm around my shoulder, looking at the bodyguards, a menacing grin crossing his face. ":You men are with him to protect him while he is here . . . what happens to him happens to you." The threat vanished from his face and a real smile appeared as Esperanza, his longtime mistress, skipped across the tarmac and almost jumped into his arms.

"We just relax tonight. We leave for the ranch tomorrow morning," Rafa said to me.

"How are we going?" I asked.

"Private plane; Jorge Perez and his son Junior are to be our pilots."

That night we settled into a hotel in Barranquilla and all had dinner together; I watched Jorge Perez and Junior get blasted on Chivas scotch.

"Enough of this shit," I said, and rose to go to bed. Fernando Loperra and Jaime Pecas, my bodyguards, also rose and proceeded to walk up the stairs behind me.

"What do you guys think you're doing?" I asked as they filed into my room.

"We must also sleep now, Señor Max, if that is what you are doing."

"This is my room! What, are we all going to sleep together?"

"In a way, Señor Max," Jaime answered in a slurred voice. "We will sleep on the floor."

"But there isn't even a rug on the floor."

"That is of no importance, Señor Max. If someone were to bust in and try to harm you, they must first step over us. We wouldn't be much good if we were in another room, would we?"

"Suppose I wanted to pick up a hooker and get laid?"

"We wouldn't mind, Señor Max. We know about such things."

"Well, I would mind. But suit yourselves," I grumbled, and went to sleep listening to a chorus of drunken snores, wondering what the hell good they would be if anyone really did break into my room.

In the morning they shook Rafa awake and we headed out to the airport with them, bleary-eyed and mumbling. We arrived at the airport and went directly to the civil section.

"Rafa, I ain't flying with your hotshot pilots. I'm not getting in the plane with them," I said.

"Max, you worry too much," he said, "It's Jorge's plane. These guys can fly. They're terrific pilots." He pushed me through the door as Jorge and Junior slid into the pilot and co-pilot seats. "It's only a ten-minute flight."

"But look at the goddamn weather!" I said, pointing to a sky above the mountains that was as black as death.

"Storm's going the other way, Max," Rafa lied.

Jorge and Junior, grumbling at each other, started up the plane and I shouted to Rafa. "Aren't these guys at least going to do a pre-flight check?"

"Naw, they probably did one yesterday." Rafa grinned and broke into a laugh. "If it's your time, it's your time, Compadre, no one can tell me any different. Remember Chino?" he hissed.

I sat back quietly and shut my mouth as they began to taxi toward the gas pump. I saw it but couldn't believe it—a chain-link fence off to the left. We were heading straight for it.

I started to yell, but it was too late. The plane came to an abrupt halt as the left wing collided with a galvanized-pipe fence post.

"Shit! Shit! Shit!" Jorge yelled, and shut down the engine. "You wait!" he said to his passengers as he climbed out to look at the damage. I watched him through the window as he gently fingered the crushed metal. There was a small V now in the wing. He shrugged and yelled to us, "Get out! Everybody out of the damn plane, and come here."

We did as we were told and gathered around him. "Now push, push like hell," he said. We pushed the plane until it was clear of the fence.

I ran my finger down the wing and into the two-inch dent. "Don't worry," Junior whispered to me. "I seen him fly planes in a lot worse condition."

"Great! Just great!" I said, and climbed back into the plane.

We continued to the gas pump, and took on fuel. Jorge taxied to the runway, still no pre-flight or instrument checks, absolutely nothing.

Jorge contacted the tower. "Ready for takeoff," he said.

"No, you're not," the tower responded. "Nothing takes off until that storm clears."

I looked ahead through the cockpit window and all I could see was black, like a black sheet had been laid over the sky and landscape ahead of us.

"I'm leaving," Jorge yelled into the microphone to the tower. "And you ain't stopping me, *hijodeputa.*"

"Permission to take off denied. You must stay where you are." The tower was yelling now as well. "We'll call the authorities."

"Call your mama if you want, you ain't stopping me!" Jorge shouted. Junior was convulsed with laughter.

Jorge rammed the throttles full-ahead and we screamed down the runway and were airborne, heading directly for the black void that lay ahead of us.

"You assholes!" I screamed at Jorge and Junior. They only turned to each other, smiled, and shrugged.

"Que importa!" I heard Jorge mumble. "It's not important!" This only made Junior laugh more. I looked over at Rafa and Esperanza; he had his head on her shoulder and was sleeping like a baby as she stroked his head.

The blackness of the storm loomed directly ahead of us, broken only by shards of lightning that split the sky with bony yellow fingers, followed by deep booms of thunder.

Suddenly Rafa was awake. He took one look out the window and barked, "Turn this plane around!"

Esperanza started to scream, "We are dead, we are dead!" Her voice reverberated inside the small cockpit.

"Shut up!" I yelled at her, then turned my attention to the pilots. "Turn around! Put this damn thing down!"

Jorge and Junior grinned at us, ignoring our cries. "What you worried about?" Jorge asked us.

God must have been watching our tiny plane that day, because like a miracle, a small white hole opened up in the center of the blanket of black. Rafa and I both pointed toward it at the same time over Jorge's shoulder.

"I see it," he said quietly, as Junior pushed our hands out of the way.

And as calmly as if he were driving a car on a quiet country road, Jorge headed for the hole and we passed through it slick and easy, into a beautiful blue cloudless sky on the other side.

We flew on in silence for five minutes. I watched the rolling hills and the beautiful lush green meadows pass under us. And it suddenly dawned on me that we were over the land of the Ochoas. "Is that the ranch below?" I asked.

"Yes," Rafa answered.

"How big is it?"

"Three hundred, maybe three-fifty."

"Three hundred acres? No, no that can't be right."

"Three hundred *thousand*, Compadre. Now that we are over the mountains, their land stretches as far as the eye can see."

On a far-away hillock I saw huge gray forms moving together. They disappeared from sight. "What were they?" I asked Jorge and Junior.

"Elephants, Señor Max. They are the Ochoa elephants."

We were flying low, Jorge and Junior looking for landmarks to guide them. They flew like they were on a strafing run, but all the time they continued playing with us, turning around to talk to us, joshing each other, telling jokes. Suddenly ahead of us was a beautiful paved landing strip; the radio room was in the hacienda. Jorge took the plane up and circled the strip while he talked to the ground crew and asked permission to land. Rafa explained that in approaching the Ochoa ranch everyone did exactly what they were instructed by the air controller. If the Ochoas did not want you to land, you didn't land—not if you wanted to live.

"What is that?" I asked Rafa, pointing at a large arena.

"A bull ring. Fabio Ochoa is a bullfighter. That is where he practices with the famous Costa Brava bulls, the finest fighting bulls. They bring them in from Spain."

The huge, sprawling main house passed below us and several large Chickee huts appeared on the edge of the lake. The lake was about thirty acres and a man-made island of about five acres was being built in the center.

"And that island, what is that for?" I asked Rafa.

"For the lions and tigers." Rafa smiled.

Finally, we were given permission to land. The strip was in perfect condition, better than the airport in Barranquilla, and longer—almost the size of a commercial strip. It was designed for the Ochoa jets.

As we hit the runway, the heavens opened up and the rains came. The main storm had passed, but Mother Nature wanted us to know she could still have her way. The tarmac was suddenly a shiny black ribbon in the wilds of Colombia.

A truck was waiting to meet us; it was a new white Chevy Sierra pickup with a double set of rear tires and an elongated cab. Fabio Ochoa and another man jumped out of the cab. We were all standing there in the rain getting soaked as Fabio introduced me to his brother Jorge.

"Ah, nice to meet you. You are Rafa's compadre, you are welcome here," Jorge said, holding the door open for us to get in. Esperanza slipped by and climbed into the rear of the cab. "Rafa, you and Max get in, and Fabio and I will ride in the back of the truck."

And they did. We sat safe and dry inside the cab as we rode to the Chickee hut where we would have lunch. I studied them through the rear window of the cab as they sat with the rain drenching them. They were so different. Fabio was thin, light-complexioned, with long light hair, twenty-four, maybe twenty-five years old. Jorge was older and darker, heavyset, stocky, with a small spare tire around the middle. His dark hair was plastered to his face by the rain. With his thick moustache, he looked very Latin, almost Indian. Jorge was big for a Colombian, maybe five foot seven, an inch or so taller than his brother.

Neither was the image of what they were to become: billionaires. But they were already among the mega-rich, and it awed me that they would sit in the back like that, in the rain, while we sat inside the cab. They comported themselves like gentlemen, not like Rafa and his gang of ruffian killers and thieves from the barrios.

The Chickee hut was huge and round, thiry feet in diameter, with a beautiful marble floor and a generously stocked bar, complete with ice machines. The servants were working feverishly to set up the buffet tables and carry the food down from the house on covered trays. Tray after tray appeared as we settled down at a long table. There was no seating order. Dry shirts and pants were brought by the servants for the Ochoa brothers and they changed into the fresh clothes in the bathrooms.

We rose together after we got the signal and walked to the opulent buffet table laden with pork chops, ribs, roast beef, chicken, and red beans. And they all cheered when they saw the fritanga. All but me, that is. Fritanga is diced entrails of pork and cattle fried together in one pan. Intestines are not high on my list, so I passed, and picked up plenty of arepas, thick tortillas made out of white corn.

The rain suddenly stopped, as abruptly as it had begun.

Around the table there were glasses of soda and cups of coffee. No one drank alcohol of any kind, out of respect for the Ochoas, and no one was doing any dope.

No one except Carlos, "Crazy Carlos" Lehder. He didn't eat, drink, or sit with us; he circled us like a man possessed, in his own world, oblivious to what we were doing. The fat marijuana joint never left his mouth as he puffed away. His head was enclosed in a cloud of smoke; his face was only visible when he walked fast enough to get out of the smoke cloud. I didn't know why he was there.

After the meal, on an unspoken signal, the group dispersed until only Rafa, myself, the two Ochoa brothers, Esperanza, Pablo Correa, and Carlos Correa (no relation to Pablo) remained at the table. Pablo Correa was in his late thirties, very dark with graying black hair. Carlos Correa was perhaps twenty-six years old, with sandy brown hair and a light complexion; he did not look Latin. As I was to learn, both Correas would be important to my operations.

Rafa was careful to mention again that I was his compadre, and that gave me instant acceptance. Rafa was validating me, sponsoring me, and to a Colombian that meant he was putting his life on the line. It was Rafa's ass if anything ever went wrong with me. My nickname "Compadre," roughly translated, means blood brother.

Crazy Carlos did not join us but he kept circling the table.

Jorge started the conversation. "Our production now is more than it has ever been. We have warehouses full to the ceiling, and our distribution network in the United States is growing. Our biggest problem is getting more shipments into the States, and that is the reason we have asked you to come here."

"Can I go see the horses?" Esperanza asked Rafa. She was already bored with the conversation. Esperanza was very pretty, a petite brunette with flashing dark chocolate eyes. She was short, but had an hourglass figure and a lot of energy, especially energy for fun. As Rafa's mistress she was allowed to sit with us; if she had been his wife, she would have been sent to the main house.

"Yes, go to the stables and ask the stable hands to show you the horses," Rafa said offhandedly, turning his attention back to Jorge and Fabio. Everyone at the table had known Esperanza for years as Rafa's mistress.

"We must move more weight," Jorge said. "We are backlogged. We must get it up to the States as fast as we can."

"How much more?" I asked. I knew they were looking to me for answers.

"Double, triple at least what we are currently doing."

"More planes, more pilots, more each load . . ." Rafa said.

"Yes," Jorge said. "Can you do it?"

I looked at Rafa and took my cue from the nod of his head. "We will need a little time," I said.

Jorge and Fabio leaned closer, to be out of earshot of circling Carlos Lehder. "If you need another fuel stop or drop-off point, you can use Norman's Cay, Carlos' island in the Bahamas. It is near Bimini, only forty miles from Florida. He controls it totally, and the Bahamian government helps him. For a small fee he will let you stop there. He has boats that can cross the Florida Straits."

I looked at Rafa, who was now staring at the zombie-like Carlos as he continued in his never-ending circle. We were thinking the same thing. What the hell do we need Crazy Carlos for, and who would want to be under his power? But now I knew why Lehder had been invited to the meeting.

"What's a small fee, Jorge?" Rafa asked.

"A thousand a key."

Rafa smiled. "No, thanks. I got enough fuckheads of my own. Besides, I think someday he will go too far. That Nazi blood from his father and all the dope he takes will explode and take us with him. No. I got plenty of trouble. I don't need a low-life like Carlos to screw me up."

While Rafa was talking I was thinking: It's easy. We're flying in never less than a thousand pounds a flight now. We double it, and we're bringing in a ton a week. And it should be no problem to make two flights a week.

Jorge Ochoa rose and quietly walked over to Carlos, using his hand to clear a passage through the fog of marijuana smoke that surrounded him. He was out of earshot, so I didn't hear what he had to say to Carlos. Carlos was important to the Ochoas at this point; his landing strip on Norman's Cay was a major drop-off point for Florida and a refueling spot for aircraft to continue on to the Carolinas. I didn't like Carlos. He was an avowed Nazi fascist and his brain was scrambled from doing too much dope. I knew, even then, that the Ochoas would dump him the minute he was no longer of value to them. He was a living embarrassment.

Jorge rejoined us, and Rafa turned to me. "So, Compadre, you think we can do as Jorge asks?"

"No problem. The more Jorge produces, the more we bring up. I'll get it into the States. Instead of a plane coming to Colombia once a week, it will be twice a week. We will recruit more pilots, get more planes, more landing strips. We can do it, because we have the one thing we need, something I've never had before."

"What's that?" Fabio asked.

"Unlimited funds. Makes almost anything possible." I smiled, and they all laughed. "If somebody's got a pair of balls and is not afraid to do the work that's got to be done, like our pilots . . . then it can be done."

"Eh, Rafa, I like this hombre, your compadre. He talks positive, solves the problem. A good man you got here," Jorge said.

There was never any talk about selling the coke. There was no business like it. These men had never heard of the word "marketing." Selling was not their problem; the market was already strong and seemed insatiable. Just produce the stuff and find a way to get it into the USA, that's all. It was a seller's market then and it continued that way for years. And the price was high in 1981—$35,000 a key, wholesale.

I knew why they wanted American pilots. After my flight to the ranch with Jorge Perez and his son Junior at the controls, there was no question in my mind. With four hundred keys a load, it was $14 million in gross revenue per plane to the cartel. And they didn't want some doped-up Colombian who hits a chain-link fence on the ground before he even takes off.

"It is settled then. Enough of business," Jorge said. "Why don't we have a small tour of the ranch. Would you like that, Compadre?" Jorge smiled.

Basically, the main buildings of the ranch were on three levels. The Chickee hut, where we were, was on the middle level; the house was up on the top level and overlooked the entire compound. The airstrip and bull ring were below us, so we looked out over the ring and the lake. It was a big lake, some thirty acres, fed by clear natural springs. The picturesque setting was disturbed only by the rising clouds of dust from the dump trucks that were moving like an endless insect convoy down a needle causeway to the center of the lake, where they spilled their contents and hurried back to get another load. They barely missed each other as they came and went on the narrow dirt road. The ever-rising dust gave the illusion of a fire burning in the middle of the lake.

Jorge and Fabio were standing now; three open Jeeps were waiting for us, and the white pickup that had brought us to the hut for lunch was there also, idling, four armed bodyguards sitting in the truck bed.

"Before we go, show our new compadre your prize, Jorge," Fabio said.

Jorge walked to the bar and reached up for a picture that hung on the wall of reeded grass. He brought it back and handed it to me. "That, my friend, is an albino buffalo, born right here on the ranch. He is the pride of my new herd, an extreme rarity and great good luck."

"Good luck for him that he was born on your ranch, where he can still walk free with no fear," I said.

There was a silence as Jorge stopped to study my words. Then he smiled, his thick moustache rising into an even broader smile. "Yes, yes, I'm going to like this new compadre of yours, Rafa. Now let's go for a ride.

We all piled into the Jeeps. For the next two hours Jorge drove Rafa, Fabio, and me around his ranch. He took us across the green Colombian veldt and showed us his herds of antelopes, gazelles, and American buffalo that roamed as wild as they would have on the plains of Africa and America before civilization took over and moved them out. When we got to the wooded higher ground, we saw herds of giraffes nibbling the tops of trees.

On a rise just above his "secret lake," Jorge handed us each a pair of high-powered binoculars so we could see the elephants and water buffalos as they splashed and played in the lake, rolling in the mud like high-spirited children after a long-awaited rain.

I watched through the glasses, standing above the animals, leaning against the Jeep. Disbelieving: me, Max Mermelstein, a Jewish boy from Brooklyn, deep in the gut of wildest Colombia, surrounded by armed bodyguards, watching a herd of wild African animals playing in a private lake, with a gang of wild-assed Colombian *narco-traficantes* at my side.

"Hey, Compadre, what do you think?" Fabio said, a big smile on his face. "This is Jorge's game. Animals and motorcycles. I have other interests to amuse me."

"Don't you listen to him, Compadre. He loves animals and takes extra pains to make sure the vets and their staff do a good job of taking care of these beasts, eh, Fabio?" Jorge said. "And, Compadre, if you know of anyone who can get wild animals, call me. Whatever they cost, don't worry, I'll pay. Especially cats: lions, tigers, panthers, jaguars, leopards . . . the big cats, the bigger the better."

"The island?" I asked.

"Yes," Fabio said. "The island you saw being built is Jorge's island for the cats. It will be ready in a few months, and it has been designed specially for the cats."

"Let's hope the fuckers can't swim," I said.

They laughed. "That's good, Compadre. Hey, Rafa, your friend is funny," Jorge yelled to Rafa. "Very funny."

Rafa looked back at us, not smiling. I got the feeling he resented my befriending the Ochoas. I was his friend, his possession, here only because of his invitation. I decided I'd better cool it a little with the Ochoas and stay a little more formal.

Jorge drove us back to the main house, which seemed to sprawl forever. It had been designed by his sister, who was an architect. The house was on one level, with square angles like a bunch of boxes put together with no imagination. A stark concrete bomb shelter was what it looked like to me. The best thing about the house was the red Spanish tile roof.

A veranda spanned the rectangular form of the building, running completely around the entire house. There were at least forty bodyguards scattered around the house, and although they were all armed with automatic weapons or sidearms no one paid any attention to them. The house was full of the hustle and bustle of women and children.

I stopped on the veranda and fingered one of the hammocks. They were everywhere on the veranda, hung between posts, from the ceiling beams, everywhere, like a maze of fishing nets hanging in midair. "What are these for, the hammocks?" I asked Rafa.

"For the bodyguards; it is where they sleep at night. They even hang them across this entrance to the house."

I just shook my head and walked into the foyer. Rafa was anxious to leave. He had told me in the Jeep that his parents lived nearby and he wanted to visit them. And I knew he wanted to be with Esperanza, but had to go along with the Ochoas to be polite.

We walked into a massive living room, about forty feet square. It was beautifully furnished in modern chrome and glass; the ceiling was high, maybe twelve feet. The floor was a pattern of black and white marble squares.

In the middle of the living room sat a mechanical bucking bull. I decided that the old saying was true: The only difference between men and boys is the size of their toys. These guys would play with anything! The first one up was Rafa, who, on the third buck of the bull, landed with a thud on the marble floor. I passed when it was my turn and watched as bodies flew in every direction, crashing one after another into the furniture or onto the floor. The only one who managed to stay up on the bull was Jorge Ochoa. Fabio said later that Jorge had seen the bull in a Texas bar, bought it, and rode it every day he could.

Everyone was buoyant and happy from the exercise, but I knew Rafa was now very anxious to leave.

"Jorge, thank you for lunch, but we must be going," Rafa said, shaking Jorge's hand.

"No, Rafa, that is too bad. I was hoping you would stay for dinner."

"My parents are expecting me this evening."

Jorge smiled. "Ah, that is something I understand. Parents must come first; look at all they have had to put up with us as sons."

As Jorge and Fabio saw us to the door, Jorge said he'd walk down to the airstrip with us.

"Not me," I said to Rafa. "I'm not flying with that madman and his son, not me. I don't ask God to favor me twice with miracles."

"So, Compadre, you flew with Jorge and Junior, and now you know why we like the American pilots. I understand. If you want, you may take the Chevy Sierra truck and drive," Jorge said. "Please. I would be happy if you take it."

"The bodyguards?"

"A separate car for them will of course be included."

"*Gracias*, we will. Now I must find Esperanza," Rafa said, taking off for the barns that housed the Paso Fino horses that the Ochoa family was so famous for breeding.

"While Rafa goes for Esperanza, would you like to see something? Do you like motorcycles?" Jorge asked.

"Yeah, I do," I answered.

"Good. Then I will show you my collection."

With Fabio we walked to a barn near the airstrip. I could see that it had been recently built, metal walls on a concrete pad. Fabio slid back the doors and inside were at least twenty Harleys of every color and configuration. They were lined up in a long row, like bikers do when they congregate at their favorite bar.

"Holy shit," was all I could think of to say, but my wonderment pleased Jorge and Fabio.

"I like the Harley Davidsons best because they are big and powerful and easy to modify. Too bad you are leaving. I would take you for a ride, Compadre," Jorge said.

"They are very beautiful." Two men were polishing them, while another three men worked in the small garage in the corner of the barn, rebuilding one of the bikes.

"These are only a small part of my collection. I have a warehouse twice this big in Medellín full of bikes like these, over a hundred. I have them flown in every time my planes go to America. They land on one of our private airstrips. It is better that way. No need to pay too many taxes to the government, eh?"

"No, no need at all." I smiled. I could picture Jorge out on his thousands of acres together with his bodyguards, roaring across the plains and up the mountain roads on these Harleys, chasing the wild animals when the spirit moved them, going as fast as they dared, the clean Colombian air in their faces. Jorge's nickname was El Gordo, "The Fat One"—an affectionate term, but I could see in my mind Jorge's ample tummy flopping up and down as the motorcycle bumped across the terrain. The image made me smile.

My smile was short-lived. "Okay, Compadre, let's go." Rafa stuck his face in the door, his arm around Esperanza. As was the custom, she did not go up to the main house where the Ochoa wives, children, and relatives gathered. A mistress never did.

I climbed into the rear seat of the twin-cab Chevy pickup and Rafa and Esperanza got in the front. We started our journey following a narrow dirt road; dust billowed up behind us just in front of the Renault that was trailing us. Fernando Loperra and Jaime Pecas, the bodyguards, were in the Renault. While Rafa and Esperanza engaged in small talk and lovers' play, I watched the lush Colombian landscape flash by: beautiful rolling hills, tropical jungle foliage born in the rain forest, long flat blankets of treeless green, pampas, with cattle grazing and wild horses skittering away at the sound of the truck rolling past at high speed.

For over two hours we rolled nonstop. Then suddenly Rafa slowed down and I saw two huge cement pillars ahead of us, like squat, fat, gray monoliths in the middle of nowhere. We stopped just short of the barricade chain. A guard shack stood nearby and I saw the door open. Three men emerged, all carrying automatic weapons. Rafa stuck his head out the window; the leader recognized him and smiled, pulling the lever.

The cement pillars supported a heavy iron chain that had been welded solid. It was the thick sturdy anchor chain you would find on a battleship. The chain dropped slowly into a ditch so that we could pass. The truck jostled as the tires rolled over the rough surfaces of the chain.

"What the hell was that about, Rafa?" I asked.

"We are just now leaving the ranch," he answered, smiling. He revved up the truck and headed down the road.

It had never dawned on me that for the last two and a half hours we had been on the Ochoa ranch.

"I can't believe this is all theirs," I said.

"And they have many more ranches. They have four breeding farms for the Paso Finos alone. But Las Lomas, near Medellín, is the most famous; that's where the high-priced animals are kept."

I whistled under my breath in astonishment. "Have they always been rich?" I asked.

"No, they started small, like us. They had a couple of restaurants in Medellín called Las Margaritas. But they have always had show horses. It was Juan David and his brothers who founded the business that has made them so rich. I am told Juan David started it to keep up the show horses. Fabio loves the fighting bulls; Juan David loves the show horses. They are both expensive hobbies."

Ironic to think that their careers in the cocaine trade began as a result of a need for money to support their hobbies. "All this wealth in five years," I muttered.

"Sí, all in the last five years. Compadre, now it is your turn to drive. I am tired and Esperanza wants to nap." Rafa turned and winked slyly as he brought the truck to a halt.

I switched places with them, took the wheel, and pulled away. The road was straight, with few side roads. I drove for about twenty minutes and Rafa said, "Hey, Compadre, you just keep the nose of this truck pointed in the same direction. No detours, okay?"

"Okay," I said, and glanced in the rearview mirror. All of a sudden they disappeared out of the mirror. Then I saw clothes flying, a brassiere, shirt, underpants. A moment later it felt like the truck was hitting bumps, but there were no bumps in the road. Then I heard groaning. The road suddenly twisted and I came upon one of the few curves.

Up in front was a military roadblock.

I slammed on the brakes. Rafa and Esperanza thudded against the seat as their bodies rolled forward with the force.

"Hijodeputa!" I heard Rafa yell.

The lieutenant in charge walked over to my window and asked for my driver's license. I handed him my Miami license. A Florida driver's license in the middle of the Colombian wilderness. He couldn't believe it.

"What the hell are you doing here with this? Out! Get out! Keep your hands in the air." As I got out, he peered into the rear seat to find Rafa and Esperanza bare-assed, trying to get their clothes back on. He held back a smile and ordered them out. The rest of the platoon had already gathered around the bodyguards' car, and they had them spread-eagled on the hood. I saw Rafa check his wallet and slip out a handful of bills and stuff them in his shirt pocket before he zippered his pants.

"Apurense," the lieutenant said to Rafa. "Hurry." But he said it softly; by this time he had figured that Rafa might be a drug lord.

Rafa asked to speak to him privately, and I saw his hand slip into his pocket and pull out the sheaf of bills. The lieutenant glanced at them, took them, then stuffed them into his pocket. The lieutenant escorted Rafa, Esperanza and me back to the truck and signaled to the others to release our bodyguards.

Rafa waited impatiently for me to climb into the rear of the cab, so that he could take over the driving. A scowl was on his face.

It was near dark when we arrived in Sincelejo, a medium-sized town with dirt roads. Cattle walked undisturbed down the main drag. Rafa told the bodyguards to check into a hotel and then took us to his father's house. It was one of the few houses with an air-conditioner.

The first thing Rafa's parents did was fight with him because he had brought his girlfriend instead of his wife. It wasn't much of a fight, because, as Rafa later explained to me, his mother hated his wife. But she had to scold him—it was the custom.

Even so, Rafa's mother kissed Esperanza and hugged her, whispering in her ear as she showed her the bedroom she would be sharing with Rafa, "He should have married you. I told him not to marry her. She's a bitch, a real bitch. Maybe someday I will shoot her." She said it loud enough for everyone to hear.

We were all exhausted from the day's activities, so we went to bed early. But just as I put my head on the pillow there was a knock on the door. It slowly opened, creaking on its hinges. Rafa's father stuck his head in and said softly, "Hey, Compadre, you asleep yet?"

"Not yet."

"Good. I got something for you." He walked into the room, closing the door behind him.

He showed me a .45-caliber automatic with a silencer attached.

"What the hell is this for?" I asked, wondering if he was going to shoot me.

"You can't sleep in the house of Rafael Cardona Salazar without a gun under your pillow."

"What?"

"Keep it. Just stick it under your pillow," he said, dropping the pistol on my stomach, on top of the sheets. I lay there dumbfounded as he left, closing the door softly. I turned on the night light and examined the gun. It was a solid chunk of rust. I don't think it would have fired if I'd wanted to use it, but the old man had spooked me enough so that I got up and cleaned the thing.

The next morning we breakfasted early and just before we left, Rafa's mother called me aside and whispered, "Now, you be careful for yourself, and you look after my son. He graduated from high school with a degree in drug dealing and racketeering, you know. It's in his blood, so you look out for him and for yourself. He worries me." I was stunned; I had never heard a mother talk about her son that way.

Rafa announced to the bodyguards when he picked them up at the hotel that our destination was Cartagena, not Barranquilla. He went back to his father's house, called Jorge and Junior, the pilots, who were then in Barranquilla, and told them to pack our bags and fly everything to Cartagena and meet us.

Six hours later, after an endless string of dusty back roads, we arrived in Cartagena. Rafa checked us into the finest hotel, the Capillo Del Mar, which overlooks the sea. We were all looking very ragged from two days on the road. He looked at Esperanza and me after he signed in and said, "You two look awful. Let's go shopping."

Cartagena is an expensive town, and all I could find were Christian Dior silk-and-linen slacks at $200 a copy. Rafa bought me four pairs, and silk shirts and Ferragamo shoes. He bought Esperanza dresses, anything we wanted, as much as we wanted. Rafa was generous when he felt like it.

We went back to our rooms to shower and dress for dinner. The bodyguards had moved into the room connecting to mine; maybe this time they could be useful, I thought. I had been without a woman now for several days, so after we returned from dinner I sent one of them out to find me a hooker.

An hour later he came back empty-handed and said, "Sorry, señor, but it is late, almost one in the morning. Everything is closed, there is nothing."

"Screw you, screw you both!" I said, and started to leave.

"Sorry, señor, but you cannot leave alone. If Rafa finds out he will kill us. We must go with you."

"Well, if he doesn't kill you, I will. You are not going with me, and if you try I'll beat the hell out of you both," I said, slamming the door behind me.

I grabbed a cab in front of the hotel and told the driver to take me to the best whorehouse in Cartagena. I sat and watched the town of Cartagena pass by the taxi window. It is a beautiful city and was the major transshipping point for the Spanish conquistadors in the sixteenth and seventeenth centuries. It was from this city that they sent back to the Old

World the gold and silver they plundered from the Aztecs, Mayans, and Incas. Many of the buildings are of the old Spanish architecture, reeking of history and strange tales.

Finally, the cab stopped in front of a plain wooden building and the driver got out. I watched him knock on the door and eventually a little cubbyhole opened up. He signaled me to enter.

The madam brought out six or seven pretty girls. "Which one do you prefer, señor?" she asked, smiling.

"They are all pretty," I said, finally picking two of the girls. "I want them for this evening, both of them. How much?" I always took the girls back to my turf. I didn't want to get caught in strange territory with my pants down, an old habit from Brooklyn that I had never lost.

"Two thousand pesos each," she said. About eighty bucks U.S.

Back at the hotel, I went upstairs to my room and knocked on the connecting door. The bodyguards, guns drawn, answered the knock, sleepy-eyed, their hair tousled from sleep. "Here, hombres, here's a present! Can't find anything in town? Well, here's a nonexistent hooker from a nonexistent whorehouse," I said, ushering one of the girls into their room. "Have fun!"

In the morning the pilots arrived with my clothes and baggage. They explained that they had had some minor mechanical problems. I didn't ask what the problems were; I was afraid to hear the answer.

Rafa drove me to the Cartagena airport and escorted me to the departure gate.

"Compadre, you know what to do, eh?" he asked.

"More flights, more pilots, more planes," I answered.

"Yes. And now we have given our word to the Ochoas; it is binding. There can be no problems, *comprende*, Compadre?" He was smiling, but there was menace and death in his eyes.

"*Comprendo*, Rafa. I understand."

I walked to the waiting plane that would take me to Miami, and I didn't look back. I was already busy thinking about George Bergin and how I would get the pilots activated.

CHAPTER SIX

*

The New Order

I bounced back from the Colombian visit full of enthusiasm for my new horizons. Maybe it was all those animals and the billionaire lifestyle that excited me, but any doubts I might have had about my future work in coke smuggling were gone. I was in. I began to figure how I could become indispensable to the cartel and in the process make myself very rich.

I would set up an efficient new transport system of planes, boats, stash houses, and delivery methods that would work as smoothly as a well-oiled machine gun. Sure, the "game warden bust" was a fluke, but it magnified that most obvious flaw in Rafa's air operations, the coordination between pilots and ground pickup crews.

With my visit to the Ochoa ranch, I now knew much more about the hierarchy of the organization. I sorted out in my mind the general areas of responsibility within the overall operation. The Ochoa brothers oversaw the transportation facilities for the rapidly emerging cartel. Crazy Carlos Lehder and the Norman's Cay landing base he had created in the Bahamas had until recently fitted into the Ochoa transport operation, which was why Jorge and the others put up with his antics and drug use.

But Lehder's operation, successful in the late 1970s, had been seriously compromised by 1981. The *Miami Herald* had thoroughly exposed it and the Drug Enforcement Administration kept the secluded island under surveillance. The Ochoas needed new and imaginative air operations in the future. This is where Rafa, with my support, would become an integral part of the cartel's transport system.

My main job was to set up the coke flights from Colombia to the United States. Carlos Correa, owner of the airfield in Colombia's north-ernmost town of Acandí, would be instrumental in our landing, loading, and taking off again for the flight back to the U.S. with two to four hundred kilos. Then it would be my responsibility to get the cash back to the cartel in Medellín, where Pablo Correa, as chief of money laundering, would receive the bundles of bills and put the currency into Colombian and Panamanian banks.

Pablo Escobar, whom I hadn't met on my first visit to the Ochoas, filled two important functions on behalf of the leadership group. He was in charge of political corruption, bribing the police, military, and politicians to keep cartel operations flowing smoothly; and he had the primary responsibility for locating and importing the chemicals needed to manufacture the product for the tropical snowstorm I would soon be unleashing in Florida. Ether and acetone were needed in huge quantities if the demand in America was to be met.

Then there was the matter of enforcement—equipping and training the army of cartel-controlled terrorists, who were becoming increasingly more active in Colombia and the United States. There were always judges to be persuaded to act in the best interests of the cartel, and overzealous police and military officers and even the odd honest politician who could not be bribed. These types only responded to death threats against themselves and their families. This activity was becoming the province of Rodriguez Gacha, "The Mexican," a specialist among the cartel enthusiasts in the act of violence.

Rafa and the other main figures moving the cartel's product usually picked their own personal shooters from old and trusted acquaintances. However, The Mexican always had a cadre of assassins to provide additional firepower when needed. The wicked little city of Pereira, about halfway between Medellín and Cali, had for generations been a breeding ground for whores, pimps, murderers, and assassins of all types, who provided the various warring factions in Colombia with their most ruthless shooters.

Rafa let me know that in addition to transport I would find myself purchasing guns and ammunition for Gacha, looking for ether and acetone to send down to Escobar, and assisting Pablo Correa on the money-laundering front.

I beeped George Bergin on the phone a few days after getting back from the Ochoa ranch. I intended to get together with Russell and the elusive Skip Coltin to have a long discussion on air operations. I wanted to remind Russell that flying illegals into the Miami area was a hell of a lot easier then handling 250 keys of coke. Once the illegals hit the ground running, they were on their own. In the case of a few million dollars' worth of coke, the landing in the U.S. was just the beginning of a complicated pickup and delivery chain.

"I've got bad news, Max," Bergin led off when he answered my beeper call. I was waiting for his call at a pay phone near Miami Lakes, where we had just moved.

"I'm listening, George."

"Skip's dead."

"How? We didn't have anything going down." Then I asked, "What about Russell?"

"Russell wasn't with him. It was an accident. A stupid accident. If Skip had pre-flighted his plane, it wouldn't have happened. The aileron control cable slipped off its pulley. He had been having trouble with it before. He couldn't control the plane and it dove in."

I snapped back, "Yeah, I remember Russell telling me when I talked to him after the meet with Fabio. I remember it so clearly now that you tell me this. He said, 'Skip's so used to those Eastern mechanics doing everything, he won't even pre-flight his own Cessna 210 when he flies it. I do all the pre-flight when we fly south, or it wouldn't get done.' Can Russell handle a flight next weekend?"

"He's kind of shook up about losing Skip." After a pause, he continued. "But I know a couple of kids, hot pilots with the kind of experience you're looking for, who can take over."

"When can I meet them? The Ochoas are red-ass to move their goods. 'America's insatiable demand' has them all worked up."

"I'll set up a meet and beep you." George hung up abruptly.

I thought about Skip, whom I had never met. His death proved the necessity for a vigilant security and safety campaign. I also thought about Jorge Perez and his son Junior. Latinos were impossible pilots, a point the Ochoas understood, which was why they hired only Americans to fly their multimillion-dollar payloads. Yet even a good American pilot like Skip could make a fatal error.

There wasn't much I could do except drive around and wait to hear from George. I didn't want to be anywhere near Miami Lakes when I returned the beep from a pay phone. I spent the next couple of hours inspecting shopping centers, hotel and restaurant parking lots, and other secure and convenient transfer points.

About midafternoon my beeper went off and I stopped at the first pay phone I saw, jumped out of the car, and called George at the pay phone number that showed on my beeper screen.

"We'll meet with two guys who can handle all your work from now on," he said. "We're going to Trail Bowls on the Tamiami Trail tomorrow afternoon at three P.M. Fifteen hundred hours," he added, so there would be no misunderstanding.

I repeated the instructions and hung up. Driving for fifteen minutes through the Miami streets, I spotted another convenient pay phone and beeped Rafa. He was back to me in several minutes.

"Okay. We've got a meeting set up with Bergin and a couple of new pilots. Three tomorrow afternoon. At Trail Bowls on the Tamiami Trail. Pick me up at two thirty."

"That's good, Compadre. Fabio has called three times today asking about when we start flying again."

"Tell him we'll have some word about four o'clock tomorrow afternoon."

When I finally arrived home at five o'clock that evening like any other working man, I felt a sense of satisfaction. Cristina looked gorgeous to me. "Do you like your new home, Cristina?" I asked, after giving her a hug and a kiss.

"It is beautiful. Come sit out on the deck with me. Luis and Consuelo have already met some neighborhood kids their age. We are all happy."

The deck looked out on a scenic view of the lake. Sitting there with my pretty wife, I felt content. I tried to rationalize my new position with Rafa. "You know, sweetheart, we're going to be living as well as any Fortune 500 corporate president."

"But their business and yours are not the same," she pointed out.

"There's not that much difference. It's all supply and demand; buy cheap, sell dear. Some executives sell cars, breakfast cereal, entertainment—I bring the consumer a little recreation, relief from boredom or stress, a rush of euphoria." I grinned at her. "You don't like what I'm saying, do you?"

She frowned. "No. Now you sound like the Ochoas and Rafa."

Even though she had introduced me to the people I was working with, even though they were her people, she didn't like me being involved in coke.

"Hey, like Jorge Ochoa said, there's more profit in providing a little harmless high for uptight *norteamericanos* than in all the oil companies in America."

At two thirty the next afternoon, Rafa and his two shooters picked me up. "Compadre," he greeted me. "I just talked to Fabio. He will be waiting to hear about this meeting."

I waved goodbye to Cristina and climbed into the car. We reached Trail Bowls a little before three, walking into a deafening clatter of bowling balls knocking over wooden pins on forty alleys. On the wall to the left of the door was a bank of telephones.

"Hey, Rafa, what a place to make calls. You can hardly hear yourself, much less what the guy next to you is saying."

"Sí, Compadre. I will call Fabio from here when this meeting is finished."

To the right was a row of pinball machines, and beyond them, pool tables. We turned toward the restaurant and after I bought us each a cup of coffee Rafa and I took a table close to the wall where his shooters stood.

I had just lit up a cigarette and started on my coffee when I nudged Rafa. "Here we go."

George Bergin entered with his two youthful friends. After looking around and spotting us, the three sauntered over to our table.

"Meet Mickey Munday," George said.

We were introduced to a six-foot-two cracker with a red moustache.

"Hi, Mickey," I said, standing up and shaking hands. Rafa kept his seat and waved.

Mickey was wearing a long-sleeved loose shirt, baggy slacks, and a baseball cap that featured a "Mobil" patch on its peak. A mass of red curls billowed from under the cap and dropped to his shoulders.

Chewing bubble gum, he stood awkwardly as Bergin introduced his other companion, a lanky youth about my height, five foot nine, with blond hair, blue-green eyes, his face spangled with freckles. He wore Nike running shoes, jeans, and a sports shirt.

"Meet Jimmy Cooley, as hot a pilot as ever dropped into the 'Glades," Bergin said proudly. "Jimmy's the main pilot here. Mickey's specialty is keeping the planes in top condition. He runs the ground operation."

"Have a seat," I said. Then we got down to business. Our conversation was protected by the constant racket from the alleys. "You guys ever been down to Colombia?" I asked.

Jimmy Cooley spoke for the two of them. "No, but we can learn the way. We've flown a hundred times outta all parts of Jamaica, carrying maybe a thousand pounds of ganja a pop. Colombia wouldn't be no problem for us. Farther away, of course, so a smaller payload, when it all balances out with gas and weight. But what you guys got is worth fifty times more than pot, so it would still be more profitable."

I translated for Rafa. Jimmy's recitation of their capabilities and experience in his born-and-bred Florida redneck accent was punctuated by the snapping of Mickey's bubble gum.

As I would learn after working with them a few months, they both loved danger. Jimmy was into fast cars. He was once stopped doing 130 mph by the Florida state police. Mickey's passion was fast boats. He loved to rip through the narrow canals in an 80-mph cigarette boat.

"What kind of a plane do you fly?" I asked Jimmy.

"We got access to anything that's needed, but our own bird is a twin-engine, 230-mile-an-hour Navajo."

"How much is your plane worth?" I asked.

"Complete with the avionics, modified engines, and some other goodies we've put in it," Mickey answered, "I'd say it was worth all of a quarter mil."

"What kind of a load could you carry on a six-to-seven-hour flight?" I asked.

Jimmy looked at Mickey, who cracked his gum thoughtfully. "Well," Mickey the logistics man said, "we could put in one more extra tank. We'd have to, of course. Jamaica used to be two and a half hours but now that them Jamaicans got this new government that don't cut a deal with Fidel, we gotta fly all to hell and gone around Cuba. Three and a half to four hours it takes, so we already put in one more forty-gallon tank. Wouldn't take much to put in another."

"What kind of payload are we talking about?" I asked.

After another spate of furious gum chewing, Mickey came up with a figure. "Most we could do is a thousand pounds. That'd be pressing it, but hell, Jimmy don't mind, depending on the pay scale, of course."

I translated for Rafa. "Around four hundred keys a flight."

"Course, we got no problem renting a bigger, faster plane," Jimmy interjected. "I been looking at this turbojet that'd move more than a ton of your snow. Plenty of range, go up to thirty-five thousand feet."

Again I translated for Rafa. His eyes widened at the possibilities.

"How many flights a week could they make in their own plane?" Rafa asked.

I asked the question in English and Jimmy answered. "We could do it twice a week. We got us some crackerjack pilots. Almost as good as me," he added. " 'Course, the money's got to be right."

Rafa laughed at Jimmy's modesty when I translated. "You tell them not to worry about the money. There's going to be plenty, more than they can ever spend."

"Even you don't know what a hot pilot with unlimited money can spend," I replied, and then translated for Jimmy.

"Well, what kind of bucks are we talking?" Jimmy asked.

I glanced over at George, who nodded. "I guess George laid down some figures, Jimmy. You want it from me too?"

"Yeah, that would be cool."

"Okay, then. You get thirty-five hundred a key for as much as you can carry. Isn't that what George told you?"

"Yeah. And he gets a grand a key out of that just for the introduction."

I sensed it was time to straighten these kids out a little. "Just so everybody knows how this works"—I looked from Jimmy to Mickey and back—"George is guaranteeing you. Anything bad happens to a load and his ass is on the line. I mean, look behind you. See those two Latinos leaning against the wall?" Mickey and Jimmy looked and turned back to me. "They're shooters. They love their work. And after they find George, they go looking for the pilots. So George, see, is performing quite a service. Okay?"

"Yeah," a chastened Jimmy replied.

"So you bring in, say, a four-hundred-key load once a week, that's way over a million dollars on your end, and George walks with four hundred thousand. You like those numbers? Beats the hell out of flying pot up from Jamaica, doesn't it?"

"Yes, sir," Jimmy replied. "It sure do."

"What did you make? Maybe twenty-five grand a trip?"

"Something like that."

"Even after all your expenses, maintenance, new engines regularly, you're making more money than the head of General Motors, and when you bring in two loads a week you can add on the salary the head honcho at Standard Oil pulls down. Okay?"

"Yes, sir."

"Call me Max. Everyone else does, except the Colombians. They call me Compadre. Now Rafa has some questions to ask you."

As I translated Rafa's interrogation of Mickey and Jimmy, we learned more about their operation. Jimmy was considered a daring pilot, and Mickey had a meticulous sense of logistics. Mickey handled all ground operations, from mechanics and landing zones to pickups and deliveries. From the time the engines started turning in the U.S., on through the landing and takeoff from the supply point, until the final touchdown on some access road or clearing in the Everglades, Jimmy was in charge. One of their trusted pilots flew with him.

It would be a six-and-a-half-hour flight to the pickup point we had chosen on the last trip I made to Colombia. Acandí was just a few miles from Colombia's border with Panama on the Caribbean coast. Relief at the controls was important.

After about an hour of translated conversation accompanied by the cracking of bowling balls knocking down pins, Rafa was convinced we had found a good replacement team for Skip and Russell. He abruptly stood up and gestured for me to follow him. We walked directly to the telephones.

"This is very good, Compadre." Rafa was jubilant. "Better than the way we did it before. Put the call through to Fabio for me."

Even standing beside Rafa as he rattled on in Spanish with Jorge, I could hardly pick up the conversation in the echoing din of the bowling emporium. I made out that Rafa was calling for a test run, say 250 kilos, before trusting the new flying team with a 400-kilo load, and I gathered that Jorge, who also got on the phone, gave the go-ahead.

"Okay, here's how we're going to do it." I translated Rafa's terse orders when we arrived back at the table. "The pilots leave early Friday morning, two days from now, and return Saturday or Sunday. We will take the load from your ground organization on Monday. I'll work with Mickey on that. By the way, they're sending 250 keys on this flight. If all goes well, it will be 400 from then on.

I noticed a disappointed look on George's face. "What the hell's wrong with you, George? So you do a test run and only make $250,000?" I glanced at Mickey and Jimmy. "You guys got anything against pulling down $875,000 after George's take on your first flight with us?"

"Hell, no, Max!" they answered in unison.

"Tomorrow afternoon," I continued, "a Colombian pilot will arrive at the airport here on a commercial flight from Colombia. He will be your guide for this first trip to Acandí. He'll show you how to find your way in. Acandí is the best location for originating coke flights from Colombia, and we'll probably be using it for at least the next few months."

"I only have to be shown once," Jimmy said confidently.

"That's what we want to hear," I said. "Now Rafa wants Jimmy to meet Carlos Correa on this first trip. He is known as the king of Acandí. He handles most of the coke going in and out of Colombia these days.

Carlos personally owns the Acandí municipal airport and controls the military and police in the area."

"What about mechanics, if Jimmy has a problem?" Mickey asked.

"You'll have to bring anything you need with you. Later we'll try to get some spare parts and tools stored at the strip."

"Is there much traffic into Acandí?" Jimmy asked.

"One commercial flight a week. But Carlos brings in an average of five flights of his own a week. That's what pays for making it the best airstrip for our purposes in Colombia."

"We'll be ready to go on Friday," Mickey assured me. "How do we get together with the guide pilot?"

"When Rafa and I pick him up we'll take him to the airport Sheraton. Meet us at the hotel at about four. There'll be a suite reserved in my name. Just ask for the key and come right up." I turned to George Bergin. "Any questions, George?"

George smiled and shook his head. He had much to smile about—unless he or the boys screwed up.

"Okay, see you guys tomorrow." Rafa and I stood up and the meeting was over.

I took George Bergin aside and quietly asked him if Russell Hodges still wanted to fly for us.

George flashed a pained, gap-toothed grin and shook his head. "I don't know what you said to him the last time you talked, but between that and his buddy's fatal plane crash, he's split the scene, quit while he was ahead." He paused thoughtfully. "Russell's the only one of us I know who saved every cent he made. The last thing he said to me was that not you, not me, not the state of Florida nor the Bahamas would ever see him again. Ever!"

"Well, good luck to him then," I answered. "He was a pretty good guy. I hope life treats him well."

Outside, I watched Mickey and Jimmy pile into the tow truck which was apparently their daytime vehicle of choice and drive away, followed by George Bergin. I hope this is the beginning of a sharp operation, I thought, then climbed into Rafa's car.

With the first totally Max-directed mission coming up, I found myself in a state of excitement dampened only by the gnawing awareness that if anything went wrong I was second in line, after Rafa, to bear the brunt of the Medellín cartel's wrath. A fatal wrath.

The next day Rafa and I met the late afternoon flight from Barranquilla and picked up the guide pilot. I was happy to see it wasn't the Colombian pilot that only a merciful Jehovah had prevented from killing us all. Hernando was his name, a young, respectful man, and he spoke passable English. We took him to the nearby Sheraton Hotel. Up in the suite we had rented, Jimmy, Mickey, and George Bergin were waiting, charts spread out over a large table in the living room.

After shaking hands with Hernando, Jimmy ran a pencil line from Miami, out across the Bahamas north of Cuba and Haiti, and then south through the Mona Passage between the western tip of Puerto Rico and the eastern tip of the Dominican Republic. From there a straight southwesterly course would take them close to Acandí, where Hernando would show them how to navigate into the airstrip.

Thursday night I started sweating. I didn't know what time our men would be taking off or when they would land in Colombia. If something had to go wrong, I thought, let it be on the leg down. Once the Colombian cargo had been loaded aboard the plane, the accountability was on my shoulders.

On Friday Rafa and I briefly visited the new stash house I had rented just a few days before my visit to the Ochoa ranch. Chava was there, the man living with her having gone off to "work." The remote-controlled garage door opened smoothly. All was prepared for what would be a relatively small first stash.

"Things look good here, Rafa. Now let's go see Edgar Blanco."

We drove to Kendall and located the Ochoa town house, which was indistinguishable from the hundreds of others that lined the wide streets of this development.

Edgar Blanco was in his early thirties, blond hair, blue eyes, about my height. He was certainly as unlikely-looking a Colombian drug dealer as you could find. In his sports shirt, Sportif shorts, and Topsiders, he looked all-American.

Until I came along, Rafa ordinarily had taken an entire load to his stash house and then delivered the Ochoas' share to Edgar a day later. This didn't make sense to me. Well over half of every load was owned by the Ochoas. They sold the extra space on the flights to other Colombian distributors who dealt in five- to ten-kilo loads—they seldom sold to the same individual twice. I knew that finding these miscellaneous characters, delivering the stuff, and collecting their money was the biggest problem we had. Rafa had become one of the main importers as well as the transportation boss for Jorge and Fabito.

"Compadre," Edgar greeted me. "I have been thinking about your proposition, and I talked to Jorge this morning."

"What did he say?"

"He told me to make the decision and he would back me." Edgar smiled broadly. "And since you are right, that most of every shipment is ours, I will go along with you. We will pick up the loads when they come in, take out our share, and deliver the rest to you."

"Thanks, Edgar." The less I had to transport and stash, the safer I was. It was a nice shortcut. Already I had formed a plan to rent stash houses by the month through a real estate agent I found named Joan Campenella of Vintage Homes Realty. Before we were through, she would also be selling guns to Rafa for export to Colombia on the down legs of our flights.

I spent Saturday afternoon driving around Miami with Rafa, expecting my beeper to go off at any moment. We were both nervously awaiting notification that the plane had left Acandí.

Hours passed. Then the beeper startled me and I saw the code number we had been waiting for come up on the screen.

"That's it!" I said. "Ten number sevens." I drove to the nearest pay telephone and put through the call to the Ochoas' office in Kendall. In moments I was speaking to Edgar.

I listened a moment and then flashed a triumphant smile at Rafa. "The plane left Acandí a half hour ago."

I looked at my watch. Seven thirty. The plane would be landing sometime after midnight. With the shooters' sedan behind us, I drove Rafa back to his house. His wife, Odila, a plain, petulant little Colombian girl, was waiting for him. I knew that the moment he was in the house he'd start freebasing.

That night I lit cigarette after cigarette. Cristina watched me uneasily. I had resolved never to tell her anything about the business, but she knew something was up. Wisely she didn't ask.

I couldn't sleep until after midnight. I had no sooner closed my eyes, it seemed, when the phone rang.

On the other end Mickey's voice rang out, "Congratulations!" Then *click*.

I pulled myself out of bed and looked at the clock. It was three thirty. I dressed and headed for Rafa's house.

It took fifteen minutes to get there. There were lights on inside as I walked up to the door and rang the bell. Odila, her eyes smudged with fatigue, let me in. "He is sick tonight," she said simply. She led me to the sitting room in the back of the house. Rafa was sitting on the floor, a box of Marlboro cigarettes beside him.

As out of it as he was, Rafa knew the reason for my visit and grinned broadly. I repeated Mickey's salutation in Spanish. *"Felicitaciones!"* Then I added, "The new era has begun. I'll work out the delivery and Edgar's pickup on Monday."

There was no sense sitting around with Rafa when he was coked up. He was capable of anything, so I said good-night to a sad Odila and left.

My first transaction, the beginning of what I liked to think of as "the new order," began late Monday morning.

By midmorning on Monday, Rafa had sobered up from the freebasing, and we drove over to Denny's on NW 67th Avenue. We took a window seat overlooking the parking lot and ordered coffee. Mickey soon arrived in the tow truck and parked in front of our window. A few minutes later two cars drove up. The drivers locked their cars and walked into Denny's, sitting at the far end of the restaurant from us.

Mickey, carrying a copy of the *Miami Herald*, walked in and sat at the table with Rafa and me, laying the folded-up paper beside me.

"Hey, how was the fishing?" I said it to Mickey, and called for more coffee. As we talked about fishing and forty-pound test line, I slipped my fingers between the folds of the newspaper. They touched two sets of car keys. I closed my fingers over the keys and casually moved my hand from the table, dropping the keys in my pocket.

After a few minutes I stood up and left Denny's, walking across the parking lot to the McDonald's opposite. Inside I saw Edgar Blanco drinking coffee with two men, his drivers. I walked into the men's room and up to a urinal. Unzipping my pants I placed the two sets of car keys on top of the urinal as Edgar walked in and stood at the urinal beside me. Neither of us made any sign of recognition. Then I zipped up my fly and walked away as Edgar reached over for the keys and pocketed them.

I ordered a cup of coffee at the counter and watched out of the corner of my eye as Edgar handed each of his men a set of the keys. Soon all three left. I walked out of McDonald's in time to see Edgar's two drivers back out of the parking slots beside the tow truck.

I tried to conceal my elation as I stepped back into Denny's and slumped into the chair between Mickey and Rafa. All of us had to restrain ourselves from exploding with the triumph we felt as we talked about fishing, women, and boats.

After about ten minutes I ended the small talk. "I gotta move out. I'll be in touch." Rafa and I walked out and got in his car.

By now another driver had come and picked up Mickey's two men who delivered the cars, their trunks loaded with coke-filled duffel bags. Mickey, furiously chewing a wad of bubble gum, drove off in his tow truck.

The following day we drove over to southwest Miami for the first of many weekly visits to the Ochoas' office in the Kendall town house. There we made arrangements for delivering our part of the load to my latest stash house and picking up the cash in twenty-, fifty-, and hundred-dollar bills for smuggling in their share. In all, it would take about three days to deliver the goods and get all the money from the people who had bought space for their keys of coke on the flight.

CHAPTER SEVEN

*

California Cowboys

It was the late summer of 1981 and, for once, things in my life had settled into a regular rhythm, almost a harmony. Once or twice a week I went to breakfast with Mickey Munday or Jimmy Cooley, shot the breeze with them, and picked up a load. I never touched the dope, just made sure the switch went okay, collected the money later, and paid the pilots. I was working, tops, two hours a week.

I did a lot of fishing, mostly chartering boats in Miami and the Keys. I loved to fish; it took my mind off everything, including the magnitude of what I was doing. The air operations were going well; we never brought in less than four hundred keys a load, almost nine hundred pounds of pure-grade cocaine—87 percent pure or better. The stuff was being sold for about thirty-five grand a key on the street, wholesale, so each load was worth about fourteen million bucks to the cartel. Double that if we did two in a given week. Rafa couldn't believe his good fortune.

He still scared the hell out of me. He was freebasing whenever the spirit moved him. And it bugged him that I had so much free time.

My free time didn't last very long. Rafa walked into my house one morning with that traveling look in his eye and said, "Pack your bag, Compadre."

"Where we going?"

"California."

"What's goin' on?"

"We're working on a new route to the West Coast."

"I thought that was Juan David's territory."

"Juan David has asked for a little help."

"But they've been getting stuff out there."

"Using mules. Using their people to carry the shit out there from Miami."

"Is George Bergin coming?"

"Yes. We leave tomorrow." Rafa smiled. He loved to do things on the spur of the moment: just think about it a little, and do it. He liked keeping it all in his head, keeping control, and keeping me off balance.

On the flight out to Los Angeles, Rafa slept. He had been freebasing steadily the night before. George Bergin carried his 151-proof Myers's with him, and poured it into his Coca-Cola. He filled me in on Morgan Hettrick, whom I was about to meet. They had been old pot smugglers together, and their friendship went back twenty years. For five hours, with the help of the Myers's rum, I heard about George and Morgan and the good old days.

When we landed, Rafa and I waited while George rented a car on his credit card. Then at my insistence I drove the car out to Oxnard. I didn't want George drinking and driving. We checked in to the Hilton, and drove directly from the Hilton to Camarillo.

"The plane should be in by the time we get there," George said as we started out.

"What plane?" I asked.

"The plane that left yesterday for Colombia, Compadre," Rafa said, smiling.

"How come nobody told me?"

"You didn't need to know before, and now you do," Rafa said.

"Why now, then?"

"Because you're going to be running this deal," George said. His breath was strong and sweet-smelling from the rum; it permeated the car like a fog. "Turn here. This is Camarillo. The airport is straight ahead."

"What are they flying?" I asked.

"Cessna 210s."

"They fly single-engine planes from California to Colombia and back? I can't believe it."

"Yeah, thirty-six hours of air time, no sleep. They're Californians, what can I say?" George shrugged.

"They're crazier than Colombians," I said.

"Here's the airport, and there's the hangar." George pointed to a hangar at the end of the runway. The airport was strictly for private planes.

"Nice setup," I said. Morgan Hettrick obviously had the entire hangar solely for his business. "He must do all right."

"He's been doing all right for years. Ran guns for Somoza, built some experimental aerospace parts under NASA contracts, and he was involved with the original design for the Lear Jet with Lear himself, at least according to Morgan. He's been in aviation for a long while," George said, as we all climbed out of the car.

The three of us walked into the offices and I came face to face with Morgan Hettrick. The minute I saw him I knew we would not get along. He was a big ugly grizzly bear with tortoiseshell-rim glasses—thick, like the bottoms of Coke bottles. I guessed him to be in his mid-fifties, a little over six feet, and around two hundred and sixty pounds. But the most distinctive thing about him was his stink. Stale sweat. Behind him his wife rose and walked over to us to say hello. She seemed to inhale a little deeper as she passed her husband.

She too was past fifty, a stout, belligerent woman, almost a mirror image of her husband. I knew I wouldn't like her, either.

"We just heard from the boys," Mrs. Hettrick said. She knew Bergin, and could understand why Rafa was there, but she was staring hard at me. She had cringed at my Jewish name when George Bergin made the introductions.

"They called six hours ago from Texas," she continued. "Should be here any moment."

She walked over to her husband's desk and picked up two framed photographs. "This is Buzzy, Morgan's son, a terrific pilot." She waved the photo in the air. "And this is Jimmy." She put Buzzy's photo on the desk and clutched the second photo to her ample breasts. "Jimmy, my boy. He's the co-pilot."

"Yes, dear." Morgan smiled at his wife and walked over to a huge map on the wall. He described the journey to us. "The boys fly down the Pacific side, staying low and almost following the coast, then they cross into Colombia at Buenaventura, pick up the shit at Montería, and fly back up the other side, the Atlantic; same basic drill—fly close to the shoreline, low and slow. Through the Yucatán and a straight shot across the Gulf of Mexico to Texas, refuel, and then cross-country to our little setup right here in sunny California." He smiled at us. While he was talking I'd had to move away from him, his smell was so strong. His wife saw me back up and moved in even closer, almost cuddling him. Her nostrils flared, inhaling as she looked at me defiantly.

Morgan slipped away from her embrace and went to look out the window, passing Rafa and George Bergin as he went. They both crinkled their noses.

It wasn't missed by his wife. She looked directly at me. "You know, Mr. Mermelstein? You know what I like? A horse runnin', lathered up.

There's nothing sweeter than the smell of a horse sweatin' after a heavy run. That's what I tell Morgan, ain't it, honey?"

"Yeah, that's them, right on time." Morgan Hettrick pointed to a speck in the sky.

Ten minutes later the single-engine Cessna 210 was down, and we were introduced to Buzzy Hettrick and Jim Crowder, the pilots. Crowder was slightly retarded, and had that distant look in his eye. Bone-deep fatigue had settled into both men; thirty-six hours in the air cramped up in a small plane would do it to anyone. I helped with the unloading, and noticed four of the duffel bags were open. "What's this?" I said to the slow-witted Crowder, pointing at one of the open duffels.

"That's our oxygen tent," Buzzy said, as he walked over to me, smiling. "We unzip one of them duffels, shake it up, stick our heads inside and breathe deeply, two or three big breaths, and we're good for another few hours."

"Maybe so," I laughed, "but you guys sure look like hell."

"Yeah, we ain't going to win no beauty contests," Buzzy said, punching Jimmy Crowder on the arm.

Rafa pulled me aside and asked me to drive the rented car into the hangar to load it. As I brought the car up to the plane and the hangar door closed behind me, I saw George Bergin move toward Rafa and heard him yelling.

"Rafa, what are you doing with that car?"

"Loading it," Rafa said, staring hard at George.

"No chance. This car is rented in my name. You're not using it. Go rent one under your own name!"

"You're making a thousand a key and you won't use your car?" Rafa asked.

"If we get busted they'll put me away forever," George wailed.

"If they bust us, we all go away forever, anyway. What the hell difference does a car make?" Rafa snarled. The hangar went dead quiet.

Morgan Hettrick was a wary animal, an old soldier of fortune. He had seen Colombians in action before. He knew Rafa would kill George right there on the spot, blow his brains out. Hettrick broke the pregnant silence. "Hey, you guys, take it easy. Use my car." He pointed to a big gray Cadillac.

"You sure?" Rafa said.

"Yeah. What do I care. If you get stopped we're all going to the slammer anyway. What difference does it make if the car's in my name or not."

Hettrick shrugged his massive shoulders in acceptance of his fate, the flesh rolling down his massive body like a wave in a waterbed.

After the Cadillac was loaded, George Bergin told Rafa he would meet him back at the hotel. But Rafa, with murder still in his eyes, ordered George immediately back to Miami. George knew he was eyeball to eyeball with the grim reaper and immediately slid into his rental car and drove out of the hangar.

Morgan Hettrick handed me the keys to his Cadillac and said, "Drive careful. I love this car and I need to get paid for the hundred keys in it. This Caddy is now worth $450,000 to me," he quipped, patting the trunk.

"I'll take those car keys," Rafa said. "I'll drive."

"No, Rafa. I'm driving," I said.

"Why?"

"Number one, you drive like a maniac. Number two, you're upset, so you'll drive even worse than usual. And number three, you're a dark Colombian with a fuzzy head of hair. All we need is a state trooper to stop us because of the way you look."

Rafa waited a second before answering, deciding what he should do, then he smiled. "Okay, I'll be the navigator."

We got in the car and took off, the map open between us.

"Where to?" I asked.

"The Marriott at the airport."

I was glad George Bergin was gone. I knew that when Rafa sat down later at the hotel, had a few drinks to celebrate, and thought about the scene in the hangar, he would have taken out his gun and shot Bergin.

We drove to the Marriott and left the car in the parking lot. In the restaurant, Rafa made the connection with the pickup man, Rafael Esmeralda, and his son Juan, who eventually joined us just long enough to pick up the car keys. Juan, like most of the Colombians in the trade, was young, in his mid-twenties. His father Rafael was the biggest supplier in the Los Angeles area and boasted of his heavy-user customers in the movie business.

Taking the car keys, Esmeralda disappeared for an hour and a half. When he returned he said, "It's done," and handed the keys back to Rafa.

"What about my money?" Rafa asked.

"It'll take a couple of days. I'll call you."

Rafa just shrugged. On the way back to the Hilton in Oxnard, Rafa said we never had to worry about Esmeralda, Juan David Ochoa personally guaranteed him. At the hotel we called Morgan Hettrick to let him know everything was okay and we would have his money in a couple of days.

Two days later Esmeralda brought us shoeboxes full of money in the parking lot and handed them to Rafa. We took the money out to Hettrick in a duffel bag, $450,000 in hundreds, fifties, and twenties. Rafa thought we should play a little trick on Hettrick. He hated Hettrick's smell, he said it reminded him of the barrio when he was a kid. So we bought a stick of Right Guard deodorant and stuffed it into the bag. Hettrick opened the bag, took one look at the deodorant, picked it up and threw it over his shoulder. "This shit is for fags. I like it natural, and so does my old lady. Any objections?"

"Just count the fucking money," Rafa spit out at him.

After Morgan counted the cash they planned the next pickup for two weeks later.

Rafa said, "Max will be back next week to help."

It was the first I had heard that I would be returning to California. "Alone? Just me? Thanks for all the notice," I said.

"You want to bring somebody, bring somebody. But I'm not going to be with you. You know the people. It'll keep you busy, Max. All you been doing in Miami is sitting around and jerking off," Rafa chuckled. "This will expand your education. Besides, it's for Juan David, and we do what the Ochoas ask, eh, Compadre?"

Two weeks later to the day I was back in California with one of Rafa's boys and the delivery went smoothly.

On the third trip I decided to bring Cristina along with Edgar Diaz, a great gofer, delivery boy, and bodyguard. Rafa trusted him implicitly; he was sent with me both times previously because he knew the people in California, and we believed this job was going to be an easy turnover. It turned out to be a nightmare.

Morgan Hettrick had moved to the Mojave. He liked the desert, it was more isolated, and it was easier to control who was coming and going. Cristina, Edgar, and I flew out to Los Angeles and checked into the Marina Del Rey. Morgan came to the hotel and gave us directions to his new hangar. I made a practice run with Edgar Diaz and we set up to be out at the field to meet the delivery at ten the next morning.

The next day Edgar and I drove out in a rental car to meet Morgan's boys. We picked up the dope and loaded it into Morgan's Cadillac. Edgar drove, and I followed in the rental car. Back at the Marina Del Rey, I called Edgar Blanco, who ran the office in Miami, to tell him I had the stuff.

"Who gets it?" I asked Blanco.

"Three people."

"What the hell do you mean, three people? Edgar, it's only supposed to be one person."

"Well, it's three people. You've got to make three separate deliveries."

"How do you expect me to make three separate deliveries? I'm here in a goddamn hotel with my wife!"

"Compadre, no one asked you to bring your wife, and it ain't my problem. You're out there, you deal with it."

So Edgar Diaz and I made three telephone calls, and waited. Three cars showed up as the hours passed, one at a time, and pulled in next to the Cadillac and we did the switch right there in the parking lot of the Marina Del Rey Hotel. It took all day and most of the night. Edgar Diaz did not sleep. He had to stare out the window all night, waiting for the pickup cars to come.

When we were finished, I was shaking so bad I almost fainted. I had just violated every rule that I had been so careful to set up: I had used the same car three times, I had handled the shit personally, and I had used the same spot for three deliveries.

It took me the next two days to calm down, and I vowed never again would I be caught in such dangerous circumstances.

I couldn't wait to get out of there and back to Miami. From the money I received, I took out $12,000 for personal expenses and stuffed the rest into two garment bags. We carried the bags onto the plane and placed them into the overhead compartment. There was $450,000 in cash hanging over my head for the entire trip home.

After that trip, Hettrick boosted his loads up to two hundred kilos a trip, and I changed everything. We set up safe houses, hired a full-time employee, and bought a fleet of cars, so that it was just like our Miami operation.

And that's how we got started in California, which was to become the cartel's greatest market. A stinky wild-assed seat-of-the-pants pilot and his Smilin' Jack kids and a bunch of coked-up Colombians who had trouble planning their breakfast.

It seems so strange from my vantage point now. I can still see Edgar Diaz standing at that window in the Marina Del Rey, staring out into the California smog, waiting for the pickup cars to come. And I can still see Morgan Hettrick tossing that stick of Right Guard over his shoulder.

Like yesterday.

CHAPTER EIGHT

*

Jumping Bail and the Tampa Bust

It was September of 1981 and the boys were getting cocky, things were too good. Everybody was making the kind of money that made you thumb your nose at even the wildest lotteries.

I would sell five keys to some Colombian for $30,000 a key, or a total of $150,000. By the next day the Colombian had adulterated my pure stuff, just off the plane, by 20 percent, adding enough quinine or amphetamine (better known as speed) or inesitol (powdered vitamin B) to produce six cut keys. He sold the six kilos he had created, claiming it was "pure" stuff, for $30,000 a key, making a quick profit of $30,000 in a day or two.

Some other lowlife Colombian bought the cut key and made it into a key and a half by further adulterating it. Then he sold this hashed-up kilo and a half to black street dealers in measures of one-eighth of a "pure" key, selling twelve one-eighths of a key and pocketing his profit.

The street peddlers took their one-eighth of a key and added more cut to double it to one-quarter key, then sold it on the street by the gram, a quarter key becoming 250 grams, for $80 to $100 a gram.

The money derived from the pure stuff we brought in from Colombia kept a huge coke-hungry army of dealers and petty pushers driving their fancy cars around the slums of America's cities.

Edgar Blanco, working out of Miami, was the cartel's main man for the entire United States. He was calling the shots, and life was sweet. Edgar distributed the pure cocaine to his recognized main dealers in the major cities of the country. Nobody closely associated with the cartel dealt in anything less than multiple kilograms of coke straight from Colombia. We never even saw street peddlers.

I helped Edgar launder the money, picking up anywhere from three to ten million dollars in cash from the money houses and loading it on our flights to Colombia. Word went down to the Ochoas, who notified Pablo Correa that the money was on its way; when it was received we were notified. Cash was always bundled into packages containing exactly one hundred bills. Whether they were twenty-dollar bills or one-hundred-dollar bills, they were always packaged in bundles of one hundred of the same denomination. This made counting the money easier. I had found that one million dollars in clean hundred-dollar bills exactly filled one shoebox.

Of course, all the money wasn't shipped back to Colombia. The cartel also acted as a bank for legitimate Colombian corporations. Edgar had chief tellers and even officers at select banks in Miami on the cartel payroll who would accept large cash deposits without reporting them. Then when the coffee or sugar or cement company needed more than the paltry $25,000 they were allowed to spend in dollars outside Colombia, they could go to one of the cartel's banks in Miami and negotiate whatever size narco-dollar checks they wanted—in the millions if they needed it—to buy plant equipment. They would then pay the cartel, through Pablo Correa, in Colombian pesos. The cartel was fast becoming the mainstay of the entire Colombian economy.

From time to time Jorge Ochoa would call me and tell me to contact some Colombian businessman and hand him three million dollars, or five million, or whatever. I would meet the person and drive around while he counted the money and gave me a receipt for it. Back at whatever house I was using for an office at the time, I would call Jorge in Colombia and tell him that the money had been delivered and I had the receipt. Needless to say, I did not like keeping such incriminating pieces of paper in my possession. As soon as the money was paid in pesos to Correa or the Ochoas, I was notified, and I immediately destroyed the receipt.

Edgar Blanco enjoyed life. He had a beautiful thirty-six-foot twin-screw Bertram cabin cruiser tied up at the Dinner Key Marina on Biscayne Bay. It seldom left the dock. Edgar's chief recreation was smoking pot while sitting in his boat, named, none too subtly, the *Captain White*.

In late September, Edgar decided to take a week off and head out to California for some fun.

On the flight to Los Angeles he thought he would have a little extra fun; he lit up a big fat joint and proceeded to fill the first-class cabin with the heavy, unmistakable aroma of marijuana.

When the flight landed, Edgar was met by airport police. They found two grams of coke in his pocket and a couple of joints. They sped Edgar off to jail and charged him with possession, an immigration violation, and imperiling an interstate flight.

Gabriel Jaime Herrera, who at the time was the Ochoas' accountant and was destined to become the cartel's main man in Panama, called me and said, "Max, we got trouble, big trouble. Edgar Blanco has been busted. What can you do to get him out of the slammer?"

"Leave it to me," I said confidently.

By this time I had met a knowledgeable young Miami all-purpose lawyer named Martin Senior. He and his partner Bill Joyce could do the legal work themselves or find a specialist to do what had to be done. The cartel, unlike the Mafia, did not have lawyers on retainer. It fell to me to go out and hire the legal help to do the job. We paid top dollar, so there was never any shortage of lawyers to call upon.

I was carrying $100,000 in cash when Marty and I flew out to Los Angeles to handle Edgar's case. Marty called a California attorney, who expedited the bail hearing. Bail was set at $50,000. It turned out that Edgar had been deported once before. Unlike Florida, which had recently tightened its regulations on dope charges, California accepted a $50,000 cash bond. It would be another couple of years before California learned about Colombians.

When I delivered Edgar to the Miami office, a call came in from Jorge Ochoa. "Get your ass on a plane, Edgar," he said. "You're coming home." And that was the end of Edgar's reign as the cartel chief of operations in the United States.

I figured that Edgar's name was probably on some government holding list, so I used my passport to buy a ticket and pick up a gate pass, gave them to him, and watched Edgar jump bail on the next flight to Colombia.

Edgar's replacement was a man called "Tocayo," which basically means a person who has the same name as someone else. It would be like an American introducing two people with the same name, saying, "This is George and this is Ditto." His real name was Jorge Luis, and so there would be no confusion with Jorge Luis Ochoa, they decided to call him Tocayo.

Tocayo moved in and took over Edgar Blanco's job. He proceeded to make personnel changes he felt necessary. Mostly he wanted to get laid and thought he was God's gift to women, so he brought in a lot of pretty

Hispanic girls to do jobs that were formerly done by men. That, together with his bad judgment, proceeded to play havoc with the whole operation.

Tocayo's Miami operations started to get busted. Not mine. I wasn't the only transportation source, I was just the only one that didn't get caught.

It was when Tocayo started doing business with the Cubans that he ran into trouble with his coke flights. The DEA had managed to infiltrate an informant into a group of Cuban pilots, and the cops were waiting at the private airport when the plane with Tocayo's load of 250 kilos of coke landed. The agents followed the two delivery cars directly to the stash house and arrested everyone in sight. But they missed one person, who ran off and called Tocayo.

One of the traffickers arrested was Margarita, who had recently been divorced by Pablo Correa. The fact that she had been married to Correa until the year before gave her some status—enough to make Tocayo jump, anyway. Another woman, named Adriana Posada, and a kid by the name of Julio Cesar, were taken in with her.

It was the third bust that Tocayo was responsible for in a month. He called me to say that these people had gone down and he wanted my lawyers to get them out of jail. I told him to get lost.

I had had trouble with him only the week before, on a California load he was in charge of. I called him to get the list of deliveries that were to be made. I was already annoyed that I had to find three different customers. After the deliveries were completed, I called him up a second time to tell him everything was fine.

"No, it isn't," he said. "I made a mistake on one receiver. Go get the fifty keys back from this guy and deliver it—"

"Just a minute! You outta your mind? I made those deliveries once and I'm not looking for those people again. I'm not delivering that shit again. You're crazy."

"I made a mistake. You gotta do it."

"Well, I ain't doing it. You want it done, you come out here and do it yourself."

"I'm going to call Jorge," Tocayo screamed.

"No, you won't, asshole. *I'm* calling him." I slammed down the phone and called Jorge in Colombia. I explained the situation, telling him the guy didn't know what he was doing, he was going to get someone killed.

"Don't worry about it, Compadre," Jorge said. "I'll straighten it out, you go back home." And so I did.

When Tocayo called to ask me to help him out after the bust, I wasn't anxious to help, but I met with him anyway.

He was panicked about the arrest of his four people. "Just get them out, Max. I'll pay the bills. I'll be responsible."

"No, man. Your word sucks as far as I'm concerned. It's no good."

"Well, whose word do you want?"

"I want Jorge's word."

"You got it, Max," he says.

"I got it when the *real* Jorge says I got it—not you." I pointed to the phone.

Tocayo spoke to Jorge and when he was through explaining the situation he handed me the phone.

Jorge told me, "I will guarantee what has to be done. Get them out of jail."

"I'm worried," I said. "I'm worried about the whole goddamn operation."

"Compadre, do not worry, Jota is on his way." Jota was the only name I ever heard for Gabriel Jaime Herrera's replacement. Later, together, these two men would oversee billions and billions of dollars as the two financial officers of the cartel.

"Consider it done, Jorge," I said, and hung up.

I called Martin Senior; he and Bill Joyce went immediately to the jail where the prisoners were being held. With all the confidence of high-priced lawyers, they asked for Tocayo's people by name. That was a mistake. A hush fell over the room. The Colombians had not been allowed a phone call yet. No lawyers had been notified. No one even knew that these people had been arrested. So how the hell did these lawyers know?

Nobody told the cops they had missed a perpetrator hiding in the stash house, who had called Tocayo. The lawyers had shown up a little too soon and set off alarm bells. Picking up on the strange vibes, Marty and Bill backed off immediately. They went for coffee to think it out.

Bill, an expert in immigration law, returned to the jail and quickly learned that the Colombians were charged with immigration violations and were being held by the INS. The drug charges had not been filed yet by the DEA.

Bill called me with a brilliant idea. "All they are doing now is holding them as illegal aliens," he explained. "The DEA have been dragging their feet in making out the paperwork on the drug charges. They believe that your friends will be held by the INS. But with illegal aliens, we have the right to demand an emergency deportation hearing."

"So?" I asked impatiently. "What does that mean?"

"It means we go down there, demand a hearing, and tell the magistrate that they admit their guilt as illegals and they want to be deported; that they want to leave the country, voluntarily, and have purchased tickets for the next flight. All you have to do, Max, is bring airline tickets showing a Miami departure as soon as possible. What do you say?"

"Sure, let's do it," I answered.

The lawyers set up an emergency deportation hearing right then and there and we rushed Tocayo's people before the magistrate.

That's the way the law is written. The Colombians could not believe it; in their country this would take weeks. The judge looked over the documentation and airline tickets, slammed down his gavel, and said, "So ordered!" The INS had to personally escort them to the airport and onto the plane. The agents shoved them on board and slammed the door behind them.

I smiled to myself at the image of the DEA men flying down the corridors of justice with papers in hand and discovering that the four Colombians were already out of the country. I had learned through experience that these federal agencies never liked to talk to each other, so I just used it against them. I think the DEA scratched their heads a long time after that, trying to unscramble what the hell had happened.

It took the courts a lot longer than it ever should have to realize that you don't give a Colombian bail; no matter how high you set bail, it's not going to be high enough.

In November, Jorge Ochoa asked me to bring the pilots down to Colombia to meet with him. I spoke to Mickey and Jimmy, but they refused to go to Colombia; they wouldn't fly in a commercial airline and get their passports stamped. They did not want the exposure. I explained their problem to Jorge and he suggested that we meet in Panama. Jimmy still refused to get a passport, and I agreed. He did not want anything filed with the government that carried his photo.

Mickey was a different story. Since he was ground crew, he felt more relaxed about it. So, on November 4, a couple of days after my birthday, we flew to Panama and checked into the Holiday Inn in Panama City. I had reserved a two-bedroom suite. This Holiday Inn was special; not only was there a casino attached to the hotel, there was also extra security on the sixteenth and seventeenth floors. There was a security desk right where the elevator stopped on both floors, and the beefed-up security gave Mickey and me a warm feeling.

At one thirty the next afternoon, the cab driver we had adopted drove us to the Ibero-Americano Bank and we opened accounts. Mickey and I each deposited five thousand in ciphered accounts, numbers only, no names. When I returned to my room there was a message from Edgar Blanco. He had left a room number in our hotel. I called him.

"Ah, Compadre, good to hear your voice. We are all here; we'll meet you downstairs."

"When?"

"Immediately. In the lobby, sí?"

"Sí," I said, signaling to Mickey that the meeting was on.

Minutes later we were in the lobby. Edgar greeted me with a great hug and a kiss on each cheek; he remembered California, and me making his bail. "Hey, Compadre, come and sit with us."

Edgar introduced Mickey to Jorge, and Jorge introduced us both to the man sitting next to him. "This is Pablo Escobar."

I studied him carefully as I shook his hand. Escobar was the boss of bosses, El Jefe of the cocaine trade. He was wearing jeans and a striped soccer shirt. He was tall and thin; of course, everyone looked thin to me in those days, when I weighed almost two hundred and fifty pounds. Pablo had wavy hair and a moustache; he could have portrayed a stereotype Latin lover in a film. Women would find him handsome. He was conservative in his greeting, very confident, talking in a low voice, precise and cool. He had been a car thief in his younger days; now he was a billionaire.

Jorge spoke first. "Is everything going well? Are you being treated right?"

"Yes," I said. "They are looking after the repair kits well and the spare parts are being taken care of at each landing strip."

Mickey spoke up and we spent the next fifteen minutes talking about airplane maintenance, routes, any problems we had. It wasn't until this was over that they really got to the point.

Pablo Escobar opened up the subject. "Why can you not increase the loads and put more than four hundred kilos on your planes? Either we must do this or we must run more flights; our warehouses are filling and the distributors are screaming for more cocaine."

Mickey said, "I'll try to run more planes; more than four hundred keys could break us. I'm afraid of what the weight might do to the planes, and we do not want to use bigger planes. I'll see if we can make more flights. We will do our best."

This seemed to satisfy Jorge and Pablo. They understood that we, like them, also wanted to make more money and we would do what we could.

The meeting ended after about an hour, and Edgar stayed with us while Pablo and Jorge made arrangements to leave on their private plane.

There was no question in my mind that they could supply as much product as we could fly. We all knew that we were going to be richer than in our wildest dreams, and it made us high, naturally high, thinking about all that money we were going to make.

Edgar headed off for the downtown duty-free section of Panama that specializes in selling electronics, and he spent about $30,000 on electronic toys, peeling off wads of bills to buy TVs, stereo equipment, and cameras. He then made arrangements to have it flown back to Colombia on the cartel plane that was carrying Jorge and Pablo. The plane would land on one of their estates and no duty would have to be paid. The normal duty on these items in Colombia is 300 to 400 percent.

Edgar joined us that night for dinner in the hotel. Afterward I asked him, "Where do you want to go?"

"I want to get laid," he answered.

"Me too!" Mickey chimed in.

"Me three. Let's go," I said. We all jumped into the back seat of the waiting cab.

For the next three hours we got the full tour of the whorehouses of Panama. The red-light district there is one of the sleaziest in the world, awash in filth, squalor, and degradation; a place where you can buy or see any type of perversion sick minds can invent. For two dollars and up, you can get anything you want in that fetid underworld. And General Manuel Antonio Noriega got a commission on every decadent, indecent, and delightful act that took place there.

We entered a few of these places, places where you wouldn't place your hand on the bar for fear of disease.

The cab driver finally took us to the best the city had to offer, a little place called the Blue Grotto. There, we selected three beautiful girls and returned to the Holiday Inn. We partied the night away, switching girls between Edgar's room, Mickey's room, and my own. We all got our money's worth.

At eleven the next morning Mickey and I caught our plane to Miami. Once I was back home, I had time to think and I realized that the main reason for the meeting was that Pablo Escobar had wanted to meet me. These men of the cartel acted on a personal basis. They said they operated on a business level, but they wanted to know who they were dealing with, and when it was necessary to be personal, they could be personal. They had it down to an art, as I was going to find out when they finally forced a murder contract on me. You couldn't say no to the cartel and live.

On November 12 the incident that changed everything in cartel thinking occurred. Marta Ochoa Nieves, the young sister of Jorge, Fabio, and Juan David Ochoa, was kidnapped from Colombia's University of Antioquia by a group of M-19 communist guerrillas. A ransom of $15 million was demanded by the rebels. The Ochoas refused to pay.

"I am truly sorry to hear that, Jorge," I said when he told me about the abduction. "I wish there was some way I could help."

"There is, Compadre," Jorge replied. "A new closeness has sprung up among all of us in our business. The cartel has never been as strong as it is now. We are united. We are now truly working together. What happened to Marta can happen to any family in our business. I have formed an organization, at least two hundred and twenty-five businessmen so far. We are about to issue a manifesto that we will no longer tolerate ransom kidnappings by guerrilla groups trying to finance their revolutions. Each member of the organization has contributed two million pesos to create an armed force, which we are calling MAS, Muerte á Secuestradores." Death to Kidnappers.

Jorge went on, his voice taut with emotion. "Pablo Escobar and 'The Mexican,' Gacha, have organized the men and are buying guns. We are asking you to send in a heavy supply of arms and ammunition on the down legs of all your flights. The manifesto will soon be issued. We will drop leaflets over the soccer field in Cali just at the start of the game between Cali and Medellín."

"We have three flights scheduled before December. The next one is scheduled for this weekend and it will be full of what you need."

"Thank you, Compadre. I knew we could count on you."

"Again, Jorge, let me express my sympathies, and my willingness to help. And please don't forget that come December, when we have supplied you the guns, all my people need to take some time off to relax and let the government heat blow off."

Within hours I had the word out that I was purchasing weapons. My supplier, the well-stocked Continental Arms Company, came through immediately and and so did my other sources, all legal purchases. Three days later I filled Jimmy's plane with all the Uzi and Ingram assault rifles and riot guns it could hold. In my zeal to accommodate the Ochoas I probably overloaded the plane, but Jimmy pulled it off the field into the air and the first delivery was on its way.

Two more shipments of guns went down in November. I calculated I had armed the cartel's new terror organization with at least a hundred machine guns, including the fearsome Mac-10s, sixty Browning high-power 9mm handguns, and fifty thousand rounds of ammunition.

By the end of November we had started to pick up all kinds of radio traffic. We had two radio rooms monitoring DEA, Customs, FBI, Coast Guard, and Miami police frequencies. We noticed the government agencies were changing their radio frequencies more often. We would lose them for a while, even though our people were sitting at the HF radios day and night. The usual six-hour lulls in official radio communications were now becoming one-hour lulls. Traffic was getting more intense. And as we moved into December, busts were reported in the newspapers every few days. We even heard that AWACs, the special radar-equipped surveillance planes, were being brought in to monitor drug runs. I had established a window, a course heading into Florida for a specific time on a specific night, and our pilots came through. But the Customs and Coast Guard planes were definitely in the air looking for us. The window was being narrowed.

On several occasions they spotted smugglers, not our people, and interdicted the planes, sideslipping at them, getting on their tails, calling for more planes to help, and forcing the smugglers to land, as the feds dropped in on top of them.

The government was putting on a big effort. I could feel it; so could my pilots. There was trouble in the air. With December upon us, all the government agencies were looking for their appropriations money. They wanted to burn up the money they still had in their coffers and try to make splashy headlines in the process. The pilots figured it out too, and came to me.

"Max," Jimmy Cooley said, as he swung his worn Nikes up onto the coffee table. "I got bad vibes, the heebie-jeebies, and so does Mickey. Don't you, Mickey?"

Mickey grunted his assent and said, "Yeah, Max. We brought in nineteen tons in thirty-eight flights over six months. We're worn out."

"I thought you guys never got tired. I've heard you especially never got tired counting your money, at a million a flight."

"Money ain't everything! I don't know who told you that shit about us, but I can tell you, we're drag-ass dog tired and I mean the whole fucking crew. We're beat," Mickey said. Then he smiled. "Don't get me wrong, we like counting the greenbacks. We just need a break."

"Hey, guys, I'll do the best I can. I'm tired too."

The next day I called Rafa in Colombia and he said, "Hey, Compadre, good news." I hoped he was going to tell me that Marta Ochoa had been released. But no. "I got another load ready. Send the boys down."

"Rafa, can we hold off?" I asked plaintively. "The boys don't want to make another run. The Feds are out in force and my flyers are beat."

"What do you mean, they don't want to make another run?"

"Like I said, they're tired and there's too much heat right now, all kinds of air traffic, and the airwaves are full of angry government voices. The government is pushing hard and the boys don't feel safe in the air."

"Hey, Compadre, it's what they get paid to do," Rafa said.

"If I tell them to go they'll go, but—"

"I'll talk to them here and see what I can do," he said, hanging up.

Jorge called me back and asked me to come to Panama for another talk.

The next day, December 4, I was on a plane to Panama. I checked into the Holiday Inn, only Jorge wasn't there. Edgar Blanco and Juan David Ochoa were waiting for me in the lounge.

"Where's Jorge?" I asked.

"He didn't come."

"What do you mean, Jorge didn't come? He called me and told me to get down here. What does this mean? My men are tired and there's trouble in the air with the government."

Edgar gave me a long hard stare. "The negotiations with the M-19 rebels are getting serious. We have kidnapped many of them, including the wife of their leader. We are not going to pay ransom. If Marta is dead, we'll pay in lead and blood."

Juan David said, "I understand you are tired. Let's go upstairs to my room and call Jorge."

We marched up to Juan David's room and got Jorge on the line. Juan David explained everything in great detail to Jorge. When he was through, he covered the receiver with his hand and spoke softly to me. "Jorge says he's sorry, but as long as there are no mechanical problems and you can make it, he wants you to go. We will need all the weapons you can ship down and all available cash possible."

He said goodbye to his brother and hung up. He spoke calmly to me, like a confidant. "Compadre, we have too much inventory backed up in the warehouses and this is the best season for us. Christmas and New Year's parties in America are very festive, and partying means profits, for us, for all of us. We also need the cash for next year's production. Our estimates for the next year are astounding. I am very sorry, but Jorge is right. We need to fly and we need you to do at least four hundred keys."

I sat in silence and listened to Juan David, the oldest Ochoa brother, who had actually started the family coke business to support his love of training and breeding Paso Fino show horses. He was semi-retired now, but still maintained his California share of the cartel action. He looked much like his brother Jorge, except he was thinner and older. There was a certain sadness in his face. His wife had committed suicide and, it was said, he never got over it. She was a heavy coke user and freebaser; the rumor was that she hated the business but became addicted to the stuff, until she finally blew her brains out. Juan David was a careful man, much more reserved than the rest of his family. He was polite, but guarded. Every word was carefully weighed and measured before spoken. He had a goatee and a moustache at this time; at one time or another, they all had beards and moustaches. They changed their appearance as often as they could. It went with the business; we all did it.

There was no threat extended to me, not even a veiled threat. But there was no question in my mind that if I refused, my outfit would never have flown for them again. They would have terminated my operation, and maybe my life. If they asked you to do something for them, you simply did it, that's all.

These were insidious men, ghostlike authority figures who never displayed their power; they didn't have to. I knew by the way people acted around them that they controlled everything and everybody in their web. When I watched Rafa with the Ochoas and Pablo Escobar, there was never any doubt that they controlled him. They could strike fear in Rafa's heart with a single phone call.

I returned to Miami and put in a call to Mickey and Jimmy. "Meet me at the B.K. east," I said.

An hour later we were at the Burger King on 163rd Street and Biscayne Boulevard. We settled down in a booth with our Whoppers and I told them the bad news. "We're going" was all I said.

"Oh, shit!" Mickey said as his teeth sank deep into a double Whopper. "Oh, sheeeeit," he repeated slowly, with his mouth full.

On December 12 Jimmy took off on his second flight in his new 400-mph Conquest turbo jet. He had paid close to a million dollars for it. It could carry five hundred kilograms, so he earned almost all of it back on his first flight. I had jammed it full of guns and ammo on the down flight, along with several million dollars in cash to be recycled in Colombia.

On December 13 I got the dreaded call from Mickey. It was four in the morning. "We got problems, big problems." It was our little code for disaster.

"You on your way over here?"

"Affirmative."

I immediately called Rafa, who answered in a sleepy voice. This time the message wasn't my normal "Congratulations." It was a single word that I uttered: "Problems." That was all I had to say. Thirty minutes later he was sitting in my house, in his pajamas and bathrobe.

"How bad is it?" he asked, sleepy-eyed but alert now.

"Big time. Looks like we lost it all. Mickey should be here any second."

Just then Mickey rang my doorbell and I let him in. He had not slept since the day before, and looked like death. Flopped on the couch, he told us how he had been listening to the operation go down on the police radio and had followed the intercept from the beginning, but he did not have all the details.

"Max, Jimmy called me after he landed. They kept the plane, so Jimmy had to rent a car to get over here."

"He's on his way?" I asked.

"Yeah, but he's coming the slow, complicated way, the old highway across the Glades, to make sure he ain't followed. He's got Harold, his co-pilot, with him."

At ten thirty that morning, Jimmy Cooley showed up at my house. He looked awful. He had just flown fifteen straight hours and been chased all over the skies by the cops. He had not slept in two days.

"Where's Harold?" I asked.

"Home. I dropped him at home."

Jimmy sat down on the floor with a cup of coffee and spread aviation charts on the floor in front of him to explain. "The first mistake was flying the Conquest turbo. We were flying too high and too fast. We penetrated American air space at thirty thousand feet, which automatically means that the Air Force sends up a couple of F-16s to make sure we are not invaders. Right away the Air Force jets track us and they figure us for smugglers.

"It don't take a genius to figure out what we're doing up there, flying in at four hundred miles an hour at thirty thousand feet with no flight plan, does it?" Jimmy asked no one in particular, handing me his cup for a refill. I poured it for him and handed it back. "They called in the cavalry. They called up a couple of Customs planes to join the pursuit, then the DEA sends up two Blackhawk choppers, and suddenly we're a real target and everyone in the fucking world is chasing us."

"What did you do with the dope?" Rafa asked.

"I'm telling you, for Chrissake. It was unreal; it took them two hours to force us down. They chased us back and forth over Tampa Bay. Hell, twice they broke the sound barrier. There must be a million broken windows in Tampa."

"There are," Mickey said. "I heard the Tampa news on the radio. The glass-cutters will be working for the next six months replacing the damn windows."

"We found clouds and disappeared into them. We tried going north and then east. We threw some bags out over Disneyland, for Chrissake. We tried everything but we couldn't shake them. We'd shake the jets, and the choppers would stick with us; we'd lose the choppers, and the Customs planes would be up our ass. The only way I could throw them off was to speed up and lose the choppers, then slow right down to a hundred miles an hour and outslow the jets. They couldn't throttle down anywhere near that. All the while I'm doing this, Harold Johns is tossing the duffel bags out of the plane."

Jimmy Cooley pulled an aerial chart toward him and stuck his finger on Kissimee, right where Disneyland is located. "Four bags were tossed right here. There are going to be some happy campers down there tonight if they find them." He traced his finger across the chart to Tampa Bay and the Gulf. "The rest of the shit wound up here, somewhere in the Gulf of Mexico and Tampa Bay."

"Did they see you ditch the coke?"

Jimmy nodded vigorously.

"They took a lot of photos. I could see them in the chopper clicking away with their cameras."

"So, after you dumped all the dope you let them force you down."

"Yeah, we were sure we couldn't lose them, so we landed at Tampa Airport, and a fucking Customs plane landed right behind us, right on us so we couldn't take off again if we wanted to. They were armed, and madder than hornets. They searched us, handcuffed us, and searched the plane. And they found jack-shit, not even any residue. So all they could do was cite us with some bullshit FAA violations, like not responding to the tower, which they did, and they kept the plane. We stuck to the back roads. We weren't tailed. I even checked for a helicopter tail."

"Not too smart of Harold to go home," I observed. "What else?"

"They gave us subpoenas and checked out our pilot's licenses and said for us to leave the plane for further searching, that's all. But I don't like it. I'm beatin' feet for a while. I told you, Max, that we shouldn't fly this month, but nobody listens to little ole Jimmy, he's just up there flyin' for a living."

I looked over and watched Rafa as he carefully marked down the coordinates of where they had dumped the bags. He looked up at me and said, "Compadre, get up to Tampa and see what you can get out of the newspapers, see what you can hear on the news. I've got to get those newspaper clippings down to Colombia to back us up or we are all in deep trouble."

Jimmy said, "Well, I got a feeling I'm in deep trouble already. So like I said, I'm beatin' feet, hittin' the bricks, boys. I'm headin' for parts unknown till this blows over. I feel the heat and I don't like it." He smiled that slow redneck grin of his and pulled back the peaked cap on his head. Even his freckles looked tired.

"Yeah, you do that, Jimmy. Just keep in touch," I said.

I went upstairs to Cristina; she looked at me and said, "Where are we going?"

"Leave the kids with the baby-sitter. We're going to Tampa for a few days."

Cristina smiled and shook her head hopelessly. Twenty minutes later we were on our way.

As we drove into Tampa, I turned on the radio and it was all over the news: "An air chase between the Air Force and drug smugglers occurred last night. Hundreds of windows were broken in Tampa by the sonic booms of Phantom jets breaking the sound barrier too close to the city."

Cristina took one look at me and my interest in the story and she knew why we had to come to Tampa in such a hurry. She just sighed and stared out the window. Later that afternoon it came out that local fishermen had found some duffel bags floating in the Gulf and turned them in to the local police. The bags were full of coke. That was news and it made the afternoon paper, page one. Cristina and I picked up the papers, spent the night in the Tampa Marriott, and headed back to Miami the next day.

The pilots were in the shithouse now; Jimmy's instincts had been right.

Back in Miami I gave Rafa copies of the newspaper stories, and he headed to Colombia. That same day I got a call from Jorge Ochoa. I wanted to ask about his kidnapped sister but there was enough trouble without bringing up Marta.

"What happened?" he asked.

"What do you mean, what happened? I told you we weren't going and you said *you're going* and we did what you said and we got it good."

"You're right, Compadre. I have no one to blame but myself."

"Rafa's on the way down with the newspaper story. He'll let you know what happened. They got Jimmy's toy, that Conquest he loved so much."

"We should have stuck to our regular planes, slower and lower," Jorge said.

"Right," I said. "But it isn't all bad news. We learned an important lesson today."

"What's that?" Jorge asked.

"Coke floats," I said, and laughed. There was a long, pregnant silence. I could hear almost him thinking on the other end of the line until he understood.

"Expensive lesson," he said.

"Cost of doing business, Jorge. We all lost our asses today."

"Well, Max, I can tell you one thing that has come out of this. We will never again fly our loads into Florida in December." He said it with a sigh.

And the cartel never again flew cocaine into Florida in December, at least not while I was with them.

As I suspected, Harold Johns, Jimmy's co-pilot, made a big mistake. He had stayed at home because he didn't think that they would be able to do anything without evidence, and nobody got to him to warn him. He's still doing time in the slammer. I heard they abused him badly and put so much pressure on him to turn over his people that he tried to commit suicide in jail a couple of times. He never talked.

Jimmy survived the Tampa bust. He was smart, he never drove a car. He always had his girlfriend drive, or one of his pals. He knew that a lot of dopers are pulled in on simple traffic violations when the cops check the crime computer. And he was one hell of a fast driver. He finally went down in 1986 in "Operation Beacon," a government operation I assisted after I became a witness. Jimmy flipped immediately after he was captured. He gave everybody up, on the spot, and became a witness against them.

Jimmy will be out sometime around 1993 if he is a good boy. And I believe he's got plenty of loot buried.

I believe that because one day I asked him to give me some money back for an operation that went sour because of a mistake the pilots made. He said, "I got to go get the shovel."

"Come on," I said. "What are you talking about?"

"It's buried."

"You're out of your damn mind."

"No, Max, it's buried."

And sure enough, when he brought me the money it had that unmistakable smell of freshly turned earth.

Those boys were basic, real Florida crackers with good common sense. They didn't believe in banks, and that's probably why they still have their dough. You can't chase a paper trail if there's no paper.

CHAPTER NINE

*

John Z. DeLorean
and Disaster

Up until the Tampa bust at the end of 1981, the organization I was running for Rafa and the Ochoas was a smoothly functioning and fast-growing machine that had dumped nineteen tons of Colombian snow in South Florida and nine tons in California. Besides Jimmy Cooley, I kept six pilots flying the airways from Colombia up through the windows I had opened into the Miami area. Morgan Hettrick had three pilots bringing the coke into the Los Angeles area.

I had bought for cash a nice $240,000 house in upper-middle-class Miami Lakes. Rafa had paid half a million for his in a more exclusive neighborhood where he could look into the backyard of Governor Graham's brother. The pilots all lived in houses that reflected comfortable though by no means out-of-proportion incomes. We were playing it cool and cautious all the way.

I gave a Halloween costume party to celebrate my daughter's October 31 birthday and my own on November 1. Everybody was there and, Colombian style, they were all carrying their guns. Even I dressed up like a cowboy and packed a .44 single-action revolver in my holster.

There was much to celebrate. The money was rolling in. Rafa in particular, who was personally importing up to twenty keys a flight, was becoming a multimillionaire. George Bergin, too, was making a huge fortune. The only shadow hanging over the group was the fact that Edgar Blanco was no longer with us. He had been popular, and his successor, Tocayo, was considered an obstinate idiot.

Edgar's younger brother, Alfonso Blanco, who was working for the cartel, was at the party with his very pretty and shapely young wife, Marina.

The party was swinging into high gear when George Bergin called for quiet, saying he wanted to make an announcement. He was wearing his regular clothes—a bum's costume—and waving an arm for attention. His other hand clutched a time bomb of 151-proof rum and Coke.

When the room finally quieted down George announced that, effective the next week, he was retiring. In December he would sail off in his forty-two-foot ketch for Grand Cayman Island, where he expected to live for the foreseeable future.

There was considerable cheering, although some of the Colombians, including Rafa, muttered that there were only two ways you got out of this business and we all knew what they were. George continued to toss back rum and Cokes and mingle, brushing up against the women. Then he made an irreversible error in judgment. He put his hand on Blanco's wife's rear end and squeezed. She let out a shriek. Pecas, seeing what George was up to, whipped out his gun and pointed it at George, waving everyone else to get out of the way. There was no doubt that he fully intended to kill George, and there was also no doubt that a lot of people there wouldn't have been upset, particularly since we owed George a pile of money.

Instantly, I drew my .44, strode over to Pecas, and put the barrel to his head. I pointed out that he was a guest in my house and I would have no shooting for any reason. It took a few minutes to talk some sense into him, but slowly he put his weapon back in the waistband of his costume, and the other guests, who had all reached for their guns, relaxed. It took a while, but the party finally resumed. George Bergin never knew how close he had come to being blown away.

In December I took two boxes full of hundred-dollar bills down to George's boat. He was ready to set sail for Grand Cayman and wanted the money we had been holding for him so that he could deposit it in a bank there. An indication of the size of our operation by 1981 was the amount of cash I handed to George Bergin as his share: two million dollars.

The Tampa bust brought us to our knees. By January 1982 we had lost 427 kilos, Harold Johns had been arrested, and Jimmy Cooley was moving around the country in a Winnebago, a fugitive, shifting from place to place like a nomad.

Mickey and I went to work reorganizing the entire Florida operation. We tore down our organization first, liquidating warehouses, getting new warehouses, bringing in new equipment, adjusting personnel. Basically we needed a fresh start.

We knew now that coke floated, and we did a lot of sitting around bullshitting and brainstorming. Mickey told me about all the pot he had brought in from Jamaica in the old days and how a lot of times they'd drop the pot in the water to be picked up by boats below.

And I said, "What about a water drop for the coke?"

"Hey, I'm game for anything," Mickey answered.

"Can it be worked out?"

"Well, if we package it right and we drop it without too much of a shock, maybe it will be all right, maybe it will work."

I nodded. "I'll talk to the people down south and see if they are willing to go along with an operation like that."

Rafa was in Colombia. I called him later that afternoon and laid out the idea to him.

He said, "I don't care if coke floats or not. I just want you to bring the shit in. I don't care how it gets there!"

"Well, do you want to try it or not?"

"I'll talk to the Ochoas about it and let them make the decision."

Rafa spoke to the Ochoas. If we came up with something we thought would work, they told him, they would give it a shot.

So Mickey and I set the wheels in motion and began to plan for a water drop. But first we had to finish cleaning up the existing air operation, and that's what we did for most of January.

At the end of January, Rafa called from Medellín, where he had been living since the Tampa bust. Although Odila had been permanently at their Miami home she was with him in Colombia now. She needed some sort of oral surgery and wanted it done in Colombia. Rafa asked if Cristina and I would come down to visit him. We decided to meet in Cali, the beautiful city where my wife was born. Her family still lived there. Rafa was pleased at the opportunity to get away from his wife and be with Maria Monzano.

Marta Ochoa Nieves was still a captive of her abductors, and as a result of the joint effort by all the drug lords throughout the country to stamp out kidnapping, relations had never been better between the Cali and Medellín traffickers.

We played tourist when we first arrived in Cali, visiting the elegant Palmera area and the old city, shopping and relaxing. We both needed to unwind; 1981 had been a hell of a year.

But after a few days of rest I was ready to go again. Rafa did not show, so I called his house over and over again, always getting the strained, confused replies: he's drunk, he's freebasing, he's delayed at his ranch, he can't make it. Finally, I gave up trying to reach him.

It was Cristina's birthday and she wanted to do something special, so I decided that's exactly what we would do.

I called Nelson Urrego, lab owner and friend, and asked for his help in planning a party for Cristina.

"Let's take over a whole disco," Nelson said.

"You call the shots," I said, and slipped him five thousand dollars.

"Hey, I'm calling the shots and you pay the money? I like that, Compadre."

The party took place on a Friday night at Los Años Locos, "The Crazy Years." It was the newest, trendiest disco in Cali, and we took it over for the night. Cristina was thrilled. She was like a teenager, primping and chatting. It was wonderful to see her that way. She had invited all her old friends and family.

We had a dance band that played salsa and Colombian music. When the band took a break, a group of female impersonators took over. They were good, and the guests loved it. The people—fifty or sixty had turned out—looked great, festive, dressed in their finest clothes and on their best behavior. There was plenty of food and drink, as much as anyone wanted.

The party was a great success and diversion for me. But there was something preying on my mind, something that I had to tell Rafa. The Tampa bust had made it clear to me how real this was, and what the stakes were. I didn't want to go to jail, and I was tired of it. I wanted out of the business.

Rafa finally called two days after the party and said he would be in Cali that afternoon.

He arrived, and we had our talk. To my surprise, he was extremely lucid, perfectly tuned in and aware of every little thing around him. I didn't know whether it was from the drugs, or from a new combination of drugs, or because he was just coming off the drugs. But his eyes were clear, sparkling and unblinking. He stared at me and listened.

I told him I wanted out. I was tired and nervous, especially after the bust. I wanted to get on with my life. I had just bought my house; I had paid cash for it. But I could always earn enough money as an engineer to put food on the table and a roof over our heads. I concluded my long speech with, "Rafa, I will set up the water-drop operation and train someone to take my place."

He was not buying it. He just sat there staring at me, his eyes like two black coals burning right through me. "You're dead, Max," he said. "You just don't know it."

He let a silence hang between us, then went on. "There are only two ways you leave this business, in a cell or in a box."

And that was all he said. We met again later, and he told me he was using another route until I pulled myself together, but I'd better get back in business again, fast. We were all losing too much money. With that he went to find Maria Monzano. The romance between the two godparents of my daughter typified the new Cali-Medellín relationship. Total cooperation reigned. Men from Cali and Medellín were standing shoulder to shoulder and gunning down potential kidnappers. Cali coke was being shipped on Medellín flights to the States. The beginning of a turf war between the Cali traffickers, who traditionally controlled New York, and the Medellín "snowmen," who coveted the northern market, was called off. This spirit of peace and cooperation between the traditional rivals boded ill for the guerrillas.

And sure enough, I had been home only a week when Rafa called to tell me Marta Ochoa had been released by M-19 and not a peso of ransom had been paid. Indeed, it appeared that some sort of alliance between the drug lords and the anti-government rebels had been reached. Product would be more plentiful than ever from both Cali and Medellín. I forgot all thoughts of quitting.

I was no longer involved with California. Rafa had his brother-in-law, Bobby Montanez, running that operation. So I was surprised when, in early February, a call came through from Morgan Hettrick, right out of the blue.

"Hey, Max, how are you? What's going on?" Hettrick asked.

"Not bad. What about yourself?"

I was careful in speaking to Hettrick. Bobby had told me that he was under suspicion for income tax evasion. And Hettrick had basically shut down operations out there because of an ongoing investigation of his operations. I treated the call as if the line was tapped, and I now believe it was tapped.

"By the way, I need fifty aviation tires. Can you help me out?" Hettrick asked. By fifty tires he meant fifty kilos of cocaine.

"I don't know what you are talking about," I said. "I'm retired."

"What about Rafa? Where's he?"

"He's in Colombia."

"Do you talk to him anymore?"

"No, we've separated. We had an argument and I don't want to get involved anymore. I'm retired."

"Okay," Hettrick said. "Do me a favor if you see him. Let him know that I need fifty tires."

"If and when I see him, I'll pass on your message."

And that was our conversation.

The next day Rafa arrived from Colombia and I said, "Morgan called. He wants fifty tires."

Rafa smiled, and his whole disposition changed. "Oh, yeah? Fifty tires, huh? I could use the money. I got some stuff coming in on one of the Ochoas' other routes."

"Be careful, this guy is under investigation."

"Naw, I'm not worried about it. If Morgan says he can handle it, he can handle it."

"Well, be my guest. Do what you got to do," I said, shrugging my shoulders. "But I ain't getting involved in this one."

Two days later Rafa reappeared and said, "I spoke to Hettrick, and I'm going to supply him."

"You're going to supply him with fifty keys?"

"No, I'm going to supply him with only twenty. Hettrick told me they're for some guy who says he's a big shot. The guy manufactures cars."

"Cars? What cars?" I asked, curious now.

"That new stainless steel car that's on the market, the one where the doors come up like this." Rafa stood and raised both his arms over his head, like a butterfly closing its wings.

"You're talking about John DeLorean," I said.

"Yeah, that's the name."

"What the hell is a guy like that doing involved with you?"

"I don't know. All I know is, it's him that wants the fifty keys from me."

"You going to meet with these people?" I asked.

"Yeah, we're all meeting on Grand Cayman Island. I'm going to bring Marta. We're going to let George Bergin set up the entire deal down there. We'll do the money end in the Caymans, Bergin will do it. He's tight with the banks there."

"When do you go down there?"

"In a couple of weeks. I'll let you know."

He did, and I made the charter arrangements, private jet to Grand Cayman for Rafa and Marta Ochoa Saldarriega. She was a first cousin to the Ochoas and a cocaine queen in her own right.

He spent about a week in the Caymans. Whe he returned, Rafa told me what happened down there, over a Chivas on the rocks at my house.

"We met at the Holiday Inn, where I was staying. Hettrick brought DeLorean with him, to meet George Bergin, Marta, and me," Rafa said. "They introduced this big, good-looking guy to me as John DeLorean, and we met a couple of times. We agreed on a price, and I told him only twenty keys this shipment; he pays on time after delivery, then I'll send him more."

"And?" I asked.

"He agreed, and we worked out the details for the delivery in California."

A pained frown came over Rafa's brow. "I had one problem down there. Marta got coked up, out of her mind, and borrowed Bergin's car and hit a tree. It was a miracle she wasn't killed, not even hurt. She was high on freebase. They put her in jail and wouldn't let us bail her out. When I left yesterday, she was still locked up."

"You left with Marta still in jail?"

"George Bergin has some good contacts; he'll get her out. I told Bergin if he tries to touch her I will kill him. I told him to get her out and put her on a plane. I got to make some money, Compadre. I'm sending the twenty keys."

"How? How are you sending it?" I asked.

"I'd like to fly it out."

"You'd better talk to Hettrick about bringing it out there himself, because we can't find Jimmy and my guys just aren't ready. We aren't set up yet."

"I'll send Rodrigo Restrepo in the blue Chevy." Rodrigo was Rafa's cousin.

"Okay, that'll work," I said.

We had modified the blue Chevy with a *caleta*, a hiding place. The back seat was removed and a metal compartment was welded into the trunk and sealed. The result was that a ridge extended about twenty inches into the trunk. Everything was recarpeted so that it looked original. If you opened the trunk you could not see that anything had been modified. The compartment was closed and the seat replaced. There was a special solenoid switch up under the front seat. The compartment only opened if the solenoid button was pushed. We paid five thousand dollars a car to have them modified.

We stuffed the twenty keys, each marked with the letters RCX, into the compartment, and Rodrigo Restrepo drove the Chevy to California.

Rodrigo turned the load over, car and all, to Steve Robinson, Hettrick's man, and grabbed a plane back to Miami.

A few weeks later I was sitting at home and turned on the national news. DeLorean had been busted. The bust was being shown right there in my living room. An undercover agent was standing holding a kilo in each hand, and right across the tape in big bold letters was written RCX. The RC stood for Rafael Cardona and the X was for Max; it was our code to identify our own inventory. Hettrick had set DeLorean up for a sting.

And there was more. They actually showed DeLorean on videotape accepting the dope.

We followed the DeLorean trial closely, and after he was acquitted, Rafa said, "Now I've got to collect for my twenty keys. The bastard still owes me and he's going to pay. One way or another, I will collect."

And I always believed Rafa would collect, one way or the other, just as he said he would.

Part Three

* *
*

WIDENING THE WINDOW

CHAPTER TEN

*

Mayhem in Mexico

For the first two months of 1982 we slowly reassembled our crippled delivery operation. Every hangar, warehouse, and vehicle was changed. The Conquest turbo jet that Mickey and Jimmy had paid nearly a million dollars for had been seized and Jimmy was nowhere to be found—fortunately for him. Mickey and I were alone now, trying to build up a new group. We lost several who were afraid that if Jimmy, a fugitive, was caught he would tell everything he knew. The ones who stayed needed plenty of rest and relaxation after the heavy flying schedule we had carried out during 1981. I was trying to set up fresh, uncompromised routes into Florida. Mickey and I were also working out the intricacies of packaging coke for water drops somewhere out in the Bahamas. Rafa was back in Medellín.

I actually luxuriated in my enforced vacation from coke smuggling. There were no financial problems, I had plenty of money lying around. When Rafa called in early March and suggested a trip to Mexico, I jumped at it. I had already been planning to call my friend Raul Falciola in Mexico about some hunting.

Raul and I had done a lot of hunting together in Texas; he was glad to arrange the visit for Rafa and myself. Rafa brought Maria Monzano, and I brought Cristina. Raul met us at the Nuevo Laredo airport and drove us through the town, which was no more than a slum. The American air base across the border had been closed, and Nuevo Laredo suffered from all the other financial problems Mexico had created for itself.

Raul's family farm was about thirty-five kilometers south of Nuevo Laredo. The place was a huge tract of sandy desert covered by sagebrush and mescal cactus. Cattle and donkeys spotted the countryside. The farmhouse itself was a three-bedroom adobe structure. In the center of the living room was an open hearth, a sort of indoor barbecue.

While the women unpacked, Rafa and I talked with Raul and his ranch manager, Flaco. We decided to drive around the property that afternoon and sharpen our shooting eye on jackrabbits and wild turkeys. In preparation for this trip, a friend of Raul's had smuggled in several hunting rifles for us.

The pickup truck was rigged for hunting, with a shooting rail around three sides of the platform and a seat on top of the cab for the lookout. The pickup roared over the desert floor and stopped short whenever a jackrabbit appeared. I shot the first one on the run with the 220 Swift I was carrying. Each time I shot a rabbit, Flaco jumped out of the truck and collected the carcass to feed to the dogs.

We did this for about an hour, until we came to a long stretch of flat terrain. The truck stopped and Raul smiled as he pointed at an almost perfect natural landing strip. He had been waiting for the perfect psychological moment to show it to us. No one said a word, as the light began to dawn on Rafa and me.

The strip stretched in a straight line for eight hundred meters, with a natural impacted surface which blended perfectly into the surroundings. It could easily be lengthened and would be impossible to spot from the air without markers. Rafa's excitement was contagious; he fell in love with the place and before we left we were calling it "our airstrip."

The next afternoon we drove back to Nuevo Laredo and flew on to Dallas, where Cristina, Maria, and Rafa spent several hours shopping in the Galleria before we returned to Miami.

Rafa left for Colombia the next morning to talk to all three of the Ochoas about the airstrip. Their enthusiasm was as great as his, and they told him to check it out for immediate use. He called me from Colombia and instructed me to meet him in Cancún, in Yucatán. I made a reservation at the Sheraton Hotel in Cancún, and I took off from Miami that afternoon.

By the following evening there was still no sign of Rafa. I called Cristina, but she couldn't locate him. I called Colombia, but nobody knew where he was. It was two more days of sitting in the hotel, surrounded by jungle, before I finally reached Odila at their house in Medellín.

"Where is Rafa?" I shouted in frustration.

"Rafa is not well. He's asleep," she replied.

"How long has he been freebasing?"

"Two days. He will be awake tomorrow."

"Tell him I've been waiting for him in this jungle for three damn days!"

"I will tell him," Odila promised, and hung up.

The following afternoon the phone rang and Rafa's happy voice rang out. "Compadre, how are you? I'm sorry, I had business to attend to, I couldn't get away."

Obviously he wasn't going to tell me he'd been blasted for three days and sleeping it off one more day.

"Hey, where are you?" he asked.

"You told me to meet you in Cancún. I'm in Cancún!"

"I don't want you in Cancún. We're supposed to meet in Monterrey."

"Then why didn't you tell me Monterrey?" I shouted.

"I'll fly up there tomorrow. You leave now and meet me tomorrow afternoon at the Monterrey airport."

Good soldier Max was at the Monterrey airport in industrial northeast Mexico at two o'clock the next afternoon. To my surprise and shock, Odila stepped off the plane with Rafa. Also in the party were his two top shooters and Victor, a Peruvian laboratory technician, a high-class cook.

"Come, Max," Rafa said pleasantly. "For the rest of the day we relax. Tomorrow Fabio will fly here and we will go up and inspect our new airstrip."

I was getting bored sitting around hotels, but I passed the time with Rafa and his entourage, all of whom I knew, and the next day at noon we were all at the airport when Fabio landed in his cream-colored twin-engine Navajo. We were introduced to Ruben David, Fabio's new Colombian pilot, and then we went back to the hotel. Fabio and Rafa wanted to fly up to Nuevo Laredo in the Navajo, but I flatly refused. There was no way in God's creation I was going to get in that airplane with a Colombian sitting in the pilot's seat. My experiences flying with Colombian pilots were all too fresh in my mind.

We decided that Fabio, Rafa, Odila, and I would make the four-hour drive the following morning to Nuevo Laredo, and Ruben David would fly up with Victor and the two shooters.

It turned out to be a pleasant drive, with Fabio in top form, running through his repertoire of jokes. We arrived at about one o'clock, and I checked us all into six rooms at La Hacienda Motel on the main highway from the United States down through Mexico. Then I finally got Rafa away from everybody else.

"Why did you bring your wife?"

"She wanted to come," he answered lamely.

"Why bring a sandwich to a banquet? This is the best town to screw around in outside of Panama."

"I didn't know."

"Well, you're stuck with her."

"She wanted to come back to the United States now that she's had the operation in Medellín. She didn't trust Yankee doctors."

"What was the operation?" I asked.

"Why do you think she is so quiet and eats nothing but soup? Her jaws are wired together."

"You beat her up again?"

"Not this time. She had something wrong. She isn't feeling well, Max. I've got to stay with her."

I couldn't believe such out-of-character consideration. "Well, you stay with her. I'm going out."

The group gathered for lunch. No business was discussed; we all knew why we were in Nuevo Laredo. Fabio kept up his barrage of jokes in between the gossip from Colombia and Miami. Raul Falciola, my buddy, joined us that afternoon and became acquainted with Fabio, who, if all went according to plan, would become a big paying customer at Raul's ranch.

Fabio reported he had just received a phone call from Pablo Correa, the money launderer for the cartel, to whom I had sent about $50 million in cash on the down legs of my flights in the last year. Pablo had decided he would also fly up from Medellín and let his pilots have a look at the airstrip.

Early the next morning we received a phone call from Pablo at the Nuevo Laredo airport. Customs did not want to let him into the country. Raul and I went out to the airport and found Pablo and his two Colombian pilots being held in the Customs compound of the airport.

After a long confidential palaver with Customs, Raul reported what had happened. As Pablo and his pilots had checked into Customs and Immigration, they were asked the purpose of their visit.

"We came to swim at the beach," Pablo replied.

"What beach? You are in the middle of Mexico. Where do you think you are?"

"Cancún," Pablo answered, his two pilots nodding.

The Customs and Immigration agents stared at them suspiciously. "You are in Nuevo Laredo," they informed the Colombians.

After considerable persuasion on Raul's part, and a couple of hundred dollars distributed by me, we rescued Pablo and his pilots from the Mexican airport authorities and brought them back to the motel, where Fabio was waiting.

Young as he was, Fabio was a family man and a disciplinarian. There was no drinking that night, and those of us who would have liked to go to Boys' Town, the most celebrated red-light district along the Mexican border, refrained.

At nine o'clock the next morning we started out for the ranch in two rented cars, Raul leading the way in his pickup truck. Raul's aunt and uncle greeted us at the house. They were aware of the reason this delegation had arrived, and were more than happy to greet us. Suddenly the ranch showed signs of becoming a highly profitable property.

We left Odila at the house and took a ride out to the field. Fabio was thrilled with the airstrip and its strategic location. Already he was imagining his pilots flying loads of up to one thousand kilos of Medellín cocaine into this Mexican border strip and American pilots landing and taking off, transshipping the Ochoa product to Florida and California. The airstrip was almost exactly midway between the two destinations.

From Rafa I learned that he planned to bring in a thousand kilos each week from Colombia. That would be just over a ton. It never ceased to amaze me that there was no limit to the amount of cocaine that could be sold wholesale in the United States, at prices ranging from $30,000 to $40,000 a kilo.

"We will need underground fuel tanks and landing lights," Ruben David said. "Even in daylight this place is almost impossible to find."

Rafa walked over to Raul. "You are the engineer. How much will it cost to make an 1100-meter strip and put in the fuel tanks and lights?"

Raul figured for a few minutes. "Between twenty and twenty-five thousand dollars," he replied.

Fabio peered into Raul's eyes. "Done. The money will be turned over to Max in Miami, and he will get it to you. How soon can we start operations?"

"One month from the day I get the money, you can bring in the first load in your Aerocommander 1000," Raul answered decisively.

We headed back to the house and told Raul's aunt and uncle the news, to their obvious delight. Rafa and Raul were already discussing how much would be paid in landing fees as we drove back to La Hacienda Motel.

The first thing I did at the motel was put a call through to Mickey

Munday and tell him to get himself to the Hilton Hotel in Laredo, Texas, the next day, and I would call him from the Mexican side of the border. I wanted Mickey to have a good look at the strip so we could incorporate any ideas he might have in the construction work.

Pablo, Fabio, and their boys planned to fly out of Nuevo Laredo early the next morning. Pablo was still complaining about the Mexican authorities and how rude they were. He was the only one of us who doubted the advisability of using the Mexican airstrip.

Ruben David was worried about the fuel pump on the left engine of the plane, and Fabio had the good sense to tell him to fly it alone and he would drive to Monterrey and catch a flight the next day.

I announced that I was going to look around town that evening. The bodyguards and pilots, though obviously worried about the staid Fabio's reaction, elected to go with me. We never mentioned Boys' Town, but everybody except Odila knew where we were going. Fabio and Pablo never gave a thought to accompanying us redneck campesinos, and a disgruntled Rafa was also obliged to stay back, looking after his lockjawed wife.

We took two cars and drove through Nuevo Laredo to the compound on the desert known as Boys' Town. Driving through the single gate in the fence guarded by a grinning cop in a sentry box, we looked down the streets lined with nightclubs. There must have been fifty to sixty two-story bistros inside the walled-in pleasure pasture, music blaring from each and every door. The girls waited downstairs for their customers, and then took them to second-floor bedrooms.

The biggest and best club, Papagayo, featured a pulsating multicolored neon macaw and sign that ran the width of the building. We headed for the door; we could see a number of girls in various stages of undress.

We seated ourselves around a table and ordered drinks. The girls came in all shapes, sizes, and persuasions. They had one thing in common, they were all Mexican. This was a land of equal opportunity for Mexicans only, and that restriction even extended to the whorehouses. No foreign girls were allowed to participate in whoring. But there was plenty of variety to satisfy the most jaded of desires. The women wandered over to us, sitting on our laps and perching on the edge of the table, opening their legs to expose their wares.

"Make them show you their doctor's card before you take them upstairs," Raul warned. "If it's been a whole week since they were last inspected, you'd better try a new one."

I picked out a pretty, bosomy young señorita and told her I was going to take her back to my room at La Hacienda. Her name was Maria. She asked for fifty dollars. I handed her one hundred. Maria sat with me, drinking, laughing, and offering suggestions to the others with me who were sharing rooms at the motel. Many of them stayed and did their thing right there at Papagayo.

When we left Boys' Town we had to pause at the gate while Maria paid twenty dollars to the police for a pass to leave the compound and return the next day. Maria gave me a night to remember.

The next day, with Fabio, Pablo, and their people gone, there wasn't much to do except wait for Mickey Munday to show up from Miami. We didn't really expect him to arrive until late that night, so after dinner I went up to Rafa's room. Odila was lying on the bed and Rafa's pistolocos were standing in a corner, waiting for permission to take the night off. I suggested to Rafa that he leave Odila alone and come with me and the boys back to Boys' Town. Rafa shook his head mournfully. "She isn't feeling well, and I don't want to put her in a bad mood and have to beat her up again. I will be here in case Mickey calls."

"Okay, you stay here." I walked across the room and just as I reached for the doorknob, the door burst open, popping off its hinges, and all I could see was camouflage suits and guns—shotguns and .45-caliber handguns.

"Everyone on the floor, face down!"

The last thing I saw was one of the jungle-fatigued thugs throw a pillowcase over a wide-eyed, silently screaming Odila. Then in a spasm of pain from a blow to the back of my neck, I pitched forward onto the floor, fighting back the nausea that welled up in my throat.

The Mexicans shouted, "Police! Faces down on the floor!"

They handcuffed our hands behind our backs. We were helpless. They stretched elastic bandages over our eyes and around our heads. I could hear the strange sounds from Odila as they took her out of the room. The next thing I knew a pillow had been pushed down on top of my head and I felt the barrel of a shotgun against my ear. The cops, if that is really what they were, then conferred about what to do next.

We were dragged to our feet and prodded by gun barrels. Rafa and two of his men shuffled out of the room and were pitched face down on the floor in the next room. Again pillows were jammed down over our heads and shotgun barrels shoved behind our ears. The *click-click* of the cocking mechanism terrorized us.

"Tell us where it is! Tell us where it is!" they kept shouting at us. "Tell us where it is and we'll let you go."

"Tell you where what is?" I managed in a muffled cry. "We don't know what the fuck you're looking for." My question drew a swift kick to my ribs and I groaned in pain.

Rafa was in the worst mental state of any of us. They had his wife and he was sure these assholes who claimed to be cops were sexually assaulting a woman who, with her jaws wired shut, couldn't even cry out for help. Not that La Hacienda security personnel would challenge anything our assailants did to us; the motel manager had obviously cooperated with the raiders.

An hour later, I was kicked to my feet and prodded out of the room and into another one, still blindfolded. I was rocked by a stinging blow to the temple that jerked my head to the right, then another whack jolted it back to the other side. It was petrifying to be completely blind and not be able to tell where the next blow was coming from until it landed. All the time this punishment was being inflicted on me, the bastards kept shouting, "Where is it! Tell us where it is!"

Every time I asked, "Where is what?" another painful blow slammed the side of my head.

Suddenly, I heard the door open and a harsh voice demand, "Is that him?"

A female voice replied, "Yes, that is my friend. Please let him come with me."

The male voice let go with a few obscenities and told her to get out before she was pulled in to join the others. Then the door slammed shut.

I later learned that Raul had driven up and seen the military police cars. Knowing better than to get involved, he called his cousin, a young woman, and asked her to go to the motel and, posing as my girlfriend, see what she could find out. The military police wouldn't harm a young Mexican woman, Raul reasoned.

All of us spent the night suffering intermittent beatings, and we were not allowed to go to the bathroom. Some of Rafa's men were soaked in their own urine by morning. About every hour a shotgun was pressed to the back of my head and the *click-click* of the gun being cocked reverberated in my brain.

All night we could hear room service coming to the rooms, bringing food and bottles of liquor to our captors, although they wouldn't let us have so much as a glass of water. My throat was painfully parched and it was with difficulty I spit out the blood that ran down my face. The living nightmare went on through the next morning. Desperate for water, we could hear and smell a huge breakfast being brought by room service to the raiders.

Finally I was led into a room and the bandage removed from my eyes. I looked up to find myself staring into the black eyes of the leader of this band of military terrorists. He was smiling broadly under a thin black moustache, his eyes twinkling with the fun he and his men had enjoyed at our expense.

"I am Lieutenant Ramirez of the National Military Police," he said. "You are free to go. We apologize for the inconvenience, but we were told you were drug dealers. My orders were to find the drugs. It seems it was a mistake." Then he shouted *Vamonos!* to his men and they all disappeared. We could hear their vehicles screeching out of the motel driveway.

Rafa and I took stock of the situation, and to Rafa's relief, found that Odila had been treated with respect and not been molested. But our property had been stolen; my watch was gone. When we counted up the money the Mexican police had lifted from us, it came to $30,000. Luckily I had another $2,000 hidden in my boot: I divided it up so everyone would have some cash to work with.

When I went to check out at the desk I was totally shocked to find that our tormentors had charged almost $2,000 to my room in food and liquor. Adding a final insult, the cops had left with full bottles of liquor charged to me.

"I'm not putting those charges on my card," I said indignantly. "I didn't sign for them."

An evil grin came over the motel manager's face. "Your personal guests signed these charges. Naturally you are responsible."

"That's outright thievery," I screamed.

The manager reached for the phone. "I will call for Lieutenant Ramirez to bring his men back here and settle the matter."

Defeated, I put the entire bill on my MasterCard, and we began deciding how to get out of that hellhole and back to the States. Rafa did not want to cross the border from there, so we took him and Odila to the Nuevo Laredo airport, where they would hop a plane to Monterrey and then fly into some U.S. airport. The members of Rafa's entourage would make their own way back to Miami. About all that had been left us were our credit cards.

"I'm not going straight back to Miami," I said to Rafa. "Suppose they put a tail on me or something like that. I'm going to lay over a few days someplace and let things quiet down."

"Okay, where do you want to go?"

"I'll kill a few days in New Orleans, see what happens."

"I'll meet you there. Check in at the Hilton and I'll find you tomorrow."

Raul drove me across the border to the Laredo Hilton, where I found Mickey Munday still waiting for me. "Boy, it's a good thing you didn't come over looking for me," I said. "All we needed was for a gringo pilot to walk in while the military police were holding us."

"I am very careful, Max. You should know that by now. Except for that Tampa disaster, which wasn't our fault, I don't make wrong moves. What do you want to do now?"

"I'm going to hang out in New Orleans for a few days." I was still shaking from the ordeal. "You're welcome to come with me."

"Okay," Mickey said, lazily popping a gum bubble.

Mickey, as always, had a wad of cash on him, so that night when we arrived in New Orleans we did all the tourist things, and by noon the next day Rafa had checked into the Hilton. We met to discuss what we would do next. He had Odila with him; she refused to be left alone anywhere. Both of us still had the sweats and shakes from the Mexico experience. Rafa had reported the incident to Jorge Ochoa in Medellín and advised strongly against proceeding with the airstrip. But Fabio still thought it was a great plan and was already making overtures to the Mexican authorities, regarding who to bribe.

Mickey Munday thought the whole Mexican fiasco was the funniest thing he had ever heard. He sat around in Antoine's with us, listening to us compare notes, downing amaretto and Coke.

We had fled Nuevo Laredo on Friday and by Monday night we finally calmed down. When we knew for sure that there was nobody behind us, we decided to fly back to Miami. It would snow in hell before anyone would ever again see Max in Mexico.

Nevertheless, Fabio had $25,000 delivered to me in Miami the day I returned, with instructions to tell Raul Falciola to proceed with the airstrip. Within a month Raul had built the lighted strip, complete with underground fuel tanks. As far as I know, not one cartel plane ever landed there.

CHAPTER ELEVEN

*

Coke Floats

The winter of 1982 was upon us and the organization was in disarray. We made a big effort to re-form the group, recruit new pilots, and get back into action. Rafa kept urging us to start up flying operations again, although not through Mexico. He was as sour as I was on the place and had tried to curb Fabio's plan to put the strip into operation. We had not done anything since the December 13 bust in Tampa, and we were all losing plenty of money as a result.

Until that disaster I had had the best group in the cartel. We were careful men who tried to think of everything. Hell, we even had a Colombian senator on our payroll by now. Senator Alfredo Martinez had always wanted to be a wealthy man, so he decided to go into the drug business. Rafa was happy to educate him.

The commander of the Colombian air force was a close personal friend of Martinez', and together they helped us. The deal was, we would pay them fifty grand a trip, and the air force's Mirage jets would stay grounded for three days and let us fly through our window. We never told Martinez exactly when we were coming or going; we didn't trust him enough. And for those three days, nothing military flew in our area. I never even knew you needed a key to start a Mirage jet. But I was told that Martinez would actually go to the air force base, collect all the airplane keys, slip them in his pocket, and disappear for three days; nobody would know where the hell he was. I used to smile at the thought that Colombia could have been invaded by Venezuela and there wasn't a damn thing they could do about it without the keys to their planes.

Martinez did this every week; every time we flew he got paid. The only exception was if they moved the jet squadron inland or up to another province, then we got a freebie.

Senator Martinez is still in the business. He lives in Colombia and smuggles pot into Miami. He travels with immunity on his diplomatic passport, laughing all the way to his bank in Panama. So, as we recovered from the Tampa bust the senator was screaming too; he missed his fat paycheck.

We had developed our routes carefully, and had them down pat. Going down was a breeze. We eased off the Florida peninsula and flew straight down the Grand Bahama Bank to the Mona Passage between the Dominican Republic and Puerto Rico. Then it was a straight shot west to the Sierra de Perija, the mountain range that separates Colombia from Venezuela; we stayed on the Colombian side. We would slip through this slot and shoot north to our landing strips, which were anywhere from Barranquilla to Acandí; sometimes we used one of the strips at Vera Cruz, Jorge Ochoa's ranch.

Each strip had a refueling station, if you could call it that. The fuel was stored in rusty old fifty-five-gallon drums; the fuel was famous for being dirty, so we used our own filters. Even so, the pilots were always nervous about bad fuel; a lot of pilots before us had wound up in the ocean, never to be found, because of dirty fuel. And we kept spare parts at all these locations: tires, hoses, fuel pumps, carburetors, everything we could think of. Each flight down, we brought spare parts with us and whenever a field was closed, whatever parts were at that location would be transported to our new spot.

The pilots never lingered on the Colombian side. They did not like being under someone else's control. They loaded, refueled, and headed back to the good old U.S.A. as fast as they could. The trip down was around twelve hundred miles and not so tough; the trip back was fourteen hundred miles and it was usually a ballbreaker for the pilots.

We were pros. The pilots, ground crew, and me, we loved the challenge and the money; it was all we had to think about, and it was all we did think about. A tremendous amount of logistics were involved. I spent four or five hours a day with my people, brainstorming, going over maps, picking routes, selecting equipment. We could never assume that because we had done it right once, bingo, we could do it again. We never did it exactly the same way twice. We had a briefing before every flight, everything was gone over, again and again, every detail, no matter how small, was discussed, and we didn't care whose feelings got hurt; they had to learn their part. It was like being in the military, it had to be perfect. Hell, it *was* just like war: we were putting lives on the line and millions of dollars were involved.

On the trips back, the payloads often were exceeded and the pilots had to stretch their planes to the breaking point to get airborne, pray them up. We flew twin-engine Navajo Panthers, with the six passenger seats ripped out. The fuselage was crammed solid with four hundred kilos of coke, almost nine hundred pounds, and rubber bladder tanks filled with fuel took up the rest of the space. They were flying cokebombs. We also had oversized regular fuel tanks and special wingtip tanks.

The route back to Florida was slightly different. The pilots headed back through the Mona Passage and up the far side of the Bahamas. They flew 250 miles to the east of the Bahamas, way out in the Atlantic Ocean, outside of all surveillance, and stayed out there until they were on a line with the Georgia-Florida border, then shot due west for the Florida mainland. All the heavy surveillance was in South Florida and the Bahamas, so they headed north to avoid it, simple and effective.

One of the trickiest parts was crossing the Florida Straits. Our planes flew so low that the co-pilot had to wear starlight night goggles that allowed him to see in the dark. His job was to watch for freighters and tankers in the shipping lanes while the pilot concentrated on keeping the plane fifty feet or less off the glassy dark surface of the ocean. Jimmy Cooley's worst fear was that he would run smack into the side of a big tanker or container ship and squash against it like a bug splattering on a windshield. Chances were the ship would never even have known what happened. Jimmy believed it had happened to some of his friends, who had taken off on drug runs and never been heard from again.

Storms were a problem, too. Flying fifteen hours in those kidney busters was bad enough, but when they hit a storm it was like a flight through hell. We finally put Ryan storm scopes into the planes, the same kind they use on the airliners, little television screens that show the weather that's waiting up ahead. It helped our pilots to fly around storms.

The last thing they did when they left the Florida Straits, before they hit the mainland, was to cut up the bladder tank and jettison it into the sea. The cops could never figure out how we were getting such long range from those planes. On the way back, instead of running the tanks first and then the bladder, we'd do it the other way around. All the plumbing for the bladder tanks was hidden below floor level, so no one could see the connections.

Our planes crossed over the Straits into Florida around Jacksonville, and then it was a straight shot down the center of the state.

We always had a primary and a secondary landing strip, and the ground men never knew which location they had. They always believed they had the primary, so they didn't know if they would be doing the unloading until the last minute; we liked to keep their adrenaline up. In the beginning, we used to land right on Route 27, which is Okeechobee Road, the old truckers' route. And there were plenty of access roads that ran alongside the canals and were always deserted. Sometimes we used one of them, after we cleared the bush and weeds. We timed the flights to return at dawn; there was never any traffic at that time of the morning.

The planes would touch down on access roads that ran next to isolated canals and our off-loaders would be on them in seconds. The primary and alternate landing strips were always close to each other and the pilot made the final choice; often he didn't know which one he was going to use until he was just about at Lake Okeechobee. There was constant ground-to-air communication between the ground crews. Everyone kept a sharp vigil and we had plenty of walkie-talkies. The pilot was kept well informed on ground activity.

We had about six or eight men in each location. As soon as the plane touched down, the ground crew moved in, the duffel bags were unloaded, and the plane took off again to land later at our private hangars near Opa-Locka, or at Fort Lauderdale Executive Airport, where it was quickly taken into our hangars. As we got richer, we built our own strips at Lake Okeechobee.

The dope was put into special cars that we had designated for the purpose. We had our own used-car lots and body shops, and we even owned a towing company. We used them all constantly for the operation. The preferred car was an old Marquis Brougham or an old Ford LTD. The trunks were modified in our body shops. The gas tanks were taken out and smaller tanks put in, with about a ninety-mile range. We rebuilt the entire trunk in fiberglass so that it was completely waterproof. We could get between 200 and 250 kilos in the trunk of each car, about 500 pounds. We installed special air shocks and we'd pump up the shocks to bring the car level, to keep the ass of the car from dragging. Every car had the biggest engine available, a 460 Lincoln. The cars looked like hell, but there was nothing on the road that could come close to them. Hard to believe that when they were loaded they each carried $5 million worth of cocaine.

The unloaders were highly motivated. If they did the actual unloading, they got $15,000 apiece. If they were the secondary unloaders and they didn't do anything that night except sit out there as mosquito bait, they got $5,000 for their trouble. But to make it fair, the off-loading was rotated; everybody wound up making the same amount. The drivers always got a little bit more, depending on their responsibility.

The planning was meticulous. A tow truck followed the loaded cars in case of mechanical failure. You didn't want to have to call for help if the cars broke down; you couldn't switch loads in the middle of the day.

In between the tow truck and the loaded cars was our "crash car." The crash car was our insurance policy. Usually it was a pickup truck or something big and heavy like an old Cadillac. The driver of the crash car had a bottle of booze next to him. If a loaded car was stopped by the police for a traffic violation, the crash-car driver would take a long swig of liquor, spill the rest of the booze on his clothes and the inside of the car, then proceed to run into the back of the stopped police car. The cop would go nuts and arrest what he thought was a drunken driver, while the loaded cocaine cars slipped quietly back into the traffic.

After each load was delivered to the stash house we would return the cars to the body shop and repaint them. We never used the same color twice; some of the cars in our fleet were covered with a half-inch of paint.

But our well-oiled flying machine had come to a grinding halt: Jimmy Cooley had hit the road for Lake Charles, Louisiana, Harold Johns had been arrested in his house the day after the Tampa bust, and Mickey Munday and the rest of the crew were paranoid and depressed.

Rafa had called me from Colombia back in February, before he ever thought of going to Mexico. "Compadre," he had said, "we are going broke. Can't you do something?"

"The boys are depressed and scared. They are also worn out, just like I told you and Jorge."

"We remember what you told us. What can we do now?"

"I have an idea I want to try. I want to try water drops."

"Try whatever the hell you want. I already told you it was okay with the Ochoas, just get those guys flying again. I need the business, Jorge needs the business, and you need the business, *comprende*?" And Rafa hung up.

And so it began. I knew the pilots would rise to the challenge, and the fact that they could push the coke out of the airplane and drop it into the sea removed an entire level of danger from the flight. No more touch-and-go off-loading in the Everglades. Mickey loved the idea.

The first thing we had to do was to select a good location in the Bahamas. After studying many locations, we chose Long Island. Long

Island is exactly what its name implies, a long skinny island, just south of Andros and north of the Turks and Caicos, not too far from the Florida coast, and an easy island-hopping run in a small boat. It had a scant tourist business and few inquiring eyes to worry about.

Once we picked Long Island, we had to select the exact sites for the drops. Water depths, tides, and currents all had to be studied. We had to make sure that if we did miss a duffel bag, we would know exactly which way the current was running on any particular tide so the bag would drift into the mangroves or wash up on a beach that we had under our control, instead of floating out to sea. All of these things had to be carefully planned. If the tide was coming in, the planes approached from one direction; if it was going out, they approached from another direction.

The next thing we had to think about were the boats. They had to be customized with long-range gas tanks and special bilges and holds to carry two hundred kilos. We used twenty-six-foot Duskies, ordered directly from the Duskie Corporation factory in Miami. They built in the modifications we wanted. Our specs could have been ordered by any serious offshore fisherman. There was no way the builders could know how we'd use the boats. They set the stringers as ordered, installed oversized gas tanks, and built up the transom to carry a larger engine.

These boats modified by us carried the dope in a special fiberglass compartment that ran up the center, built in our own shop. The gas tanks ran in tunnels next to this compartment, with a one-inch metal lip that covered the center coke-holding tunnel. If the cops drilled a hole in the floorboards, they would hit aluminum, then gas; it would look like any other boat.

We used these boats for two years until we started building our own in 1983. All the engines we used were brand-new, but broken in. They were the biggest engines that Evinrude manufactured. But we kept a low profile on our boats. We even changed the engine covers, putting a 140-horsepower cover on a 200-horsepower engine so it would look like a smaller engine. No detail was too small for me; preparation was everything for survival and not getting caught. These boats were not fancy racers like Cigarette boats, or Magnums, or Scarabs; we left those for the people who watched *Miami Vice*. They were too high-profile for us.

Our boats were small, open fishermen's vessels equipped with full fishing gear—used gear, not new—with ice and bait on board, sodas, sandwiches. Fish were purchased in the Bahamas, dropped in the fish boxes, and iced up. Everything, so we would look like weekenders returning from a little fishing fun in the Bahamas. All our boats were scheduled to hit Florida on Sunday afternoon, unless there was a fishing tournament. We loved making runs during tournaments. There were so many returning boats it was impossible to detect one of ours. If the tournament was returning on Saturday, we returned on Saturday. The captains kept their outriggers poised and the rods ready; if they saw something in the distance or heard something on the radio, all they did was cut the throttle from sixty miles an hour to six miles an hour, trolling speed.

And we used Coast Guard–licensed captains who knew what they were doing. They obeyed every law on the books: life jackets, fire extinguishers, proper registration and papers. Our boats would sail through a safety inspection. Cops don't need probable cause to stop a boat. They call them safety inspections, but they are really drug searches.

The next thing we had to design was a way to drop the dope from the planes. The load was going to hit the water like a bomb, at 75 to 80 miles an hour from between 125 and 150 feet in the air. It had to be protected.

So, with good old American ingenuity, we devised a way to protect it. We had special plastic bags made to order, fiberglass-reinforced with a thickness of five millimeters. The bags were a little bit bigger than a duffel bag. We made up practice coke "footballs" exactly the way they packed them in Colombia, only we used phony coke, flour, for testing. We stuffed the footballs into a plastic bag, then put the entire package in the duffel bag.

Finally, we were ready to test our package. It was a disaster; the bag leaked and the "coke" was soaked. We added two more plastic bags. The duffel was slipped, mouth first, into one plastic bag, and that bag was sealed. Then we reversed it, and packed it into the second bag, and sealed it. We wrapped heavy-duty fiberglass filament tape around the entire package. We overran the tape to make two handles on each end so that when it was floating you would have something to grab onto without piercing it. At first we had used gaffs but they penetrated the bags. So we switched to boat hooks.

The next day we dropped the bag and it worked.

The money the pilots were paid was hard-earned; they had expenses, and any losses incurred as a result of their negligence was their responsibility. So the stakes were high.

The pilots and crews started making four or five practice runs a day;

they had scheduled seventy practice runs over the next two weeks, keeping a sharp eye out for the Bahamian marine patrol. We had picked a good spot, isolated and desolate. We worked unnoticed under the sleepy eyes of the few Bahamians that passed by.

In April Mickey came to me in Miami and said, "We're ready."

He stood there grinning at me, proud of himself, indulging in his two major vices at the same time, sipping from a 7-Eleven cup of Dr. Pepper and chewing on a mouthful of bubble gum, snapping bubbles. Mickey was six foot two and thin as a rail. He always wore baseball caps and long-sleeved shirts for two reasons, because he was a redhead with freckly, light skin, and because his left arm had been broken. He couldn't straighten it out all the way, and he was self-conscious. Neither Mickey nor Jimmy smoked, did dope, or drank much booze. They got high off their jobs: if the job called for fast and dangerous, they wanted to do it.

We spoke in the hangar. There were six Lycoming engines on blocks; the engines were completely overhauled after every run. There were three identical planes, Navajo Panthers, in the hangar, all painted the same and with the same registration numbers. These boys believed in backup.

"So, is Jimmy in?"

"He's hot."

"I know he's hot. But he's the key to this operation from the air. Is he in?"

"Why don't you go ask him, Max?"

"Is he in Lake Charles?"

"Yeah. I'll give you his address."

I jumped in my car and drove for fourteen hours to Lake Charles, Louisiana, which was a busy oil area, buzzing with small planes and helicopter traffic coming in and out of the Gulf of Mexico from the oil platforms. Jimmy was hiding out in an area where he felt comfortable.

I called and asked him to meet me at Howard Johnson's.

Half an hour later we were face to face. "So, Max, what's on your mind?" Jimmy asked as he sat down with his burger.

"You know what's on my mind. We've got the first water drop scheduled for two weeks from now."

Jimmy just looked at me for a second with a skeptical eye. Then he said, "Okay, Max, you've always been square with us. I'll fly back to Miami tomorrow and fly the first one in myself. I'm bored here anyway. Wanna fly back with me?"

"No way. I'm still getting over the ride on 836."

"Hell, Max, that wasn't nothin' compared to the fun we can have in the air," he said, smiling.

His smile reminded me of the last ride I had with Jimmy on Route 836, outside Miami. We were in his El Camino, which he used to call, in his Deep South accent, his "El Kaminy with the 454." This was a monster car with a fully blown engine and a Hurst racing transmission. We were traveling on 836, on our way somewhere to pick up a boat. I made the mistake of saying, "Jimmy, I think we're being followed." "You think so, Max?" Jimmy asked, checking his rearview mirror. "I don't think so!" he muttered, and floored the gas. We were doing fifty at the time, and the car leapt forward like a cat springing. I was pressed into my seat. The tollbooth a mile ahead of us was hardly visible at first and then it was suddenly looming right there in front of us. My eyes slid over to look at the speedometer; it registered 110, and climbing. Getting through the tollbooth would be like threading the eye of a needle with a shaky hand. I closed my eyes tight as we sped right through it. All I heard was a big *whoosh*. I didn't open my eyes again until I could no longer hear the alarm bell. The highway patrol didn't even bother to chase us; we were just a blur. It was no wonder Jimmy had a full-time driver now that he was on the lam; he couldn't risk a ticket.

With Jimmy's promise to join us again I headed back to Miami.

I contacted Rafa and asked him if he had received the cases of fiberglass tape and the special five-millimeter bags that we had sent.

"Yes, they arrived here two days ago and the sample bag came as well." I had sent a bag wrapped exactly the way they were to wrap our shipment. "I have talked to Jorge and we both examined it carefully."

"So you'll remember to put the footballs in after the five-mil bag has been inserted, then wrap the outside of the duffels in two five-mil bags, sealed at both ends."

"Hey, relax, will you? It will be done right at this end, just you don't screw up your end, okay?" Rafa said. "Remember how much those boys are getting paid."

The pilots were now getting paid $3,500 a kilo, with a minimum guarantee of 350 kilos even if we shipped less. George Bergin was taking his $1,000 a key, so the pilots netted $2,500 a key. Or to put it another way, the air operation never received less that $1 million a run.

Two days later Jimmy left Miami for Colombia to pick up the load, 383 kilos. The return flight was carefully planned so the plane would hit Long Island in the Bahamas at dawn. We were ready: the boats had been built and transported, the retrieval crews stood by in flat-bottomed skiffs with their boat hooks, waiting anxiously, ready to carry the packages to the bigger boats. The tides had been exactly calculated. In case we missed any bags, they would float up on the deserted beach.

Mickey described the scene to me.

Jimmy's plane showed up exactly on time, a small dot on the horizon at first, a speck in the glow of the rising tropical sun. Soon the silhouette of the wings became visible, like a big seabird flying low along the ocean swells. Then the drone from his two engines became audible and broke the absolute stillness of the waking island.

The skiffs started to move, boatmen poling them out of the mangroves where they had lain hidden all night and easing them onto the sand flats, the poles fluffing up the sand, leaving little white puffs behind them in the clear, turquoise-blue water.

The gurgling of two strong outboard motors broke the silence as the Duskies moved into position in the finger channels. They left their engines running as they waited for the boats to bring them the packages.

Jimmy circled once to make sure everything was in position. He dipped the wings a little and veered offshore to make his approach from the northeast. The passenger door slid open and the co-pilot pushed all the bags out in rapid succession. The bags fell from a hundred feet and skipped along the surface, then split from the force of impact.

There was an audible gasp as the men in the pick-up boats watched the bags bobbing and the white powder slick start to form on the surface of the pristine Bahamian waters; 40 percent of the bags were destroyed. The coke glistened silver on the surface, as the sun rose over the Bahamas.

I was the first one to get the call from the Bahamas. Mickey was on the line, frantic.

"Max, we lost ten packages out of twenty-six, one hundred and twenty-six kilos." The loss represented over two million dollars to the cartel. "They didn't pack it right. They just covered the bags with one five-mil bag and stuffed the footballs in, like regular."

"Did you collect all the packages?" I asked.

"You're fuckin' right we did. What the hell is the matter with those dumb bastards!"

"Take it easy, Mickey."

"*Easy!* After all the work we put into this operation, all the money we laid out for boats, people! We got to pay our people anyway, Max! They gotta get something for their trouble."

I had never heard Mickey so excited; he was the most laid-back person I knew. "Hey, Mickey, calm down. I know. Just make sure you get all the packages. We don't want those sleepy Bahamians to figure anything out or we'll have to start paying them off."

"Yeah, yeah, Max, we already got that covered. We don't screw up, you know. We're not like your friends."

"Just get back here, Mickey."

"Don't worry about it. I'm leaving the boat crews in the Bahamas. I'll move them over to Stella Maris and let them go fishing."

"Right," I said, my fingers flying, punching the numbers for Rafa in Miami. He had returned for the shipment.

"Rafa, we lost it," was all I said.

He was at my house five minutes later, eyes blazing with anger. He sat across from me at the dining room table and I started to explain. "We lost the whole load; it exploded on contact with the water. And we're pissed, Mickey's pissed, the captains are pissed. We've been working for two months on this, almost every day."

"*You're* pissed! You got some nerve being pissed. We lost the load and how can we be sure it happened like they say?"

"They're bringing back the split duffel bags."

"So? Who's going to pay for this?" Rafa was standing now, shouting. "Over *one hundred* keys! Someone is going to have to make good on this! You guaranteed this would work. Who the hell is going to pay for this!"

"Jorge should make good."

"What are you talking about?"

"Look, the bags were not packed in three layers of plastic. Those assholes in Colombia just slipped a single bag over the packages. We knew that wouldn't work, we'd already tried it that way. Shit, we sent you a sample of a perfectly wrapped package."

Rafa just stared at me for a minute. I could almost see the thoughts swirling through his paranoid brain. He didn't say anything, he just called Jorge and told him what had happened. Now Rafa had to listen to what I had to listen to when Mickey called me from Long Island. Jorge Ochoa was screaming so loud I could hear him across the room. Rafa held the phone six inches from his ear, waiting for Jorge to calm down. Finally he put the receiver to his ear and said, "Here, talk to Max."

"You forgot something, Jorge," I said.

"What? What did we forget?" Jorge asked.

"The plastic sleeves for the water drop. You forgot to pack them in plastic, one five-mil bag inside and two outside, end to end." I knew Jorge was too busy to supervise these things personally anymore. "I sent you a sample package, remember?"

"I'll call you back," he said, and hung up.

Rafa and I waited in silence for fifteen minutes for Jorge to call back. When the phone rang Rafa gestured to me to take the call.

"You were right, we forgot the plastic," Jorge said. "Just do what you can. I have talked to my people. Can you send your pilot back?"

"Jimmy will need a day to sleep, then he can return."

"We'll have it done right this time."

"I hope so, Jorge. There was a lot of money put up already on our end."

"Yes. Just send him back."

I repeated the conversation to Rafa after I hung up and I could see the color return to his normally olive-colored face.

"Well, let's not screw up this one," he said.

"Hey," I answered, "we didn't screw up the last one. Some asshole down there in Colombia who makes about five hundred dollars a year did it, not us. Have them put good people on it."

"Don't you worry, they will."

Three days later Jimmy flew in the next load. It came into Little Exuma, an island located right off Deadman's Cay, Long Island.

And the same damn thing happened, the bags split on contact.

Rafa had returned to Colombia, so this time I called Jorge Ochoa directly; Rafa was with him.

"Jorge, we got the same problem as three days ago." I let my words hang in the silence. "Those guys you got down there packing have shit for brains."

"Compadre, I told them—"

"Jorge, I'm afraid you're going to have to find yourself another route. We ain't taking the responsibility for this shit anymore. My people are totally pissed off at me, nobody's making any money, and we're all taking a lot of risks."

There was a pause as Jorge talked to Rafa, then handed him the phone. "Compadre, I am putting Orlando in charge of packing," Rafa said.

"Great," I said sarcastically. Orlando was one of Rafa's drivers and gofers. But Orlando turned out to be a good man, and later became the foreman on Rafa's ranch. "Send him up to me. I'll give him a lesson he won't forget!"

"I'm sure you will. He will be there tomorrow."

Orlando arrived the next day and I took great pains to show him how to load and tie the bags. Every shipment after that was dropped without water damage.

But getting the coke packed right was not the end of our problems. Next, we had to face George Bush and his Federal drug interdiction team.

When the Vice President of the United States was placed in charge of putting an end to cocaine smuggling he came into Miami with ideas that might have worked but for the constant turf wars, mistrust, and infighting that plague the government agencies. He put together a strike force of DEA and Treasury Department agents along with Metro-Dade narcotics cops. The Coast Guard was also involved. Under Bush's direction, the most sophisticated and expensive high-powered pursuit craft was suddenly made available to the government's special task force: Black Hawk helicopters and twenty to thirty electronically equipped, high-speed Scarab ocean racers at $200,000 a crack.

But it was not a team. If it had been, the operation would likely have put me out of business. Fortunately, we could count on all the agencies and the Coast Guard fighting each other, withholding intelligence information, and even in a subtle way sabotaging each other's efforts to make the big bust that would have made one agency top dog. Bush had the money and resources and know-how, but neither he nor any other government bureaucrat ever figured out how to make competing government agencies work together.

Each of our boats had at least two HF radios connected to our "Radio Central," which was located in Mickey's spare bedroom. The room looked like the heart of a major radio station. He had the most sophisticated scanners, receivers, and transmitters money could buy, with people manning the equipment twenty-four hours a day. It was a great game for our people. When we lost the cops because they changed frequencies, we would take bets on how long it would take to pick them up again. It was never more than a few days before we had them back on the air, monitoring their every word. Now the police use military scramblers, so it's tougher, but it can still be done.

We had a second monitoring station in the penthouse of a high-rise in Haulover Cut. This location was also equipped with high-powered telescopes and night-vision glasses for visual observation. We kept it manned full time and logged every patrol that we saw. We also kept spotter planes in the air to keep a watch out when we had a load coming in.

About a month after our first successful drop, our boats were rounding the bend off the north coast of Long Island, heading west, and all of a sudden they picked up radio traffic that was unreal. The airwaves were full of excited voices. The lead captain checked in with "Radio Central" in Miami.

"Mickey, we got a lot of static around here," the captain relayed.

"Pull in your fish and take the alternate route home. Do it now! It's a big-time storm you're facing."

"Roger, ten-four," the captain said, immediately activating the alternate plan by changing course north to Exuma Sound and Nassau. The captains went to a prearranged marina, where we had the boats hauled and left on the ways for a week until the Feds moved on.

But we had made a mistake; the bilges were full of water and the plugs were not pulled, so the coke was left to wallow in pools of saltwater for a week. We lost about a hundred and twenty kilos, and that was our responsibility.

We didn't realize this until the load was brought into Miami. The mooring we used was at Maule Lake Marina at Biscayne and 172nd Street. We used this marina because the kid that was operating the forklift there was working for us. We would glide into the marina and have the forklift pull the boat and load it on our trailer, then we would haul it away. No unloading was ever done in the marina. We towed the boat to our warehouse, closed the door behind it, and unloaded it. That's when we discovered the spoiled goods.

So Rafa sent for his mad chemist in Colombia and we set up our own lab in Miami to recycle the spoiled coke. We saved about a hundred kilos out of a hundred and twenty spoiled keys.

The next disaster happened a few months later, the blue box incident.

I got a call from Mickey. "Hey, Max, I got a surprise for you. I don't know who came up with this idea, but what they are packing it in now is absolutely fantastic."

"I don't know what you're talking about."

"Go on over and you'll see," Mickey said, laughing.

A half hour later I was standing inside the stash house and I saw what Mickey was talking about: blue corrugated fiberglass boxes to house the coke. They were great. They stacked up nice and neat, one kilo to the box, they were easy to pack, they absorbed the shock, and they were waterproof.

I inventoried the load and immediately called Colombia. They gave me Jota, the chief accountant, to check the numbers with, and I said, "Jota, the new packing is great; putting it in boxes was absolutely inspired."

"Oh, that was Fabio's idea."

"Is he there? Let me talk to him."

Jota put Fabio on the line and I said, "Fabio, that was a terrific idea. The pilots loved it, not one kilo was damaged."

"That's good, because that's all we're using from now on. I came up with the idea and I had thousands of boxes made, hundreds of thousands," he said proudly.

"Well, they're working great! Adiós."

"Adiós, Compadre," Fabio said, and hung up.

And they did work great, until the cartel decided to speed up production time. Instead of taping the boxes closed, they stapled them. That was faster, except half the time the staples went right through the plastic bags inside the boxes, and we started to get some real water damage again. So I called Fabio Ochoa, screaming, and he went back to taping them.

The problems never ended, but the money was so good we could absorb almost any mistake and still come out ahead. In the five years my pilots were with me, I personally paid them over ninety million dollars.

CHAPTER TWELVE

*

The Black Widow

If there had been no Griselda Blanco de Trujillo, there would have been no cocaine wars.

My first contact with Griselda Blanco was in 1982, at my house in Miami. Rafa had invited her over. Everybody in the drug business knew her by reputation. She was known as a ruthless killer who was almost totally responsible for the cocaine wars that had been raging in Miami since 1978.

Rafa explained, "Griselda Blanco is a longtime friend of mine, Compadre. She helped save my life and I owe her an awful lot."

"She's a dangerous person, I hear."

"Perhaps. But she is having grave financial difficulties, and I feel that I must help her."

It was common knowledge that she was experiencing financial difficulties because she had been at war for so long against so many people that she had used up a great deal of her money and had little time to really work at the business. All her time, energy, and money were spent in warring.

"How did she save your life?" I asked.

Rafa told me that he had first met Griselda Blanco in Colombia back when he was a young thief, stealing cars and anything else he could get his hands on. "In 1979, Flaco's family contracted with a shooter to have me killed. They were angry about Flaco's brother, Cesar," Rafa said.

Angry, sure! How well I remembered the story of Rafa shooting Flaco's brother in the face at Livia Cardona's party just before he got me to drive the van and watch him shoot Chino.

"Griselda warned me they were coming after me. They almost got me anyway." Rafa pulled his shirt back, exposing his shoulder.

"Bullet wounds?" I asked, looking at two ugly scars on his shoulder.

"We were stopped at a light in Medellín, Colombia," Rafa continued.

"I was driving, and Pecas was sitting next to me. Somebody ran up to the car and stuck a gun in the window, and *bam! bam!*" Rafa made a gun out of his hand and pretended to shoot. "But at the last moment I had seen him coming with my side vision, maybe I was extra alert because of what Griselda had told me. I turned and was shot in the shoulder. If I had not turned I would have been shot in the chest. I rammed the gas pedal to the floor and flew away."

"And Pecas?"

"He pulled his gun out, but by then we were too far away to shoot back. Besides, the shooter had disappeared."

I was startled. I had no idea that Flaco's family had tried to take revenge for that bloody Christmas Eve. I sat there dumbfounded. The shooting had happened three years before and Rafa had never even mentioned it to me. Fucking amazing.

The doorbell rang and Cristina answered it. In walked Griselda and her entourage. In her train were Toto and Tonio, two of her shooters, and Dario Sepulveda, a famous Colombian bandit, who was Griselda's husband. And last through the door was Osvaldo, a kid I immediately recognized.

Rafa introduced me to Griselda and she turned to introduce me to her son, Osvaldo. I swallowed hard and shook his hand. Osvaldo had a slight smile on his face. I looked over at Rafa like I could kill him. He shrugged and sat down.

Rafa had already introduced me to Osvaldo a year before, in 1981. I was going to California to make a pickup, when Rafa brought this young punk to me and told me to take him along.

I had taken Rafa aside. "Rafa, the kid is fifteen years old."

Rafa laughed. "Maybe he's sixteen."

"I don't care whether he's fifteen or sixteen, he's a goddamn kid."

"He needs to be trained in the business. As a favor for an old friend of mine, do it. Teach him the business, please," Rafa had said, and simply left, left me with the kid.

But this was no ordinary kid. On the flight to Los Angeles he told me that he had already killed two people.

"You're crazy," I said.

"No, I offed somebody when I was fourteen."

"Sure. Sure you did," I said, as I looked out the plane window at the clouds drifting past, avoiding his eyes. But I believed him and it gave me the chills.

The first fight I had with Osvaldo was when I picked up my rental car.

"I'll drive," he said.

"Bullshit. You'll sit next to me, watch what happens, and do as you're told."

We went to the stash house, where Edgar Diaz, one of Rafa's men, was waiting for us. I introduced Edgar to Osvaldo, and we went to examine the car we were going to use for the first delivery, thirty kilos. We watched as the door panels covering the hidden compartments were removed. Edgar and I just looked at each other and shook our heads. There was no way that thirty kilos was going to fit into the doors.

"Let's just put the stuff in the trunk and get on with it," I said.

Which is exactly what we did. Edgar Diaz drove the load car and Osvaldo sat beside him. I followed in my car. I never wanted to be in a car if it had dope on board. We drove to the San Fernando Valley and into a parking lot, a shopping strip with a big supermarket as the centerpiece.

There was a Colombian kid waiting for us in the parking lot. Edgar Diaz gave me the keys to the load car, and I walked over to the kid and handed him the keys.

"Did you put the stuff in the compartments?" the kid asked.

"No, it wouldn't fit. It's in the trunk," I said.

"Then I'm not going to accept the car."

"What do you mean, you're not going to accept the car?"

"Hey, I'm not going to accept the car. The shit has to go in the compartments."

I walked away from the kid to straighten out my head and calm down. Osvaldo came over to me and said, "I'll drive it for the kid, I'll take him."

"No. You don't go to his stash house, ever. Where he's taking the stuff is none of our business. Use your head, Osvaldo. If we know where his stash house is located, he can accuse us of a ripoff. From this point on, it's his responsibility."

The kid came over to where I was standing and started to get in my face. And Osvaldo kept piping up. I walked to the load car with both Osvaldo and the kid harping at me, following me, and I threw the keys on the floor of the car.

"It's yours!" I said to the kid. "If you want it, take it. If you don't, I'm calling Colombia right now. I made the delivery, it's going to be paid for. Period. Any way you want to pay for it, fine. You want to pay for it in cash, you want to pay for it in blood . . . it's going to be paid for!"

"You can't talk to him like that," Osvaldo yelled at me.

My hand moved like lightning. I couldn't stop it. I backhanded Osvaldo right across the mouth and sent him flying onto the hot tarmac of the parking lot. He looked up at me, bewildered. I turned to Edgar Diaz, who was standing by my car, and said, "Pick him up. We're leaving."

After that Osvaldo behaved himself.

But I'd had no idea he was Griselda's son. Everyone in the business knew she was a very possessive woman. She was possessive to the point of insanity. Nobody could mistreat her kids. The word was that she had had girls killed because she thought they were getting too close to her boys, or she just didn't like them. I could only hope that Osvaldo had never mentioned the story to his mother.

Griselda was supposed to have caused the death of over two hundred people, and that included several of her husbands. Behind her back she was called the "black widow," because when she was through with her lovers, she killed them.

Dario Sepulveda, Griselda's latest husband, sat across from me smiling. I liked him immediately. He was handsome, about five foot ten, salt-and-pepper hair, a deep tan. He was an elegant dresser. You could tell by looking at him that he spent a great deal of time on his clothes. He was wearing silk slacks and fine Italian shoes, looking every inch the Latin lover.

Griselda was heavy when I met her. But she had been a beautiful girl, a beauty queen in Colombia. That day in my living room, she was dressed like an ordinary housewife, a kerchief tied around her hair and sunglasses propped on top of her head. She wore baggy clothing to try to hide her extra weight. It was her eyes that betrayed her. They were forever cold, ice cold, colder than Rafa's were when he was in the killing mood. But she could be as charming as she could be deadly. This I was to learn over the next year.

Griselda hit it off with Cristina. They chatted and made small talk. Griselda made an appointment to get her hair done with Cristina the next day. That first time we all met was purely social and no business was discussed.

Cristina knew Griselda by reputation, so at first she was a little standoffish. But Griselda was an actress, she could have won an Academy Award. She could con a snake. And she could have conned the Pope into being her friend if she wanted to turn on the charm.

She needed us. Rafa had decided that I would be the one delivering her merchandise and collecting her money and shipping her cash down to Colombia for more purchases. I was her lifeline to the dope. She had burned a lot of people in Colombia and her sources of supply had dried up. She was out of cash.

Griselda started spending a lot of time at my house. She cultivated my wife. Griselda didn't drive, so when she wanted to go somewhere without her entourage of shooters, she would ask Cristina to drive her there. Griselda loved the beauty parlor and would go every second or third day for a manicure or pedicure or to get her hair done, and Cristina would go with her. They grew close in the sense that anytime Griselda needed a ride or to sit down and talk to another woman on an equal social level, she would call Cristina.

But the shooters were never far away. Griselda was incredibly paranoid, so the shooters would be in the car behind or waiting outside for her; they were always in the background.

One day Griselda brought over a leather bag, about the size of a makeup case, full of jewelry. She spilled the jewels out on our coffee table and pulled out a diamond ring the size of a small egg. "This diamond belonged to Eva Peron," she said. Then she picked up a diamond-and-emerald necklace that took my breath away. There were thirty 10-carat cut emeralds, strung together with diamonds, at least forty diamonds, all between 1 and 2 carats. These emeralds were the deepest, darkest green I have ever seen. They are called *gota de aceite*, "drop of oil." They are the best emeralds from Colombia, the best in the world. The necklace alone had to be worth two or three million dollars. The jewelry sparkled, lying in a jumble on the table in front of us: rings, loose stones, brooches, pendants, earrings. The total cache was probably worth at least ten million dollars.

But no matter how winsome Griselda could be, death was always sitting on her shoulder, ready to leap.

I was having some problems with Cristina. The money was pouring in, and it was changing my personality. I started playing around here and there, and Cristina was upset. One day at the beauty parlor, she talked about this to Griselda and told her she was considering a divorce.

Griselda said, "You don't need him anymore. My sons can run that end of the business with no problem. Instead of getting you a divorce, let's just get rid of him. I'll tell one of my people to go and shoot him."

Cristina was shocked. "No! Oh, my God, no! You can't do that, he's the father of my child."

When Cristina came home that night she was still shaking. She told me about it. It helped me change my ways in a hurry. But from then on, I knew it was just a matter of time until Griselda turned on both Rafa and me.

She also wanted to blow Rafa's wife away. Odila continually tried to push her out of the business, because Griselda would try to persuade Rafa to go out with other women and Odila found out about it. Griselda loved intrigue, she loved to see people fighting among themselves. She would encourage it, then take over.

And she loved to tell stories over a couple of drinks. The stories were always about all the people she killed and how she killed them. One evening she told me why some people referred to her as La Compasionata, "The Compassionate One."

Griselda had found an arms dealer who had access to automatic weapons. She was negotiating with the dealer in his apartment, and had brought along Toto and Riverito, two of her shooters, and Diego Sepulveda, Dario's brother, and Osvaldo.

The dealer started the conversation by bragging about what a big man he was. "Yeah, I just delivered a big shipment of machine guns to Papo Mejia. He's at war with some ugly fat whore named La Gorda. And I just gave him enough arms to finish the war."

Griselda turned white, whiter than the usual pale ivory of her complexion. She stood and said, "Guess who you're dealing with, asshole. I'm La Gorda, that big fat whore, and Papo Mejia is my enemy."

Right then, the dealer knew he was a dead man.

The shooters leaped for him and held him. Griselda whipped her gun out of her handbag.

"Into the bathroom!" Griselda ordered.

They had a machete, which Griselda handed to Osvaldo. They dragged the dealer to the toilet and one of the shooters grabbed him by the hair and held his head over the bowl.

The dealer realized they were going to cut his head off with the machete. He started screaming, "Please, please, shoot me. Don't do this, you can't do this."

"Shoot you?" Griselda said. "I don't want anyone to hear the noise."

"There's a gun with a silencer under the seat of my car. Please shoot me, don't use that knife. I'm sorry for what I said about you."

"Where's your car, what's it look like?" Griselda asked.

"The black Camaro, parked right in front."

"Go get the gun," Griselda commanded Osvaldo.

Minutes later Osvaldo was back with the gun.

"Give it to me," Griselda ordered. She looked down into the pleading face of the arms dealer and pulled the trigger.

Griselda ended her gruesome tale: "We dumped the body in the bathtub and hacked it up into pieces with the machete, then we distributed it around the swamps of Miami. And that's why they call me La Compasionata: I gave him his last request."

She was smiling. I didn't know what to say when she finished, so I left to go to the bathroom.

By the beginning of 1983, Griselda was back on her feet in the business, thanks to Rafa extending her credit and to her own shrewd business dealings. Her demand was climbing and she was looking for other sources of supply.

The coke that Rafa was supplying to Griselda was his own coke. And as her business grew, she wanted more credit, but Griselda was famous for paying her debts with bullets, so Rafa kept his account with her pretty current and limited. He made sure she was never into him for more than five keys or so.

But this was not the case with Marta Ochoa Saldarriaga, Rafa's mistress, and first cousin to the mighty Ochoas. Marta lived to freebase. She started freebasing with Rafa and never stopped. Marta was a beautiful, brilliant woman and she had an unlimited source of supply from the Ochoas. Marta had a constant supply of cocaine coming into the United States and a constant supply of cash leaving—or at least she did until she met Griselda Blanco.

The freebasing superseded everything, including sex and breathing. On many occasions Marta and Rafa locked themselves away for days. They just spaced out. How they managed sex with all that freebasing I'll never know. They probably lay around and did nothing more than get high. Rafa could leave it alone some of the time, but Marta couldn't.

Slowly, like a creeping cancer, Griselda started to take over Marta, when Rafa wasn't around. When he was in Colombia, Griselda would feed Marta's habit, nurturing it and keeping her company so that Marta would start to rely on her. A person who freebases will not sit alone; freebasers are so paranoid they've got to have somebody with them.

Griselda got Marta deeper and deeper into her web, until finally Marta started supplying Griselda and was using Griselda's distribution network. Marta had an unlimited source of supply and Griselda loved it.

In the beginning Griselda paid the bills she owed Marta, then she started to stretch her credit and increase the quantities. Slowly, over a period of a year, Griselda got so overextended that by 1984 she owed Marta $1,800,000 and the Ochoas had lost patience with their cousin.

During that time Griselda settled her debt with her enemy Papo Mejia.

It was August, 15, 1983, and I was sitting in Cristina Fashions, my wife's boutique, in Miami Lakes. The two best customers she had were Marta Ochoa and Griselda. We were all in there, Dario, Griselda, and me, just hanging around talking, when Riverito, Griselda's favorite shooter, walked in and and whispered something in her ear. And Griselda said, "Bring them in."

Riverito left and returned with two obvious Marielitos, Latinos who came to Miami in the Mariel boatlift. The Marielitos are the worst scum from the prisons of Cuba. Riverito had a gang of them in Miami who did his dirty work for Griselda. These Marielitos were young and well-built, wiry, muscular guys in dirty jeans and torn T-shirts.

Griselda said to them, "The plane will be in later today," and she gave them the time and flight number. "Make sure you are there, make sure it's done today."

"Okay," Riverito said, and repeated all the details to the Marielitos. Then they left.

"You know what we're doing?" Griselda asked me.

"No. What are you doing?"

"We found out that Papo Mejia is coming into Miami and we are going to take him out."

Rafa and Griselda had both been at war with Papo Mejia for a long time. This war between them was one of the main feuds that raged on endlessly during the famous "cocaine wars" that ruined Miami for years. The war started with disputes over territory and suppliers.

"You're going to waste him at the goddamn airport?" I asked.

"Yeah, that's exactly what we're going to do."

"You're out of your mind."

"No, we're not going to shoot him, we'll use a knife."

"What?"

She reached down into her huge handbag that she always carried and pulled out a bayonet. It looked like one of those World War I bayonets, all rusty, an antique weapon.

"We are using one of these." She held it up proudly. "If we don't kill him with the first stab, the second will get him." And she started to laugh.

Four or five hours later, Riverito returned to the boutique. Griselda had gone to the beauty parlor next door for a few hours to get her hair done, but she had returned to Cristina Fashions.

"It's done, but they got Miguel, my Marielito."

Riverito explained what had happened. Riverito spotted Papo as he cleared customs. "That's him," he said, and pushed the Marielito toward him. Miguel had the bayonet in a paper bag by his side with the handle sticking out. Miguel met Papo maybe three or four steps away from the customs agent, in full view of everyone in the Miami airport. "Miguel walked straight up to Papo like he was going to meet someone else, and just grabbed Papo behind the neck and started jabbing the bayonet into him. He nailed him eight or ten times. He stuck him right through the chest."

And that is exactly what happened. Miguel nailed him with eight or ten stabs and everybody figured that Papo Mejia was dead.

But he lived.

The doctors had to rebuild him. His plumbing is all plastic and they threw him in jail for thirty years on some pending Arizona charges, but he lived. Miguel was arrested on the spot and never seen again.

A couple of days later Osvaldo came into the boutique and handed me a package.

"Send this to Rafa," he said.

"What is it?" I asked.

"Open it up and look."

I opened the package and couldn't believe my eyes. It was a gold-plated bayonet. "What the hell is this?" I asked.

"When I bought the bayonet to do Papo, I bought two of them, exactly alike. My mother showed you one of them. I had this one gold-plated for Rafa. Give it to him. Rafa also hates Papo, and this will make him happy."

And I did deliver the bayonet to Rafa, and it did make him happy. He laughed when he saw it.

Griselda and Rafa could be as generous as they were deadly. I had only known Griselda three or four months when she brought me a beautiful leather jacket from Long Beach Leather in California for my birthday. It was one of my favorite shops and she knew it. She also presented me with a goose-down jacket that sold for around a thousand dollars.

And that same year at Christmas, 1982, as Rafa was showing us his brand-new Mercedes 450—the biggest model they made, with all the toys, all the options—Griselda said, "It is beautiful. Where did you get it?"

"Forget where I got it. You like it, it's yours." He handed her the keys. "Merry Christmas!" he said, and went into his house without another word.

Griselda did favors for Rafa, particularly when they served her purposes as well. Griselda had located Nicolado, Chino's brother; she knew that Rafa had put out a contract on Nicolado's head. Nicolado had almost succeeded in killing Rafa in revenge for Chino's death, and was still trying.

She told Rafa that she had found Nicolado, and Rafa gave the order: "Take him out."

Griselda sent Riverito and his band of Marielitos to do it. Riverito was not about to leave any witnesses, so he murdered everybody in the house. Six people, four males, two females, were strangled to death; only a small baby was left alive. The Miami cops called it the "Kendall Six" murders. It's still under investigation.

Nobody mentioned it to me until Rafa said, "Nicolado has been taken care of. Griselda did it for me."

It wasn't until a long time later that I realized Nicolado was one of the six people strangled in that house.

Things were always boiling around Griselda.

Diego Sepulveda, Dario's brother, hated Griselda and spent a good deal of this time trying to engineer their separation, because he knew Griselda was only using Dario to get higher up the cocaine ladder.

When Griselda realized what Diego was up to, she sealed his death warrant. She sent Riverito to kill him in his motel room in Fort Lauderdale. Riverito put a bullet in Diego's head and made it look like he had shot himself, a suicide. But there was a witness: Edgar Diaz. Diaz was in the motel room with a woman; they were totally blitzed out on freebasing. Riverito spared Edgar and the woman. Later, weeks after the killing, when Edgar came to his senses, he told me the entire story and swore me to secrecy.

When Dario got the news that his brother Diego was dead, he came over to my house. He arrived with Griselda, Toto, and a couple of shooters. Dario was crying and Toto was completely crushed. Toto and Diego had been raised together, and they were the same age even though Diego was his uncle. They had been inseparable since they were five years old. They screwed women together; they killed together. Diego taught Toto how to kill, Diego went on Toto's first hit. They were like Siamese twins, that's how close they were. Toto couldn't talk, he was sobbing uncontrollably. He stayed that way for three days.

Nobody could claim the body because everybody was in the business. Toto's mother, Elbia Sepulveda, was called up from Colombia. She was Diego and Dario's sister. She did everything that had to be done. She identified Diego's body and arranged for shipping it back to Colombia.

Elbia spent a lot of time at my place because it was a family mourning period, and my house had become the mourning house. Griselda cried more than anyone else; she outdid herself.

Finally, Toto drove his mother to the airport, then returned to pick up Griselda and the others. We found out later that they were chased by the police, but they got away.

They weren't gone five minutes when I got a strong knock on my door. I opened it to a badge being thrust in my face and a voice saying, "Agent Fazz, DEA." I looked beyond the badge and saw eight men with shotguns standing on my lawn.

"Can we come in and talk to you?" Fazz asked.

"Al Singleton, Metro-Dade Police," his partner said, also flashing a badge.

"What the hell is going on here?" I asked after I allowed them to come into the house. Altogether there were eight of them standing in my living room.

"You know Elbia Sepulveda?" Agent Fazz asked.

"Yeah, she just left for Colombia. She's at the airport."

"The DEA arrested her at the airport. Who is she?" Al Singleton asked.

"She's just a friend that we've known for years. Her brother died and she came up to make funeral arrangements."

"Do you know any of these other people?" Al Singleton started showing me some pictures that they had taken from Elbia Sepulveda.

"No, I don't know any of them."

I let them talk to the other people in the house: my wife, a guest from Peru, and my brother and sister-in-law. No one had anything to say to the police.

I left almost immediately after they did; I was sure the phone lines were tapped. Making certain I wasn't followed, I phoned Rafa from a phone booth and told him what had happened.

"Get hold of everybody, *everybody*, and tell them to move tonight."

Everybody moved except me. I had to stay where I was until the police dropped the surveillance. I went on a short vacation down to the Florida Keys for a week, and when I got back the coast was clear.

But the killing of Diego did not help Griselda. She and Dario broke up anyway. I witnessed the end of the relationship. Griselda knew that Dario was running around with an American stripper from Fort Lauderdale and she could prove it. Her possessive, jealous side began to come out. She had him followed.

Dario hated what Griselda was doing to their son, Michael Corleone, named after Griselda's favorite movie character from *The Godfather*. Little Michael was only about four at the time. Dario agreed with Griselda that Michael would go into the business, but as an educated person, not an ignoramus like Griselda and her other three sons. None of them had been educated; they could barely write their own names. But they could count money, and that's all that mattered to Griselda.

Their last argument started in my living room. Griselda was insisting that little Michael eat his lunch and Dario objected.

"You don't want it, Michael? If you're not hungry, don't eat."

"He will eat," Griselda said.

"He doesn't have to eat."

Back and forth they went until Griselda walked over, grabbed Michael by the scruff of his neck, and started to force-feed him. Michael began screaming and tried to wriggle away.

Dario had seen enough. "You've done everything you could possibly do to this kid to destroy him," he said to her. "You won't let him go to school. You treat him like an animal. You want him to grow up and be a killer like your other three. It's not going to happen to my son. The kid will be educated. The kid will be a normal kid as much as he can be. And to do it, I'm taking him back to Colombia." Dario walked over to Michael with his two main shooters, Jaime Bravo and Cumbamba, and they took Michael. That was the last I ever saw of Dario Sepulveda.

Riverito, Griselda's main shooter, stayed with her, trying to console her. She was crying uncontrollably. In between her sobs she swore, "I will get him no matter what it takes. By all that's holy, Michael will be back!"

And she did get him back. Sometime later, Dario's car was stopped in Colombia by the police. The police pulled Dario out of the car and handcuffed him. He knew instantly what was about to happen: he was going to be executed. He took off running—away from Michael so that his son would not be shot in the hail of bullets he knew would fell him in seconds—and then the police emptied their guns into him.

Little Michael ran to the body of his bullet-ridden father and embraced him, but it was too late. Dario was dead.

I made the arrangements for Michael to return to this country. Griselda knew that I had the people who could bring Michael back to the United States, with proper passports and papers. She said to me, "Whatever has to be done to get Michael back, do it."

I used a Peruvian named Martin Silva from California; he flew to Panama, where I met him and gave him twenty thousand dollars, and he made all the arrangements to pick up Michael in Colombia. He delivered Michael to his mother in California.

Griselda had paid a great sum of money to the Colombian police to execute Dario. But she had gone too far. It was the beginning of the end for her.

I told Cristina that we wouldn't be seeing any more of Griselda. She was relieved; Griselda frightened her. And my relationship ended with Griselda Blanco as abruptly as it had begun.

After his death, all of Dario's people turned against her, and his shooters became Griselda's worst enemies. Cumbamba, "The Chin," a shooter for Rafa and Dario, led the parade. He was followed by the fierce Jaime Bravo. Soon after this, Rafa joined them and they united to hunt Griselda. They vowed that they would kill her on sight, and they meant it.

Griselda was the most vicious person I ever met in my life. Others killed because they had to; Griselda killed because she enjoyed it. You could see the bloodlust in her eyes. Death lived in those eyes.

CHAPTER THIRTEEN

*

A New Cocaine War Begins

In October 1983 Rafa called me from his office in Medellín and asked me to meet him in Panama. I told him I'd come but I wanted to bring Cristina, to treat her to the trip and a shopping spree. He said he would bring a woman too. Things were going well again, the water drops were working out at last. As always, Rafa gave me no indication of what this meeting was all about. I'd learn when I saw him.

Cristina and I laughed over our speculations as to which girlfriend he would bring. When we met Rafa on our arrival at the Holiday Inn in Panama City we saw that it was Maria Monzano again. "Thoughtful of him," I said to Cristina. "Once again we have Ana's two godparents for company." The Cali-Medellín alliance.

Rafa sent Cristina and Maria off shopping and we went into the lobby bar-restaurant to talk. Rafa's main problem was that his engineer, Enrique "Kiki" Hernandez, who had been working on his extensive ranch south of Medellín, had been kidnapped by a rebel group. Despite the fear that Gacha's MAS gunmen had struck in the hearts of the communist M-19, freelance guerrilla groups were still kidnapping the rich for ransom. Rafa speculated that Kiki had been mistaken for himself. In any case, the ransom was half a million dollars' worth of guns.

By now, Panama's Colonel Manuel Noriega had become head of the military and put his own man in as El Presidente. He had quickly consolidated power and formed an alliance with the cartel, which regularly deposited huge sums of American cash into Panamanian banks. Now the cartel began making deposits into Noriega's personal accounts in Panama and also in Grand Cayman and Switzerland.

"Compadre," Rafa said, "I want you to get to know Noriega's chief drug enforcement agent in Panama City. A woman," he added. "She is equivalent to the DEA chief in the United States, only more powerful. She reports to Noriega personally and is our contact for assistance in landing and taking off from airfields here. She is also most helpful when we need to buy guns. Noriega sells us the guns the Americans give him; he sells them at a higher price than we would pay in Miami, but the convenience in transporting them makes it worth the expense."

He looked across the room to the entrance. "Here she comes now."

I followed his eyes and saw a squat, mean-faced, dark-skinned bleached blonde of indeterminate age—anywhere from thirty-five to fifty—come across the room toward us. Immediately behind her stalked an ugly, scarfaced black man in military-looking khakis. He must have been six foot three, a giant even for a black Latino. He scowled around the dining room as he followed the woman to our table. Rafa and I stood and he introduced me to her. She sat down with us, the hideous bodyguard gesturing to the people sitting at the next table to get up and move so he could sit close by.

For the next half hour Rafa gave her a list of the weapons he wanted and arranged to have the half-million dollars in payment delivered to her. He also arranged for landing a northbound coke flight at Padilla Airport. Then he placed the mantle of cartel trust over my shoulders so that I could contact her and negotiate on his behalf in case he couldn't meet with her personally the next time he had business to transact.

It was obvious that she was highly appreciative of cartel contacts. She assured us that since she was the Panamanian government's liaison with the DEA office in Panama City she would pass on to us any information she got from the agency. When she finally left, her bodyguard shuffled to his feet and followed her out of the room. Watching her go gave me the chills. I made up my mind that nothing would ever induce me to meet Noriega's chief drug enforcement officer again.

We stayed in Panama for a couple of days. Rafa did a lot of shopping for stereo sets and baseball equipment. "You will see my ranch soon, Compadre. There are three towns on my land and I am organizing a baseball team. The work on the ranch will be completed when I ransom Kiki back from the rebels. Then I will send all of MAS after them and wipe them out." The glitter in his eye at the prospect of such bloodshed left little doubt that he would carry out this threat.

As we left the hotel to go out to the airport, Rafa told me to look for him sometime after New Year's, and then we were on our way.

Just after New Year's Day of 1984 Rafa called me from Medellín to say that he would be coming back to Miami by way of Mexico and Los Angeles. For every three trips he made between Medellín and Miami,

he did two of them illegally, to avoid having too many trips from Colombia on his passport. He had no trouble getting into Mexico; from
there the Colombians had many methods of illegally crossing into California.

Whenever he wanted to come to Miami on the sly, Rafa always called
me to announce his arrival. Odila was living full-time in Miami, and a
call to me rather than to her was a signal that he was bringing a girlfriend
in with him.

This time the girl was Marta Ochoa Saldarriaga, the woman he loved
more than any other. Part of his infatuation for Marta was the fact that
she was a first cousin of the three Ochoa brothers, the true cocaine barons,
who had as close to an aristocratic lineage as anyone in South America.
Unlike the street scum, including Rafa, that made up the core of the
major dealers, the Ochoas could trace their ancestry back three generations.

Odila resented Marta above all Rafa's girlfriends. A year before, Marta
and Rafa had gotten wasted freebasing and gone to Rafa's house. Odila
screamed bloody murder when Rafa took Marta to the bedroom. He
solved the dilemma quickly. He punched out Odila and locked Marta
and himself in the master bedroom.

When Rafa sobered up a day later, Odila threatened to leave him. It
wasn't losing Odila that bothered him, it was the loss of face in the
community and the disgust in which he would be held by the Ochoa
brothers for dragging their classy cocaine-addicted cousin into the degrading squabble of a common barrio family. With gifts and cash, Rafa
bought Odila back, promising he would never see Marta again. But that
had been in 1983, and now Rafa and Marta were coming to Miami
together.

I went to the airport to meet them and drove them to Marta's house
in the Kendall area of Miami. As soon as we walked through the door
Marta started screaming about Griselda Blanco. "I'm going to get that
one million eight hundred thousand dollars the bitch owes me," Marta
swore. "She would be out of business, broke, if I had not kept her supplied.
And now my cousins are after me to pay them."

I knew that Griselda had finally paid Rafa what she owed him, but he
had still cut her off, leaving her dependent upon Marta for her supply.
I also knew that it was Marta's coke that Griselda had sold to finish paying
off Rafa, so I doubted that Marta would ever collect her money from the
"black widow."

As Rafa and I started to leave, Marta ran across the room and put her arms around him. She was a couple of inches taller, but that didn't seem to bother either of them.

"When am I going to see you again, Rafa?" she cried, a note of despair in her voice. "Where can I reach you?"

"You have my beeper number, sweetheart," Rafa replied. "I'll always get back to you."

Both Rafa and I moved residences regularly and never kept telephone numbers in our own names. Even our cars were registered to dummy addresses so the plates could not be traced. I was careful to make sure that nobody except Rafa knew where I lived with Cristina and the children.

"Do you think Marta will ever get her money?" I asked when we were back in my car.

Rafa shook his head. "Marta shouldn't be so deep in this business. She gets messed up freebasing and doesn't know what she's doing." He laughed mirthlessly. "Who am I to talk about *her* habit? But at least I sober up and keep my eyes on things."

I asked Rafa about his engineer, Kiki.

"I delivered the half-million dollars' worth of guns from Panama, and Kiki is now back on my ranch finishing the construction and landscaping."

As he stepped out of my car in front of his house, an uncharacteristic look of concern came over his face. "I am worried about Marta. I love her, you know, Max."

"Why don't you tell her to forget the money, forget going after Griselda, and get out of the business," I suggested. "Her cousins will let her off the hook. Let them send their shooters after Griselda."

I drove back home to Cristina.

Two weeks later Rafa and I were driving around, scouting for a new stash house, when Rafa's beeper went off. He put through the call at a pay phone. There was a worried look on his face when he came back to the car.

"That was Huevo asking if I knew where Marta is. They haven't seen her for several days." Huevo, "the Egg," was one of the Ochoa family. He was looking for his cousin.

"When did you last see her?" I asked.

"We were together last week."

"Has Griselda paid her any money yet?" I already knew the answer. Griselda never paid for anything if she could avoid it.

"If anything bad happens to Marta, Griselda will have more problems than she can handle."

"You want to start a war?" I asked. "We've got enough problems already."

He didn't answer. He just stared straight ahead.

A few days later I got a call from Huevo. "I've just found my cousin's car," he said breathlessly. "It's here in the parking lot of the big K Mart store at U.S. 1 and 104th Street."

"Well, go find her," I said.

Huevo hesitated. "I am afraid to go look for her because the whole front seat is covered with blood."

"Leave the car there and get the hell out of the area. We'll have to wait and see where the body turns up."

The next day Marta's body was found in the weeds beside a canal and taken to the morgue. She had been cruelly beaten, her face was swollen, battered black and blue. There were many ways to get rid of a body; Marta's corpse was dumped where it would be found, a clear signal from Griselda Blanco to Rafa that war had been declared and he was next.

In all the years I knew him, I never saw Rafa display such cold fury as when he heard about Marta's death and the way she had been tortured. Rafa knew that Griselda had tried to beat his address out of her, and mine too. If one of us could be found, the other would be nearby.

Marta's father flew up from Colombia to identify the body. He also conducted a wake, which Rafa attended. "This will all end here," the grieving father pronounced. "We will not seek retaliation. Too much violence haunts us as it is."

Rafa was unmoved by the conciliatory words of his lover's father. "Something has been taken from me that I loved very much," Rafa told me, and he swore an oath of vengeance.

Rafa sent word out to Jaime Bravo, Cumbamba, and his entire clan of shooters in Colombia, New York, and Florida to kill on sight any and all of Griselda Blanco's people. "If you see them, blow them away!" were the orders. He posted a separate reward for whoever could deliver Griselda Blanco herself to him, dead or alive.

We were on a wartime footing.

The Broward Mall just west of Fort Lauderdale was a favorite shopping area for Griselda Blanco. It was here that Jaime Bravo made the first contact of the war. He spotted Riverito, one of Griselda's shooters. Jaime had just found out that Griselda had killed his uncle, Alberto Bravo.

Rafa described the encounter. "Jaime was in a phone booth at the mall, making a call, when he saw Riverito come through the entrance and head right toward him. Riverito didn't see him. Suddenly Jaime stepped out of the booth and confronted Riverito. 'Come on, come on, *hijodeputa*,' Jaime taunted. He beckoned Riverito to keep coming. 'I'm waiting for you.' He had his Browning high-power out and was ready when Riverito finally saw him. Riverito turned and ran, slipping away in the crowd."

When Griselda heard that piece of news about the two shooters, she took off with her sons for California and that was the last anyone saw of her until the DEA grabbed her out there. She was sent to prison and will be there into the next century, if someone doesn't nail her first while she's still behind bars.

CHAPTER FOURTEEN

*

The Coronation

February 9, 1984. Rafael Cardona Salazar, at thirty-four years of age, had finally arrived. He was no longer a mere employee of the cartel. He was about to be granted a momentous honor, one that would echo through Rafa's world like a great bell hailing his rise. He had been invited to sit on the cartel council. His ascension to the hallowed halls of the Colombian drug lords had begun.

Rafa's elevation had also raised me to an important and privileged position within the cartel. I had succeeded to all of Rafa's responsibilities in the United States, and then some. There was no area of cartel operations in which I might not be called upon to offer advice and assistance. I had helped many of the high-ranking Colombians and members of their families to escape prosecution and incarceration. I had by this time personally sent over $70 million in cash back to the cartel, with more being shipped every week. For years I had been one of the chief arms suppliers to the burgeoning army of enforcers employed by the Medellín drug lords.

At the height of his importance to the cartel in Miami, Rafa's position could not compare to the status I now enjoyed. I was frequently told that I was to the cartel what Meyer Lansky had been to the Mafia. Even though I often thought about getting out of trafficking—and there wasn't a week that Cristina and I didn't mention the possibilities, and of course the lack of them, of renouncing the life I was living and taking my family somewhere that the Colombians would never find me—I never forgot Rafa's grim warning that there were only two ways out, and I didn't like either one.

Rafa's coronation was heralded by Jorge Ochoa himself, the founder of the cartel, the brains, the soft-spoken, unassuming pundit, the legendary velvet-gloved iron fist. And to confirm Rafa's rise to the council, Jorge had agreed to stand as godfather to Rafa's new son on this day.

The christening was to be celebrated high in the green hills above Medellín. Two thousand guests would gather at Kevin's disco to celebrate the baptism of Rafael Cardona Salazar Jr.

All expenses were paid by Rafa: air fares, hotel accommodations, even personal room charges were looked after. Rafa invited people he liked, including people who were not in the drug business, our neighbors in Miami, for instance. He paid their air fare, bought a suit of clothes for the man, and paid him for the wages he lost by coming to the party. If Rafa wanted you at the party, you were sent for and you came. Before the party was over, Rafa would spend over $500,000.

Combined, the invited group represented over $10 billion in net worth. Rafa alone was worth over $50 million at that time. They called themselves Nosotros or El Grupo; it means We, or Us, or The Group. I silently called them "Apalachin Colombiana" because this gathering made the 1950s meeting of Mafia chieftains at Apalachin in upstate New York look like a Boy Scout convention.

I felt honored. When I landed in Medellín a limousine stood waiting for myself, Cristina, and the three kids, who now ranged in age from five to eighteen. The limo was not in front of the terminal, it was parked on the tarmac beside the plane. We handed our carry-on luggage and passports to Rafa's father, who was sent to meet us. He handed them to a man standing next to him. The man turned out to be the head of Immigration. As we pulled out, I watched the two men move over to the belly of the plane and separate our luggage as it was spotted on the conveyor belt. It was quickly hustled onto a waiting truck. I knew the truck would never be inspected.

We were taken to Rafa's house and twenty minutes later our bags arrived, along with our passports and personal bodyguards. Rafa's was a fine comfortable dwelling with many servants, but it was not a mansion or a palace. Jaime, Rafa's bodyguard, was in charge of security. Jaime was a full colonel in the Colombian army. He had the power to move things with a phone call or a nod. All the bodyguards carried automatic weapons or pistols stuck in their belts. No one in the drug business in Colombia moved without at least one bodyguard, especially in Medellín, the wildest city in Colombia.

It had been three months since I had last seen Rafa. Never had I known him to be so happy; the blanket of paranoia that normally enveloped him had lifted from his shoulders. He was drinking heavily, but it only improved his already ebullient mood. It was the day before the big party,

Rafael (Rafa) Cardona Salazar (*right*), my mentor and chief distributor for the Medellín cartel, with Edgar Diaz, our genial gofer. This photo was snapped just a few days before Rafa murdered Chino Arles.

On Christmas Eve of 1978 Cristina and I gave a party for her Colombian friends and relatives. As it happened, my fate was determined that night. (*L to R*) Carlos Rios, called El Bicho de Oro ("Golden Cock") for his unending amatory conquests, who eventually became one of my suppliers; Chino, killed hours later; "Flaco," formerly part-owner of the Miami disco Studio 23; Flaco's brother (in glasses), whom Rafa shot in the face that night; and (with moustache) Arturo, my wife Cristina's older brother. (The numbers were used by the Drug Enforcement Agency for identification purposes.)

THE OCHOA FAMILY

The patriarch of the family, Fabio Ochoa Restrepo, a horse breeder and trainer who was never directly involved in his sons' drug business.

Margoth Vasquez de Ochoa, the matriarch.

Angela Maria.

Fabio, the American-street-educated, soft-spoken hippie brother.

Fresia.

Maria Isabel.

Cristina.

Juan David.

Jorge Luis. (DEA photo)

Marta Nieves. As Jorge Ochoa's sister, her kidnapping served to consolidate the various drug lords into the powerful and self-protective Colombian cocaine cartel whose counterterror tactics brought about Marta's release.

THE CARTEL

Jorge Luis Ochoa.
(DEA photo)

Juan David Ochoa.
(DEA photo)

Fabio Ochoa.
(DEA photo)

Pablo Escobar Gaviria, the cartel's most violent leader. In November 1989 he blew up an Avianca flight from Bogotá to Cali, killing all 107 people aboard. (DEA photo)

Gustavo Gaviria Rivero, Escobar's cousin and one of the cartel's leaders.

Gonzalo Rodriguez Gacha, "The Mexican," who was assassinated by the Colombian government in December 1989. (DEA photo)

Carlos Lehder. (*Miami Herald* photo)

Rafa at Disney World with one of his mistresses, Stela Henao, and his brother-in-law, Bobby Montanez, who took over West Coast operations from me.

Odila, Rafa's wife, with Carolina and Rafa junior.

Halloween, my daughter's birthday and the day before my own on November 1, was the occasion for regular parties at my house. This one was at Miami Lakes. (*L to R*) Soledad Cardona, Rafa's mother; Rafael Antonio Cardona, Rafa's father; and Maria Monzano, Cali's cocaine queen.

Griselda Blanco de Trujillo, the ruthless killer and trafficker known as "the Black Widow," dancing with a Colombian newspaper reporter who had no idea who she was and thought her name was Betty.

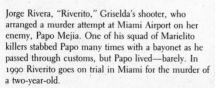

Jorge Rivera, "Riverito," Griselda's shooter, who arranged a murder attempt at Miami Airport on her enemy, Papo Mejia. One of his squad of Marielito killers stabbed Papo many times with a bayonet as he passed through customs, but Papo lived—barely. In 1990 Riverito goes on trial in Miami for the murder of a two-year-old.

Maria Monzano, the trafficker, with her husband, Elmer Tenorio. Tenorio was known as El Mudo ("The Mute"), because although Maria slept around, he never said a word about it.

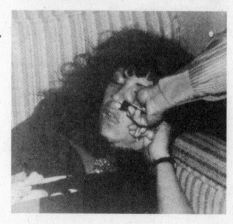

Maria Monzano, Rafa, Cristina, and I went for a vacation in Acapulco. Here, Maria is asleep and Rafa is trying to wake her up by shoving cocaine up her nose.

Outside the town of Restrepo in Colombia, where Nelson Urrego maintains a number of cocaine labs. (*L to R*) Maria Monzano; Rafa; my wife Cristina (blanked out); Enrique, Rafa's engineer; Juan Urrego, Nelson's brother; Nelson's father; and two unidentified people.

Nelson Urrego of Cali. Nelson produces the coke in his own labs, then ships it on Gran Colombiano, the Colombian shipping line. His loads average 75-100 kilos per trip. They are weighted to sink and are dumped overboard in American ports—mostly New York—where scuba divers retrieve them.

Jon Pernell Roberts, my Mafia-connected friend, who stood ready to help me find and kill Barry Seal. Jon is a fugitive today.

Mickey Munday, our ground operations supervisor.

Rodrigo Restrepo, Rafa's cousin and gofer, who drove the 20 kilos of cocaine from Miami to California to be delivered to John DeLorean. The coke was hidden in the *caletas* (hiding chambers) installed in one of our ordinary-looking Chevrolets.

Efraim Roa, the largest money launderer for the Cali cartel. Until his arrest he ran a massive operation in Cali, New York, San Francisco, Los Angeles, and Houston. His partner was the head of customs at the Cali airport.

Alfredo Martinez, the drug-running Colombian senator who kept the air force grounded when we were flying a load out of the country. This was a strategy meeting between us in an associate's New York apartment. My adopted daughter, Marisol, is standing beside him, her face blanked out for security reasons.

Carlos Arango, called Cumbamba, "The Chin," the shooter and dealer who murdered Barry Seal.

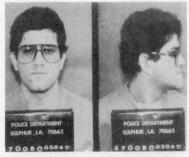

Police photo of the American trafficker Barry Seal, who was murdered after he turned witness for the government.

and his wife never left his side. She knew he was capable of slipping into a freebase haze and going out on the town to look for girls, to disappear on a binge that might last for days and ruin the party. His father also stayed by his side, gently talking to him and ushering him through the day. Rafa respected and idolized his father, and his father knew it.

The next day Cristina, myself, and the children were driven to the party high in the verdant hills above Medellín; an electric excitement crackled through the air.

Kevin's disco could hold between five and six hundred people, but this barely accommodated one-third of the guests Rafa had assembled. Kevin's was a trendy, stylish disco that looked like it belonged in Miami, not Medellín. There were few Colombians who could afford a night at Kevin's. It was built for the drug lords, their ladies and their minions.

A giant circus tent extended off the veranda at Kevin's, big as any tent I ever saw. A second canopy had been pitched off to the side. This tent was for the hundreds of bodyguards. As I observed the enormous firepower in the tent I recalled a maxim I had recently heard about this place. Medellín was a beautiful and rich valley sitting inside a mountain range like a cup. For a century it had been known as La Taza de Oro, "Cup of Gold." Since the drug lords had taken over, Medellín had earned a new appellation, La Taza de Plomo, "Cup of Lead."

The children's party came first; it began at two thirty and ran for four or five hours. Rafa singled out Ana for special attention. Ana was going on six now, and beautiful in her party dress. Rafa took her by the hand and introduced her to the other children. He could be royally charming when it suited him, and today he was in the mood. Cristina and I smiled and held each other as we watched Rafa with his goddaughter.

When the children's party was over, two orchestras arrived and set up for a night of nonstop music. The food was marched in on trays carried one-handed by liveried vassals; anything we wanted was available, including a kilo of coke plopped down in the center of the table, if requested.

The drug-hierarchy pecking order was carefully observed: the aristocracy sat inside Kevin's at tables, the lesser lights were seated outside in the tent.

It was hard to believe that this organization was born only in 1978, six years before, created out of the mind of Juan David Ochoa, the oldest Ochoa brother. He was now out of any direct dealings, although he invested in the cartel. He and his two brothers Jorge and Fabio, along with Pablo Escobar and Pablo Correa, formed the nucleus. They were the pioneers of the cartel. In the early 1980s they gradually allowed new members into the inner sanctum: Rodriguez Gacha, Pablo Gaviria, Carlos Correa, Jairo Mejia, and now Rafael Cardona Salazar.

Patrols were constantly circling the property under Jaime's direction. Jaime was a serious man. Every car that entered the property was searched, invitations were checked off against a master list, and if a guest showed up with too many bodyguards, the bodyguards were asked to leave. People arrived from all parts of Colombia: Cali, Medellín, Bogotá. More people streamed in from California, Florida, Mexico, Bolivia, Peru.

Cristina and I were seated with a few of her girlhood friends from Cali. One of the people at our table was Carlos Correa, the king of Acandí, whom I had met on my first visit to the Ochoa ranch at Vera Cruz. By now I had sent at least fifty flights to his airstrip. "Carlitos" acted like a true king in his personal fiefdom of Acandí, which consisted of fifty thousand acres. He owned Acandí and all of its surrounding area, and dispensed justice, money, love, and death as a king would in the Middle Ages.

The talk at the table stopped dead when Mono Vargas came up and embraced me, tears in his eyes. He insisted that he be seated with us. "Max, Max, my compadre," Mono said, his voice almost breaking with emotion. "I must sit here next to you and your beautiful wife if I am to truly enjoy this night. If it were not for you, I would be rotting in an American jail cell instead of breathing this beautiful cool night air of Colombia." He hugged me again.

"Tell us, Compadre; tell everyone how you got Vargas to safety here among his friends," Carlos Correa asked, even though he knew. Vargas was a trusted man. He had been Carlos Correa's main money launderer in Miami. Together they had laundered hundreds of millions.

I laughed to myself, remembering how I helped them stuff the walls of refrigerators and other household appliances with millions of dollars, four to five million per refrigerator, and send them down to Mono's import warehouse, where after the money was removed the appliances were sold at a handsome profit.

I shrugged. "I am embarrassed to tell you how simple it was. The government still has not figured it out."

"Tell them, Max," Cristina prodded, proudly wanting to hear me tell of one of my exploits most appreciated by the drug lords.

"We found out that Vargas was a marked man," I began, and silence fell on the company as I warmed to the story. "A warrant for his arrest was imminent; they were looking all over Miami for him. This is how we did it. I walked up to the Avianca counter and bought a round-trip ticket in my name. They checked my passport and handed it back to me with my boarding pass."

I chuckled and went on. "I walked around the corner and handed the boarding pass to Vargas. I waved goodbye to him as he boarded the plane. When he landed in Colombia, everything had been arranged so he could pass through Immigration without a hitch."

"Yes, the simple way is always the best way," Carlos Correa commented. "The *federales* are looking for complicated schemes and Vargas strolls by, whistling innocently, right under their noses."

"Too true," I added. "More fugitives have gotten out that way than the U.S. government has any idea of."

Dora spotted me from the nearby Ochoa table and immediately came over to see me. She had Pelusa, her husband, in tow. He and Dora owned Kevin's disco. Pelusa looked outrageous in a gold lamé tuxedo. He actually glittered when he moved, shimmering in the lights. Crazy clothes were his trademark and his obsession. "Pelusa" roughly translated means "itching powder." He made people nervous.

"Compadre, so good to see you and Cristina. How nice you both look," Dora said while Pelusa shook my hand. Dora had escaped from the Miami women's jail on the back of a motorcycle. She had been charged with possession and sale of cocaine. Dora was in deep trouble; she was hotter than hot; and after her escape everyone was looking for her. I used a private plane on the down leg of a coke run to take her back to Colombia.

"Great party," I observed, my eyes everywhere.

"Only just starting, Max. See you later, Compadre," she said affectionately. "Maybe we can find time to talk about the old times." She sailed off with the gold lamé tux in tow.

I felt complete that night, strong, powerful, elite. Not bad, not bad at all! I was the only Jewish gringo from Brooklyn in attendance, and I had the run of the joint.

Jorge Ochoa's decision to be the godfather of Rafa junior was indeed a great honor for Rafa. Jorge and his brothers were worth more than a billion dollars, with the power of life and death over everyone gathered there. It's no wonder the Ochoas were easygoing, smooth men, with impeccable manners. They were careful of their actions; they knew that one slight gesture from them could be misconstrued by a guest, who might think that he had fallen into displeasure with the monarchs and was marked for death. Paranoia permeated the high mountain air; paranoia is the sister to the white powder. Death is the brother.

The two thousand guests were treated by Rafa to anything that money can buy, the finest: Dom Perignon; quail eggs dipped in honey—the best thing I ever tasted; Beluga caviar; fresh salmon flown in from Nova Scotia; bottles of Château Lafite-Rothschild on every table; a buffet table laden with steaks, chicken, turkey, and whole roast pigs. The table was so long that it seemed to extend right into the sparkling green mountainside that overlooked the city of Medellín.

Outside, a continuous chain of limousines ran nonstop to the best hotels in the city, bringing the cocaine clans back and forth to the festivities.

The two hundred bodyguards stood on the alert in the smaller tent: men-in-waiting, soldiers standing by, ready to attend their generals when called. There was enough firepower gathered in that tent to have waged a memorable mini-war. While their masters feasted they waited like male lions, angry cats taking the measure of one another.

The kings circulated easily within their charmed circles, moving from one group to another. The Ochoa clan presided, but Pablo Escobar, a car thief and hit man only five years before, was now rated as the richest single criminal in the world; elegant and eloquent as always, Pablo did as he liked. Jota, the chief accountant for the cartel, the only man who knew everything, was there. Gonzalo Rodriguez Gacha and Jairo Mejia, both high-ranking cartel members, were there. Every one of them made a special point of coming up and thanking me for past favors and the many unusual, to say the least, services I had performed for them. They knew that in the future they would need me to perform tasks they couldn't even foresee.

Pablo Escobar had to let me know, of course, that I wasn't totally indispensable, that there were other Americans flying their product into various parts of the States. "MacKenzie is catching up to you, Compadre," Escobar laughed, and turned to Jorge. "No?"

Jorge nodded. "Sí. MacKenzie is everywhere with his planes. He has made a deal in Nicaragua to stockpile our material and then fly it into Florida, Louisiana, and Texas."

"My boys are doing okay, no?" I said.

"Oh, sí, sí, you are our compadre," Pablo Escobar hastily assured me. "The others are useful tools."

There was much camaraderie and backslapping, and the talk was constantly of expansion and ways to increase the ever-flowing stream of coke into the United States. More sophisticated smuggling techniques were discussed, along with better routes, more pilots, the use of cargo containers, freighters, even surplus World War II submarines. It was all great fun, *mucho macho* talk about exotic schemes that never would or could materialize. It was my airlift, and I guess MacKenzie's, whoever he was, that did the job for them.

A tall, gaunt man with sharp features and wearing thick glasses came up to me and laid a hand on my shoulder. "I am Kiki, Kiki Hernandez. You were with Rafa when he bought the guns in Panama to ransom me."

"That's right, Kiki," I answered, shaking his hand. "I am glad to see you are here and not with the rebels."

Kiki laughed. "I am lucky to be alive. They thought they had Rafa himself. When they discovered I was only a poor employee, they almost shot me. Fortunately they needed the guns Rafa gave to them to get me back."

"I thought MAS was supposed to have stopped all this kidnapping two years ago," I said.

Kiki shrugged. "Anyway, tomorrow I understand you will be going out to see the hacienda and grounds I created for Rafa."

"Yes, my family and I are looking forward to that."

The festivities only stopped once, fading into half an hour of respectful silence as the priest arrived to baptize Rafa's son. Junior was a good boy, smiling and gurgling as the priest said the words over him, making the sign of the cross, gently pouring tiny drops of water on his head to remove original sin, the sin of Adam and Eve. The crown prince only cried when the priest brushed salt on his tiny cupid-lips. Rafa beamed, smiling through the ceremony of baptism for his young prince, heir to his empire.

When the priest was finished and the boy was safely back in his mother's arms, the talk started again. The cartel had a problem. They had more cocaine than ever before. Tons of it were being stockpiled in the jungle, far from the eyes of any law enforcement agencies. A great secret web of jungle laboratories had been busy processing coca leaf and paste into cocaine since the previous September. They were producing four thousand kilos a month, and production soon would be doubled. A torrential cocaine snowstorm was about to fall on the United States.

The music from the orchestras filled the heavy night air, the music mixing with the women's French perfumes and the exotic scent of tropical flowers. The band played on as Jorge Ochoa explained these things to Rafa and me; he spoke slowly and quietly in a confidential way, including me as an equal, privy to his powerful secrets. I was honored. Jorge had done what no man before him had done. Making cocaine was complex. Organizing the Indians to harvest and process the leaf and paste in Peru and Bolivia and bring it into Colombia was a formidable undertaking. Tons of chemicals were required, including hard-to-get ether, and aviation fuel. Ochoa was set up to produce thirty-five tons of cocaine a year, half the cocaine that entered the United States, and he needed to get it delivered.

That's where I came in. I was given the job of opening windows in Colombian and U.S. airspace, flying the cocaine in—creating a snowstorm in Florida. Water routes were good, but they were slow and subject to busts; the bulk had to come in from the sky.

But I had it figured out. I had anticipated the need. As I sat listening to Jorge Ochoa, I knew we had to increase both our activity and our entry points: more planes, more boats, more spotters, more drop zones in the Bahamas, more entry points along the coast of South Florida right up to Vero Beach. I knew how to open these windows and that's why they kept me around. They knew I could figure these things out, organize, and administrate. If Max Mermelstein ran it, it worked.

I smiled at Rafa and he smiled back. "Keep the shit coming from Colombia, Jorge. No problem!" The more coke the Ochoa brothers made, the more we had to bring into the U.S.; the more we sold, the richer we got.

The party rolled on. Cristina and I danced until four in the morning, her classic Hispanic beauty and long dark hair shimmering in the moonglow. Never in my whole life have I experienced a celebration like the christening of Rafa's son.

The next morning Rafa wanted to take me to see the ranch he was so proud of owning. He'd been up all night and was still drunk. At nine Cristina and I and the three kids were driven to the airport, where Rafa's Cessna 310 and Cheyenne 3 were waiting. Shakily, Rafa climbed into the pilot's seat of the Cessna and announced that he would fly the plane. I helped the pilot talk him out of it and finally he left the flight deck and staggered back to the rear passenger section and collapsed. I looked around the custom interior in admiration and estimated this toy represented Rafa's profit on about eighty keys of cocaine, a fraction of one week's worth of deliveries by my pilots.

Rafa slept for the hour it took to fly over the mountains surrounding Medellín and out into the lush valley beyond, where his spread was located. We landed and taxied over to the edge of the grass. Rafa could not be awakened.

Orlando, the ranch administrator, was called. He took one look at Rafa and shrugged as he threw the small body over his shoulder like a sack of potatoes and carried it up the lawn to the house. Orlando plopped him into bed, and that was the last we saw of Rafa for twenty-four hours.

The hacienda was enormous, more like a hotel than a ranch house, with thirty-five bedrooms that formed a court around an Olympic-sized swimming pool. Each room was set up like a fine hotel, with its own TV, air conditioner, and refrigerator. The floors were marble, the bath-room fixtures gold. The roof of the hacienda was red Spanish tile, the walls thick concrete covered with swirling stucco. The view was a mag-nificent panorama of the breathtaking Colombian countryside. By the pool was a bandstand, dance floor, and a fully stocked bar, its marble top glistening in the noonday sun.

We had a nice slow afternoon, the kids splashing in the pool and Rafa sleeping off his monumental celebration. From time to time an executive jet would circle the ranch and land. Soon other guests arrived and joined us at the pool. The day eased into night and finally became the next morning.

I was elected to wake Rafa up. He came to grumpy and groggy; suddenly he snapped to alertness. "Where's the protection?" he cried.

"What protection?" I asked. "We got a couple of bodyguards inside and some shooters outside."

"Where are Orlando and Jaime? They know that when we come out to the farm, the army comes out to the farm. Jaime's a colonel, for crissake!"

Rafa got dressed and went storming out to find them. He located the two security officers near the barn. I could hear the yelling all the way back at the hacienda. Next I saw Jaime and Orlando driving the Jeep. They disappeared in a cloud of dust on their way to find the lieutenant of the local army garrison.

Two hours later Jaime and Orlando returned and reported to Rafa at the pool with his guests. "The lieutenant and fifteen men will be here tonight," Jaime announced. "They will stand watch and protect the perimeter."

Rafa removed his oversized designer sunglasses and motioned both men to come closer to him so he could whisper, "If anything bad had happened I would have killed you, *comprenden?*"

"*Sí,*" they said, and slunk away in disgrace. I pretended not to hear. Rafa slipped his sunglasses back on his face and drifted off in his hangover haze.

At five o'clock, two army trucks and a Jeep showed up. Fifteen men leaped out and awaited their lieutenant's orders. The men were soon picketed around the ranch house with orders to shoot to kill.

The next day Rafa was in good enough shape to take us on a tour of his kingdom. Cristina, the kids, and a few other guests went along for the ride. We drove in several cars for over twenty minutes, until we came to a small town.

The town was a collection of hovels, tar-paper shacks with tin roofs. There was a foul-smelling open sewer that ran off into the fields. The air buzzed thick with flies. This was pure poverty, an ultimate challenge for the Peace Corps. The people slowly emerged from their shacks to shuffle before the great Rafa. He smiled benevolently at them and asked the town elder if they had received the baseball equipment.

At first they only stared back at him. Then one of the men nudged the elder and he finally smiled, nodding at a small boy, maybe nine years old, wearing only dirty shorts. They issued an order and the boy disappeared, to return in seconds with a brand-new uniform that said L.A. DODGERS on the chest. He wore a hat to match. The little guy waved a brand-new leather Rawlings catcher's mitt and a new Spalding baseball in the air; he smiled a strange, almost retarded smile, flashing the gap where a front tooth should have been. I remembered those uniforms; I had bought them for Rafa at Sportsman's Paradise in Miami.

Rafa gestured at the boy. "Someday, maybe I get a Willie Mays off my farm, huh, Compadre?" he said, grinning at me.

"Maybe. If he doesn't starve to death first."

"Hey, these people don't mind how they live. They've lived like this for centuries." We got back in the Jeep.

"Sure," I answered, and we drove on in silence for ten more minutes until we reached the top of a high mountain. Rafa ordered the car stopped and we climbed out. The view was impressive, rolling pasture for miles and miles dotted with grazing cattle.

"Five thousand, Compadre. I got five thousand head of cattle and fifty thousand acres. Your eye can't see to the edge of my horizon. Not bad for a boy from the barrio of Medellín, huh?"

"Not bad, Rafa," I agreed. "And more to come."

"Yeah, that's good, more to come. Especially now that I sit almost equal with the Ochoa brothers. Yes, there will be lots more to come."

We drove on up another hill and down onto a long plain. I thought I was seeing a mirage at first, like a mirror shimmering in the afternoon sun, a mirror of black wavy glass. As we approached, the black mass began to rise into the air; the air was filled with thousands and thousands of ducks. Rafa ordered the small convoy stopped and four shotguns brought to him.

"Let's go have some fun, Compadre!"

The other couples and the children started to move toward the lake, but Rafa stopped them. "No, this is just for me and Max; my compadre likes to shoot. You will please wait here."

The other sightseers were left in the cars and Rafa, myself, and three bodyguards carrying boxes of shotgun shells walked to the edge of the lake. The birds had settled down again. There was no shooting unless Rafa was the shooter. We each had two riot guns, police-issue twelve-gauge shotguns. The bodyguards squatted on the damp grass beside the lake and tore open the cardboard boxes of shells and loaded the guns. The guns were handed to us and I put mine to my shoulder and waited. Rafa did the same and held his fire, almost daring me to shoot first, but I didn't.

Abruptly, Rafa started pumping rounds. He dropped the gun. He was handed a new one; now, as fast as he and I could shoot, we were handed fresh guns, locked and loaded.

The carnage went on for five minutes, until the barrels of all four shotguns were ruddy red from the firing. The birds, confused at first, flew in circles, not knowing what to do. They had never been anywhere but on this beautiful lake in the middle of nowhere. But within minutes their survival instincts kicked in and they scattered, wildly, in a thick black cloud, like a torn ink-stained blotter, disoriented and panicked.

As I looked away from the flying birds, I was amazed to see the people; they seemed to have come out of nowhere and were gathered around the lake, maybe twenty or thirty of them. They looked at Rafa questioningly. He ignored them and motioned for me to climb the tiny hillock back to the waiting cars and his less-favored guests. When he reached the top he turned and raised his hand and, ever so slightly, waved.

It was the signal they had been waiting for, the royal assent. Some of the men ran around the shore of the lake; others dove in, flailing the water as they swam, trying to retrieve the dead birds.

"They will eat well tonight," Rafa said as he climbed into the Jeep.

For the next four hours we toured the domain of Rafael Cardona Salazar. It was a spectacular feudal estate, the lord of the manor exercising total control over the destiny of his tenants.

The following morning we all flew back to Medellín. The women went shopping, along with four bodyguards. But Rafa had something else in mind for me. "Let's go for a ride," he said exuberantly, and jumped into his latest toy, a Mercedes 450 SL. Four bodyguards climbed into the gold Mercedes 380 limo, two more into the Chevy Blazer, and the final two bodyguards slipped into the front seat of the Jeep.

The Blazer and the Jeep swung out in front of us, taking the lead, and the gold Mercedes followed us. They paced their speed from Rafa's car, even though it was the third car in the convoy. As we drove, two hand grenades rolled out from underneath my seat. I picked them up and gingerly put them in the glove compartment as Rafa watched, grinning at me as though I were a stupid kid. I looked over my shoulder at the small jumpseat behind me. On the seat were two Uzis and two Browning high-powered automatics. The men in the lead and follow cars were all armed with machine guns, Uzis, and Mac-10s.

With a questioning look I motioned with my thumb over my shoulder at the hardware lying on the back seat.

"Hey, man, this is Medellín: Medellín, Colombia," Rafa chuckled by way of explanation, "and this is how you travel. Anything can happen in Medellín, any fucking thing, Compadre."

"Where we going?" I asked.

"To the beginning." He smiled enigmatically.

Our convoy sped through Medellín, weaving along the crowded thoroughfares. Heads turned as the shiny new cars zoomed by. Owning a car in Colombia is a miracle. Most of those who own them have old ones. The import duty is stiff and gas is three dollars a gallon, so the average car on the streets is vintage. You feel like you are driving in a 1950s movie or living out *American Graffiti*. Once a Colombian acquires a car, he and his family cherish it above all other possessions.

Barrio Belén slaps you right in the face like a smelly, dirty sock. As we entered the barrio, word of Rafa's presence spread as if jungle drums were beating out the news.

The barrio extends for ten square blocks of solid squalor, deep, depressing poverty, the kind that makes the Brownsville area of Brooklyn where I grew up seem like Park Avenue. This was soul-deep, totally without money, despair. A city within a city of tar-paper shacks, tin roofs, no windows or screens, open latrines, the smell of urine and feces permanently wafting through the air. These people had no time to think of anything but their ever-growling stomachs, asking only to survive to see another dawn.

This was Rafa's birthplace, and it explained Rafa to me more than any words could. It was where hell began and ended; it was the city of no hope. It was a tiny spot on earth that God had abandoned. Now I knew why his eyes were black-dead and how he could, in the same night, shoot Flaco's brother in the face, kill Chino in the van, and sleep like a baby, never thinking about what he had done.

This barrio had drained the humanity out of him. Concerns of conscience and morality were the useless thoughts of weak men, men you found dead every morning in the barrio alleys as the sun edged up over the horizon and shrill crows of roosters heralded the start of a new day.

Rafa was treated like a god in the barrio. He had done the impossible, kicked and scratched his way out of the mire. And now he was standing there in front of them, Rafa the magnificent, legend of the barrio, resplendent in his fine clothes and automobiles, protected by scowling, heavily armed bodyguards.

As the poor gathered around us, encircling Rafa in their adoration and miserable poverty, I knew why he had brought me to this spot and why he had taken me on the extended tour of his ranch. He wanted me to know his roots and how he had become the man he was: a man without conscience. For some deep-seated human reason, he needed to justify his life to me. And it was precisely because he was without conscience that he was able to climb out of this miserable place and sit with the drug lords on their councils and own fifty thousand acres of land and live in a baronical hacienda.

A man stepped forward from the crowd and spoke in a faltering, humble way as he would speak to a high dignitary. As we stood in the stinking heat, he explained to Rafa that Armando, a man who had worked for Rafa and me in the United States, had been shot the night before.

"How bad is he?" Rafa asked.

"Bad, Don Rafael, very bad. He was shot five times. He is in the hospital."

"Why? Why was he shot?" Rafa asked.

"He had sold the fat bazooka cigarettes to a crazy man and the man owed him money. Armando went to collect."

"And the man shot him?"

"Sí, Señor."

Rafa patted the old man on the shoulder and signaled us back into the cars. We sped off to the hospital.

We found Armando lying desolate in a ward, with plastic tubes sticking into many orifices of his body. He was conscious and smiled as Rafa and I walked in.

"So," Rafa said, "the bazooka business is more dangerous than the drug business in the United States." Bazookas were thick, hand-rolled cigarettes, stuffed with coca base and tobacco. They were cheap and powerful.

Armando opened his mouth to speak, but no sound came out; he was obviously in great pain.

Rafa put his forefinger to his own lips and said, "Shhhh, we will do the talking. Armando, you will rest easy now. I will see that your family has money and is looked after, and that your bills are paid. Your only job is to live. I want to brag to people that I know a man that has been shot five times, twice in the liver, and still he lived. It's good for business, it will encourage my bodyguards to take chances," Rafa joked.

Armando smiled at me and formed my name on his lips. We had done many things together in the United States. He was a reliable, trustworthy man.

"Armando, save your strength." I turned to Rafa. "Please give Armando and his family a thousand dollars from me, subtract it from my account." Armando heard this and tears welled in his eyes.

Rafa saw the tears coming and spoke to him. "Hey, amigo, I guess you didn't hear me; I told you to save your strength. Get well." Rafa walked up to Armando and touched his hand. "We must go pick up the *chicas*, they are in the plaza spending our hard-earned money. Adiós." Rafa turned on his heel and left. I followed.

We drove in silence back to Rafa's office; he was lost in thought and I couldn't get the image of Armando, another Barrio Belén kid, out of my mind. I wondered what it would be like to take one in the chest. I couldn't even imagine five bullets passing through my body. I was sweating, the sun beating down on us in the open car.

Rafa finally looked over at me as we swung into his office driveway. "Compadre, you're sweating like a pig. You should have a Coke inside." He knew that was the only kind of "coke" I'd ever touch.

The office was a circus, telephones ringing constantly, VHF radios bleating, people walking in and out. Rafa's curvaceous, sexy secretary, Estela, winked at me as she handed me a cold bottle of Coke. Salesmen kept knocking at the door, and people were coming by looking for favors. Laboratory technicians were waiting to tell Rafa their problems. There was a shortage of ether and hydrochloric acid because the U.S. government was trying to restrict exports.

I circulated, talking to the people I knew. I noticed Estela flip two passports onto Rafa's desk. Curious, I went over and sat in front of him as he turned to open the safe behind him. He pulled out four rubber stamps and started banging away on the passports.

"What the hell are you doing?" I asked.

"I'm straightening out the entries on these people."

I reached over and picked up the stamps to examine them. They were entry and exit stamps for Colombia and Panama. He smiled as he initialed the stamped passports in an unreadable scrawl.

"You have your own immigration office right in that safe?" I said, flabbergasted at how much of the "Government of Colombia" cocaine money could buy.

"Comes in handy, Compadre. You can never be too careful." He grinned, admiring the stamps. "Hey, you speak good Spanish. You know what Belén means? As in Barrio Belén?"

"No."

"Bethlehem!" he said, and stamped the passport in front of him so hard the desk shook.

Armando survived his bullet wounds and completely gave up doing or selling drugs. He became a born-again Christian. Last I heard, he was high up in the mountains of Colombia, preaching the gospel.

Part Four

*
* *
*

THE CIRCLE CLOSES

CHAPTER FIFTEEN

*

Contract for Murder

We didn't run any flights in December of 1984. The government interdiction activity was too heavy and there were still memories of the Tampa bust just a few years before—no one would fly. I was just goofing around, enjoying the slow period, getting ready for the holidays. I was bored, so I decided to take a ride to the house we were using as an office at 12542 NE Second Avenue in North Miami. Rafa was in town, so I thought I would drop by the place and say hello. We kept this address longer than any we'd ever maintained. Normally, we would have dumped it after first using it for a laboratory and later as a stash house; it had received a lot of exposure. But this house was located just half a block away from Mickey Munday's mother's house, and for some crazy reason I got a kick running the operation half a block from his old lady.

I walked in, said, "Hey, what's happening," and headed straight for the kitchen, following the aroma of my favorite coffee, Bemoka. I called it the world's most expensive coffee, because I had it imported along with the coke on the returning flights. The weight in coke it displaced was worth $3,500. I was never without a cup of it in my hand; it was my trademark and, in the stash house or in the office, they knew it. I walked in and the coffee went on.

I took my coffee out to the living room and Rafa called me over. "Compadre, come here. There is somebody I want you to meet." I walked with him into the bedroom and he closed the door behind us. A middle-aged guy stood there. "Meet Cano," Rafa said, and Cano extended his hand.

Cano can be a last name or a nickname. In this case it was a nickname for someone just starting to get gray hair. I sat down and sipped my coffee as Rafa started to explain. "Fabio sent Cano up to us on a very special mission. He needs a personal job done. The Ochoas are having some problems, Compadre," Rafa said. "Big problems. You know what's happening to Jorge, and now this guy Barry Seal has turned against him."

Jorge Ochoa had gone to Spain to open up a European front for cartel operations. He had been arrested there for false documentation and was being held in jail pending extradition warrants from the U.S. He would later buy his way out of the Spanish charges by spending six million dollars to corrupt the right Spanish authorities, their Supreme Court to be precise. But I was more interested in Barry Seal. I hadn't heard the name before.

"Yeah, I heard," I said. "Everybody knows what's going on with Jorge."

"Did you know that Seal was MacKenzie?" Rafa asked, smiling.

"No," I answered sharply. Now I was really interested. MacKenzie was the code name for an American the cartel often compared me with. He was in my league, they'd say. MacKenzie had brought tons of coke into the U.S.A.

"Cano has brought something up for you to see," Rafa said, reaching into a bag on the bed. He waved a videotape in the air. "This'll take about an hour to see. Let's go into the other room."

Rafa cleared everybody out of the living room, herded them into the bedroom, and locked the door. Then Cano slipped the videotape into the machine and we sat down to watch. The title, "Uncle Sam Wants You," flashed up on the screen.

To my amazement, it was the story of Barry Seal's life in the drug business. When Seal's face appeared, Cano yelled out, "That's the guy! Stop the machine. That's him right here!"

"What do you mean?" I asked.

"That's the guy who called himself MacKenzie, the guy who's testifying against Pablo and Jorge." "MacKenzie" had a round face, thick black hair, and a surly smile.

We settled back to watch the rest of the video. Right away my head started to whirl. Clearly, Barry Seal was not long for this world. But I still had not figured out what it had to do with me.

It was an amazing tape. The man was a pure egomaniac. He had been a Green Beret, the youngest pilot to ever captain a TWA plane, and he had become a reckless fortune-seeker with a notion of self-importance bigger than his three hundred pounds.

Seal had made the film himself with his brother-in-law, a TV producer in Baton Rouge, Louisiana, where he lived. Seal outlined, in detail, what he had done in the drug business and declared that he was now cooperating with the U.S. government. It showed the inside of the plane that he had used in the Nicaraguan deal and the famous photo the CIA had released of Pablo Escobar helping to unload the plane. I couldn't believe my eyes.

But it still didn't register. So this guy Seal was going to testify against Jorge Ochoa and Pablo Escobar—so what, I thought. We watched the tape to the end and then we went into the kitchen, ignoring the fact that all the other people were still locked up in the bedroom. Cano spoke first. "Pablo and Fabio want somebody to go out there and find him. They want that somebody to be an American. An American has to find him and do the job."

I turned to Rafa. "Why an American?" I asked.

Rafa looked back at me and his eyes were dead, that Christmas Eve dead I knew only too well. There was no arguing with him. He spoke slowly, carefully. "Baton Rouge is a small town where there are no Latins. A Latin would stick out like a sore thumb, and Jorge and Pablo want this thing to go as smoothly as possible. Compadre, you know people you can call to get it done. I don't want to know who you call; you wouldn't tell me anyway. But it's got to be done."

I got up and took a deep breath and poured myself another coffee. My hands were trembling. I tried to hide it from Rafa; I couldn't remember ever having seen them tremble before. I sat down again slowly and he continued talking.

"They want him kidnapped. Deliver him to Colombia alive and you get a million dollars. Kill him and you only get half a million." Rafa paused and looked at me for a full thirty seconds, eyes glaring. "We want you to go."

The last thing in the world I wanted to do was kill Barry Seal. I'd never killed anyone. Until five minutes ago killing was something I thought I'd never have to do. But I knew too well the consequences of saying no to the cartel. I couldn't believe the sound of my own voice when I heard the words, "All right."

"Compadre, you're doing the right thing," Rafa said. "Make the arrangements as fast as you can. They sent Cano to us because he flew into Colombia twice with Seal as a guide pilot. And he's been to Seal's house, he knows the address, he knows the cars he drives, he knows the planes he flies, his businesses; he knows locations."

Cano started to rattle off the facts for me: Seal drives a white '79 Cadillac; his secretary drives a blue Chevy; his wife drives a beige Mercedes 450 SL; the house is at 8532 Oakmont Drive, Baton Rouge, located at the end of a quiet street; Seal owns the Beechcraft business in Baton Rouge, it's located in a hangar at the airport. Cano even described the planes, down to their registration numbers.

While he was talking, Rafa was writing furiously, making a list of all the data.

Cano continued: Seal liked to eat every Wednesday at a French restaurant at the Holiday Inn, and every Thursday at a catfish place across the street from the shopping mall. Rafa wrote it all down, and when Cano was finished Rafa handed me the piece of paper. I folded it carefully and put it in my wallet.

"Okay, Compadre, so you're going?"

"Yeah, I'm going. I'll make all the arrangements as fast as I can."

"Okay. Now I got a call to make. Hang on."

Rafa went to the phone and within moments was speaking with someone. "I just talked to my compadre," he told the person. "He says that he's going to do it."

Rafa handed me the phone. "Here," he said, without telling me whom I was about to speak to.

I recognized Fabio Ochoa's polite voice. "We appreciate you doing this for us," he said. "We will consider it as a personal favor. Hang on a second, somebody else wants to talk to you."

"Compadre, this is Pablo Escobar. I want to thank you. This is something that has to be done. Please do it for us. I will put Fabio back on the line now."

Fabio spoke. "Compadre, if there is anything you need, any help, just ask."

"The only thing I need is a little money to pay expenses."

"Don't worry about expense money, it will be on its way. Somebody will contact you in a few days."

I handed the phone back to Rafa and went to refill my coffee cup; my hands were really shaking now. You couldn't turn down a request from people as high up as Escobar and Ochoa; they knew I had to say yes. Either I did it, or my family and I would be blown away. That was the reality of my situation, that was the way it was.

Go out and cold-bloodedly kill someone?

No! I couldn't do that, but I had to go along, at least look like I was trying. That, or die. I prayed to God that I wouldn't be able to find Barry Seal.

There was a big difference in my mind between dealing drugs and dealing in murder. I wouldn't deal in murder; if I could reconcile myself to murder, Rafa would have been first on my list.

I reached into my memory and brought up a name—Jon Pernell Roberts. Jon was a good customer of Rafa's who lived in Del Ray Beach. In one of our many bull sessions he had told me that he had access to the Mafia, and if I ever needed a hit done or anything like that, to call him. I had stored the casual boast away as useful information. Now I decided to activate it.

The cartel had absolutely no dealings with the Mafia. Back in 1978 an attempt to make a deal took place. The Colombians brought cocaine to the meet, the Italians brought guns instead of money and shot up the unsuspecting Colombians. That was the end of any alliance between the cartel and the Mafia.

I left Rafa and Cano at the house and called Jon on the car phone. "Jon, I got to talk to you. Meet me at the house."

"Is it important?"

"Yeah, as important as it gets."

"Okay, I'll be there in forty-five minutes."

We arrived at the same time. I let him in, told him to sit, slapped the video in the machine, and said, "Watch this!"

When Seal's face came on the screen, Jon said, "Who's the idiot?"

"That's the guy that's going to get eliminated, and you're the guy who's going to do it."

"What do you mean, *I'm* going to do it?"

"They're offering a million to kidnap him or half a million to hit him."

"Sounds fair," Jon said. "We got people who can take care of him."

We sat quietly until the video was finished. I removed the tape, made us both a drink, then sat down again. "It's got to be done properly; no ifs, ands, or buts. This is serious business."

"I'm dealing with serious people, Max. We'll probably use Barton or Barton's people. I've used them before. They took out a college professor for me in Illinois not too long ago on something that was personal."

"Okay, I know Reed Barton." Reed was a customer of Jon's and he supplied us with used rental cars, cars we needed for unloading. "Reed will be fine, if you feel he can handle the job."

"If he can't handle it, I'll get ahold of Bobby Erra, who owes me some favors. I know Bobby can do the job." Bobby Erra was supposed to be the man who controlled the Mafia in South Florida. "We're going to need expense money. Nothing up front, just expense money."

"Yeah, I figured. It's on the way. I'll call you when it comes."

"You do that, Max. And leave the rest up to us." With that he left my house.

About three weeks later I got the dreaded phone call. I'd never heard the voice before. I asked who was calling and the person said, "I'm calling on behalf of Pacho."

"Who's Pacho?"

"Pacho. You know—*El Niño.*"

Then I knew—Pacho was Fabio Ochoa's latest nickname. *El niño* meant the little boy. "Go on," I said.

"Meet me at the Chinese restaurant on U.S. 1 and 112th Street. What will you be driving?"

"An '83 blue Ford pickup. And you?"

"Don't worry, I'll find you," he said, and hung up.

I drove to the restaurant, got out, and stood in front of my truck. A young Latino, dark, maybe twenty-two or twenty-three years old, walked over and said, "Compadre?"

"Yeah."

"I got something for you. Come with me."

I walked behind him to the end of the strip of stores. We made a right and passed through a little alley between the stores that led to a second parking lot behind the restaurant. He stopped at a black Toyota, opened the truck, and pulled out a small cardboard box, about twelve inches square. "This is for you," he said. And he drove off into the night without another word.

I carried the box back to my pickup, dumped it on the front seat, and drove home. The box was loaded with twenties. It took me a long time to count it out, but it was all there—a hundred grand in used twenties.

It was only after I counted it that I understood the money was real, and it gave me an awful feeling of dread and doom; mine, as much as Barry Seal's.

I put the cash in the closet and tried calling Jon Roberts; no answer. I called him for the next three days with no luck. Then Rafa called me. "You got the money?" he asked.

"Yeah, a few days ago."

"So when are you going?"

"I'm trying to locate my people. I can't find them."

"You got the money, you should go."

"Rafa, I'm trying to get this thing organized."

"You should go, Compadre. Go now." And he hung up.

I had to move, or it was going to be my ass. So I figured I would go see Reed Barton. I drove out to the Howard Johnson's by the airport. Reed owned a car-rental agency. The office was in the lobby. His daughter Joy was there, but he was not. Joy located him in another rental office and he said he'd come right over.

When he arrived, we walked to the restaurant in Howard Johnson's, ordered coffee, and started in.

"Did Jon Roberts talk to you about some special requirements I have, Reed?" .

"Yeah, he spoke to me. I'm ready whenever you want to go, I'm ready now. Let's go out on Sunday afternoon. But I've got to be back Thursday."

"Okay, that'll work," I said. "I'll make the reservations."

The next Sunday we flew to New Orleans and checked into a suite in the Sheraton Hotel.

"The first thing we have to do," Reed said, "is check out the information that your guy from Colombia gave you and see if it's accurate, see if we can spot him."

"All right. How do you want to handle it?"

"Max, I want you to stay in the hotel. I'll go down to the lobby and rent a car, and then I'm going to Baton Rouge. You enjoy yourself here for two or three days. I'll check into a hotel in Baton Rouge. I'll keep in touch."

I wrote out all the details: addresses, cars, and businesses from the list Rafa had given to me, and gave the paper to Reed.

Reed then disappeared for three days and I fooled myself into thinking the rest would be easy. My peace of mind was short-lived.

On Wednesday Reed was back. "Come on," he said, "we're going for a ride."

We drove directly to Barry Seal's house in Baton Rouge. "There's the house," Reed said. "It's a rotten place to try anything—there's only one way in and one way out."

Next, he drove me out to the airport and showed me Seal's business, the Beechcraft dealership, and said, "I've been watching these places constantly for the last three days, and checking the restaurants on your list. I haven't seen him or anybody that looks like him."

"What about the helicopter business?" I asked.

"No deal. I haven't been able to find it."

Reed was trying to show me he had done a thorough job.

On the drive back to New Orleans that night, we decided to make arrangements to bring Reed's hitmen in from Chicago the next time we flew out there. We would check them into a hotel in Baton Rouge and turn them loose. If they spotted Seal, they would do the job.

I had been calling Rafa every day to give him a briefing. Mostly I was calling to ask him, "Are you sure that he's in this area?" in truth hoping he wasn't anywhere around.

Back in Miami I met with Rafa, who brushed aside my explanations. "We're positive he's in the Baton Rouge area," he said. "Just keep looking until you find him."

"Rafa, there was no movement, no nothing."

He glared at me. "Just keep looking, all right?"

I tried to reach Jon Roberts while I was in Miami, but no one knew where he was. As far as I could determine, he was out of town and was not answering his beeper.

So I went to look for Seal a second time. The same routine as before: Reed Barton and I flew to New Orleans, but he could only stay from Sunday to Thursday, and then he had to be back in Miami. This time, however, he called in his killers from Chicago. They flew to Baton Rouge, where Reed met them and checked them into a hotel. I knew the team consisted of two men and a woman; I talked to them only once, briefly, over the phone.

And the same thing happened. Reed and his people checked around for three days, but got nowhere. There was absolutely no movement of any kind. The newspaper was delivered in the morning and picked up by a neighbor in the afternoon. The house looked as though it was closed down. Seal's Beechcraft business was operating, but there was no sign of anyone who even vaguely resembled the fat man in the videotape. Nor could we locate his wife or his secretary. As far as we could tell, none of his cars were around.

We left Reed's people in Baton Rouge to continue the hunt, and on Thursday I flew back to Miami with Reed.

I briefed Rafa and we had the same one-sided conversation we always had on this subject: "Find him, find him, find him."

"Maybe it would help if Cano were back here with us," I said, "because we can't find the helicopter location." Rafa said he would speak to Fabio and see what could be done.

The next day Rafa let me know me Cano was on his way to Miami. Right away, I told Reed Barton to fly out to Baton Rouge, and I would meet him there; I was going to drive.

"Why are you driving?" he asked.

"Because I'm going out with a Colombian, and I'm not walking through the goddamn airport with a Latino who doesn't speak a word of English."

"Whatever you say, Max," Reed said.

I picked Cano up at the Miami airport and over the next two days we drove in my Jaguar to Baton Rouge. We checked into the Sheraton Hotel. Reed was at another hotel.

The next day I drove Reed Barton's car around town with Cano. I didn't want to attract any attention with my Jag. Cano confirmed that everything we were looking at was correct. Then we set out to find the helicopter business, which he said was right next to the railroad tracks. Using a local map, we followed the tracks for three hours, having to thread up and down the side streets, and then, bingo, we found it, a helicopter pad in an industrial area.

It was empty, thank God. The place was boarded up tight. Not one car was in the driveway.

I drove to the nearest shopping center and phoned Colombia collect as I always did, and talked to Fabio. "We found the helicopter pad, and Cano has confirmed all the other locations. But we still ain't seen him. He's just not around, he's not here. But we will keep on looking."

"Please, do what you can, as fast as you can."

"We will."

I drove Cano back to New Orleans, bought him a ticket, and put him on a plane to Miami. There was no reason for him to stay, and I wanted him out of there.

When I returned to Baton Rouge, I sat down with Barton to discuss the situation. "Just for the hell of it, let's take a ride through and see what's happening."

We drove by the house: the white Cadillac was parked on the grass behind the driveway, the beige Mercedes was parked in the garage, and the garage door was open.

"Holy shit, Reed!" I yelled. "Something is going on here, people are here!"

"Okay, Max. I'll post our people and make sure they see who is going where." Immediately, Reed got his enforcers out there and we returned to the hotel.

It was another dry lead. Barry Seal's wife was there, but it wasn't Seal moving his white Cadillac around; it was a friend. We were spinning our wheels, but I was happy. I could tell Rafa that we were on it, we were working.

"I'm coming back to Miami, Rafa," I told him. "I've got to look after my shoe business." I had started a small legitimate importing business, no ties to the other things I was doing, shoes from Spain.

"Okay," Rafa agreed. "But make sure the people stay out there. It's your responsibility, Compadre."

The next day I was at my shoe business office in Miami talking to my Spanish partner, Jose Mareno, when Rafa walked in unexpectedly. With him were Cumbamba and Bam-Bam, two of his shooters. Jose Mareno took one look at those three guys and split, closing the door behind him with a bang.

Rafa was pissed. "You've been out there *three* times. What's going on? You sure you got the right address?"

"Here, Rafa." I laid the Baton Rouge phone book on the desk, which I had brought home with me. "Here he is: Barry Seal, 8532 Oakmont Drive, okay? That's where we were." I had to get aggressive with Rafa. "And we were *at* his fucking business at the airport and there is only *one* fucking airport and *one* Beechcraft business, so we are checking the right places and Cano confirmed that."

"Fuck that," Rafa shot back. "I don't believe you can't find this guy. Why don't you just go to the house some night and take out everybody there."

"You're out of your mind. The house is in an affluent area on a one-way street, a dead end. There is only one way into the area and only one way out. The slightest shit and they seal off the street, you're dead. What you want is a goddamn kamikaze squad."

"Yeah, yeah." Rafa stood to go. He did not want to hear any more. "When are you leaving?"

"In a couple of hours."

"I'll take Bam-Bam with me. You drop Cumbamba off at the office."

"Right," I said, watching them leave.

Cumbamba looked at me hard, his chin jutting out. "Sounds like you're planning to waste somebody," he said dryly.

"Yeah."

"How come I'm not doing it? That's my job."

"I don't make these decisions," I said, wishing to God the cartel had given him the job. "All I know is they want Americans to do it, they don't want Colombians involved."

"How much does it pay?"

"Half a million to waste him." I watched his eyes grow to the size of dinner plates.

"I want a piece of this. Take me out there with you."

"I can't. I can't authorize it."

"Who can?"

"The only ones who can authorize something like that are Fabio Ochoa or Pablo Escobar."

"Then I guess I'm going to have to talk to them."

"Yeah, you do that, Cumbamba." And that was the end of our conversation.

I knew when Rafa was losing it, and he was close to losing it on this deal. I had to do something, or at least look like I was doing something. I called Jon Roberts and got him this time.

"Jon, I'm getting a lot of heat on this. You control these guys. I need your help. I want you to come to Baton Rouge tomorrow."

"All right, Max. I'll be there."

In Baton Rouge we drove around and I showed him everything, the house, the Beechcraft business, the restaurants. We even ate in one of Barry Seal's favorite restaurants one night. There was no activity, no cars, no movement.

By the next day Jon was fed up. "These people have split; I don't see anything. Let's leave Barton's guys stationed here in case he shows up, and go home."

As we loaded our bags into the car for the drive back to New Orleans I said, "Seal's house is located between the Interstate exits. We have to pass it anyway, we might as well take a swing by and see what the hell is going on."

I drove past the house, and just then the blue Chevy that supposedly belonged to his secretary backed out of the driveway. I drove a little farther, made a U-turn, and came back, slipping in behind the Chevy as it coasted down the road. I must have been too close, because she started to take evasive action. She led me into an industrial area and, the next thing I knew, when I looked in my rearview mirror she was behind me. I shot down a side street and into a strip mall. We eventually picked her up again but it didn't lead anywhere. I kept thinking, What if I do find him? What the hell do I do then?

Jon called his people, told them what had happened, and gave them the plate number of the car so they could watch out for her. We flew back to Miami.

Rafa was frantic. "These people are pushing me, pushing me hard," he told me. "You've got to go back out there. And don't leave until the job is done."

"Rafa, I am not going to do nothing but stand there and watch these other guys anyway."

"Okay, so stand and watch these other guys."

Finally I said, "All right, Rafa. I'm going out there again," and the conversation was over. Except I had no intention of going. I didn't want to kill Barry Seal; I didn't want anything to do with murder. I called Raul, my buddy from Nuevo Laredo, and told him to meet me in Dallas.

"Okay, whatever you say. I'll drive up."

We met at the Sheraton North Dallas. All I knew was that I needed to blow off some steam and get Barry Seal out of my mind. We checked into my suite and the first thing I did was grab the yellow pages and look up escort services and topless bars. I said to Raul, "We've got a week to kill, and I've got a lot of money to spend. Let's leave our signature on this town from one end to the other—let 'em know we've been in Dallas." And we did.

Rafa thought I had been in Louisiana all that time, and when I returned I told him the standard story: no Barry Seal. But he kept pushing me and I was running out of excuses.

Two months went by like that.

CHAPTER SIXTEEN

*

Dirty Cops

In April 1985, right in the middle of the Barry Seal business, I met a man I'll call Reed Benjamin of the Metro-Dade Police. It happened at my own house.

I had known Reed's friend, whom I'll call Nicky Carbone, since 1981. Nicky did repair work on our fleet of cars, the ones we used for off-loading; he provided tires, brake jobs, tune-ups, whatever Mickey Munday and Jimmy Cooley needed. He did the work at the garage at NW Seventh Avenue and 103rd Street. He also worked for Mickey on a part-time basis as the loads were coming in; he helped to off-load the planes and man the off-loading station.

Nicky knew exactly who we were, and he was always up front with us. When Mickey and Jimmy introduced me as their "business associate," Nicky knew I was the boss.

The second or third time I was in the garage, he took me into the back room, lifted the lid on a military-style wooden crate, and said, "If you ever need any of this stuff, just let me know. I've got a supplier who's well-trusted; he's part of my family."

I looked inside and whistled a shrill note of admiration. There were about two hundred pounds of plastic explosives in the box, both C-2 and C-4, mixed in together, but packed in separate packages. As an armorer in the National Guard I had taken several demolition courses, so I knew how to handle explosives. I thought Nicky was out of his mind, leaving them in the garage like that.

Nicky was a money-hungry little son of a bitch. In Brooklyn we had a name for people like him: a "half-assed wiseguy," a miniature mobster, complete with gold jewelry hanging all over him. He told me that he owned 10 percent of this garage operation, and I believed that he did. He ran the business and controlled the money like it was his own.

But there was something that made me very, very uneasy about his place. Almost every time we were in there, unmarked police cars were parked outside and detectives were wandering around. I could smell them: Metro-Dade cops, city detectives, and cops in North Miami Beach uniforms.

Finally I said, "Nicky, you're out of your mind. All of these cops walking around here like this, you're asking for big trouble."

"Nah, don't worry about those guys. Only one or two of them are assholes; everybody else is good people we can deal with."

Soon after that I started noticing a big guy wandering around in a brown jumpsuit with "Metro-Dade Bomb Squad" printed on the back in big letters. One day my curiosity overwhelmed me and I asked, "Nicky, who the hell is that guy?"

"A cop on the bomb squad."

"What the hell's a bomb squad guy doing here? You've got a load of explosives in the back room. Are you in trouble?"

"Hell, no," Nicky answered. "That's Reed Benjamin, my friend. Don't worry about it."

I just shook my head and walked away.

It wasn't until sometime in late 1983 that Nicky finally explained to me that the plastic explosives in the back room *were* Reed Benjamin's. They had been confiscated from crime scenes or stolen from the police lockup. He also told me that any arms or ordnance that I might order would be coming from Reed. I just tucked the information away in my brain for future reference.

As fate would have it, Reed's path crossed mine again. In 1984 one of our labs in Miami was busted and the cops confiscated eight drums of ether. They were fifty-five-gallon drums, and at that time ether was costing us fourteen dollars a gallon on the black market.

About three days after the bust I was in the garage, shooting the bull with Nicky, and he up and said, "You know anybody who needs a load of ether?"

"What's the story?"

"A laboratory in the Redlands got taken down, and there are eight drums — Reed's looking to sell it for a buck a gallon."

"Nicky! That's my shit!" I yelled.

"So, you want it back? Buy it back!"

I laughed, then answered, "Hell, no. The cops got the dope as well, so we got nothin' to use the ether on; we got nothin' left to process."

We used the labs primarily to reconstitute any coke that had been water-damaged on delivery or from the bilge water.

I didn't think about it again until a few weeks later when Rafa contacted me and said he needed some American guns sent down to Colombia. He also wanted automatic weapons for his shooters in Miami. Rafa told me they were having trouble with the people in Panama; they couldn't get the ordnance they wanted from them.

So I called Nicky and said, "I need to send some heavy stuff down south. I'm talking M-16s, grenades, rocket launchers, stuff like that."

"Let me see what I can find out. Give me about a week."

A week went by and I showed up at the garage. He said, "I can get you everything you want."

"How much?" I asked.

"Not here. I ain't talking about it here. Let's meet someplace else."

"Come out to my house."

Nicky knew where I lived. He'd been there once when one of my cars wouldn't start and he'd had to tow it back to the shop.

"I'm not coming out alone," he said. "I'm bringing somebody with me."

"To *my* house you're bringing somebody? Who you bringing?"

"My friend, if it's okay with you."

"Which friend?"

"Reed, the cop. He's the one that will be selling you the stuff. You want to talk to him or not?"

"Okay, bring him out tonight," I answered, unsure about the notion of a cop selling me lethal hardware.

That night I was sitting out in my yard at one of the picnic tables, just watching the road, waiting, and a big black Harley pulled around the corner, up the street, and through my gate. Nicky was driving. Behind him in an unmarked police car was Reed. In a police car! Some balls.

They parked and I waved them over. Nicky thumped his helmet down on the table, shook my hand, and formally introduced Reed.

"You know my friend Reed," he said.

"Yeah, we met at the shop a number of times. But I'd like to speak to him on a level other than his normal business level, if you know what I mean."

Nicky smiled. "That's what he's here for. You need some shit, Reed's got some shit. He can supply you with whatever you need."

Reed looked at me and said, "Anything you need that I can get, you got. What do you need?"

"Automatics, Uzis, Mac-10s, KG-9s, stuff like that."

"I can't get that now, but I've got three hundred M-16s."

"M-16s will do nicely. Are they authentic M-16s, or AR-15s?"

"Fully automatic M-16s with selector switches. The military version, not the civilian version."

"And grenades."

"No problem. I've got a couple hundred grenades in stock. I've got Browning high-powers, nine-millimeter military versions, and some 3.5 rocket launchers with twenty rounds each. I can also get a couple of Laws rockets. They're shoulder-held rocket launchers that can take out a tank. Hell, Max, you know what they are. What do you need?"

"I need some plastic, C-4 preferably, and I can use the M-16s, the Browning high-powers, and the grenades. I don't need the Laws rockets," I said. The Colombians would have loved to get their hands on the Laws, but there was no way in the world I was going to put Laws rockets in the hands of those monkeys. Too destructive.

"How much?" I asked.

He wrote out a list of the times and the per-unit prices next to them. He handed me the piece of paper and said, "This is what it will cost you."

I looked at the list and nodded. "There's something else we need. I don't know if you can get it for me or not. I need some remote-control detonators."

"What range?"

"Minimum three miles, preferably a little bit longer."

"I'll have to have those made up," he said. "It's not something you go out and buy."

"Who's capable of making them up? You have somebody capable of making them up?"

"*I'm* capable of making them up. How many do you need?"

"Twenty," I answered, awed.

"They'll cost you three thousand dollars apiece."

"Okay."

He added the detonators to the list, and handed it back to me.

"I'll get back to you, Reed."

And they took off, the big black Harley rolling down my driveway, followed by the unmarked Metro-Dade police car.

A few days later Rafa called from Colombia and I told him the total for the arms came to around $250,000, and filled him in on the deal with Reed Benjamin.

"I want it all," Rafa said.

"What about the money?"

"You are going to have to wait for me to get there," Rafa said. There was no money lying around Miami.

I should have known. It was one of those times when I had just cleaned out the money houses and sent most of the cash down to Pablo Correa to be laundered in Colombia and Panama. My score was close to $300 million in cash sent down by now, and never a dollar lost or misplaced.

Ordinarily I always made sure there was a million or two available in a money house, but Fabio had sent me a major construction contractor, Julian Sanabria Molina, who was building a skyscraper in Barranquilla and I had to give him the last million dollars we had on hand to use for making purchases of steel and other building materials. He paid the Ochoas back in pesos at a hugely inflated exchange rate; narco-dollars was the only way these legitimate businessmen could get currency for capital expenditures in the States. As a matter of fact this "legitimate" businessman Molina went into the coke business himself later and we did some business together.

I called Nicky and told him we would take it all, and Reed Benjamin got on the line. "Where's the money?" he demanded. "I'm not selling anything or holding anything unless I got the cash in my hand."

"The cash is coming, Reed. But if you have another chance to sell it, do it. I'm not going to hold you up. If you have it later, when we have the cash, we'll take it."

Weeks later, Rafa finally came up with the money. I called Nicky. "Okay, Nicky, I got the money. Get hold of Reed and tell him I want all the stuff COD. Tell him to deliver it to—"

"Hey, Max, forget it. We can't do it now."

"What do you mean, forget it? You sold the stuff?"

"No. Reed's in trouble. They busted his girlfriend for selling arms a week ago and Reed's lying low. He's got a tail on him night and day, and Internal Affairs is up his ass. He's keeping clean until her case blows over, because they've got him tied into the arms sale. His stupid Metro-Dade Bomb Squad jumpsuit was hanging in the closet of the house they busted, can you believe it!"

"Okay. I'll let Rafa know that we've got to wait until it all blows over, but I still want the stuff. Right?"

"Right," Nicky agreed.

The sequel to this story is that after I flipped and became a witness, I told the Alcohol, Tobacco and Firearms people, the U.S. Attorney's office, and Metro-Dade Internal Affairs about the entire deal, and they went looking for the handwritten list that Reed had given to me; it was enough to hang him, but they could never find the thing. I had put the list on the top of my chest of drawers, and I used to see it every day. I saw it the day I got arrested; it was there. When the police said it wasn't to be found, I volunteered to look for it myself, but they wouldn't let me.

They still won't let me, and I know the list is still out there somewhere...that is, unless somebody got to it first.

The case was investigated by Alcohol, Tobacco and Firearms and the U.S. Attorney's office. This investigation was also closely monitored by the Internal Affairs Department of the Metro-Dade Police. I was told by ATF and the U.S. Attorney's office that, without the arms list, they believed that my testimony alone against a cop's would not carry enough weight for a conviction. As far as I know, Reed Benjamin and Nicky Carbone were never indicted or charged with any crimes.

Reed Benjamin subsequently sustained an injury that led to early release from his duties on a partial disability.

CHAPTER SEVENTEEN

*

Jumped

On the morning of Wednesday, June 5, 1985, I took my usual walk around the house watching the electricians, plumbers, carpenters, and cement men—about a dozen construction workers—doing the renovations on our new home just west of Fort Lauderdale. I watched the work with a feeling of satisfaction. When completed, we would have a five-bedroom ranch house on seven acres of manicured grounds.

Jon Roberts had sent over one of his technicians to install cellular phones in my cars. Every time I talked to Jon I got a sinking feeling in my gut; he was a living reminder that the Barry Seal contract was still hanging over my head. I had run out of excuses to give to Rafa for not being able to find and hit Seal. Rafa constantly reminded me that if Jorge Ochoa lost his appeal in Spain to be deported to Colombia rather than extradited to the United States, Seal's testimony would put Jorge away for life in an American prison, absolutely the worst fate imaginable. Death was far preferable.

I tried to put the Seal matter out of my mind as I stood watching Jon's man, Teddy, installing the base plates for the phone in my Jaguar. He would also wire my pickup, a custom-built Ford Centurion double cab, with double tires, tandem axle, and two forty-gallon fuel tanks. The big tanks gave me a range of 2,500 miles. Nobody could tail me in this machine. It was always on my mind that if anything ever went wrong I could pack up the whole family and take off with them, easily outdistancing anyone in pursuit.

It was nice to have the car phone for ordinary calls, but I continued to use pay phones for dope deals.

Things were getting hot; twice in the past week I had to dump a tail. My technique was to make a fast U-turn, get behind them, and chase the chasers around town until they cut down a side street to get away. But sooner or later, I knew, it was going to go down. They'd take me. I just didn't know how soon it would be.

Just as Teddy was finishing the job, Cristina's sister Melba and her big, slow husband, Lee, a former Bronx–Fort Apache cop, arrived at our front door in the limousine I had sent to the airport to meet them. The limo was bulging with all the junk they brought with them. They planned to stay with us until they could buy a retirement home and settle in Florida. I helped them pile their suitcases in the foyer of the house.

Melba was always great for Cristina's morale and I made myself tolerate Leopoldo. Lee, as everyone called him, was of Moroccan descent, an Arab.

We already had Cristina's brother Arturo and his wife staying with us. So the house, as usual, was full of Colombians living off of us.

At about one thirty, while Melba and Lee were moving in, bag and baggage, Jon Roberts telephoned. All he said was, "Go out to the car phone and call me back."

I looked at Cristina and gave her a kind of sad smile. I had a strange instinct that something was going down as I walked out to the driveway. I slid behind the wheel of the Jag, the smell of new leather still permeating the car even after 3,000 miles. I started the engine, then dialed Jon.

"What's going on, Jon?" I asked a bit nervously. I had just landed two loads in Lakeland and I was working on a third; maybe someone had found out.

"I didn't know whether your line was bugged; that's why I said use the car phone." He paused, measuring his words. "Teddy called me after he finished installing your car phones. The cops stopped him as he was leaving the area, searched his van, and wanted to know what he was doing at your place." There was another pause and I felt my stomach knot. "Teddy showed them the order sheet and said he was just installing cellular phones. They let him go."

"I'm going to drive around and see what's going on," I said. "Stay on the line."

If the cops were really out there waiting, I could skip through the back way on foot, escape across the back lots of neighboring houses. Decisively, without knowing why, I put the Jag in gear and drove out of the driveway onto the street and into the jaws of disaster. From that moment, I knew my life would be drastically and forever changed.

As I made a right turn onto Griffin Road, east-bound, a blue Oldsmobile containing four obvious plainclothes cops pulled out from behind the trees and jumped on my tail. I grabbed the phone. "Jon, I'm being tailed." I could see the cops in the car behind me talking frantically on the radio.

I spotted eight or ten cars, some marked Broward County Sheriff's Department, some unmarked, parked sidewise in the grass on my left, their front ends looking across the highway at me. One car, lights and siren going, pulled out onto the road behind me, blocking all Miami-bound traffic. The Oldsmobile sitting on my rear bumper cut off any chance of backing out.

The two police cars farthest ahead of me pulled out into the east-bound lane, shutting off all traffic heading for Fort Lauderdale. Two more cars cut off the road in front of me, forcing me to stop. I don't know what kind of a gunslinger they thought I was, but the cops had effectively cut off any innocent cars from coming into what they obviously considered a potential killing zone.

A voice crackled through an amplifier. "Police! You're under arrest. Keep your hands in plain view and get out of the car. Do it now!"

Jon was still on the phone. "They're taking me down," I told him. I wondered if any relief was discernible in my voice. "Let everybody know!" I hung up the phone, even though to do that my right hand would be dropping out of sight for a moment below the dashboard, inviting them to shoot.

Rafa's words echoed in my mind: "There are only two ways you get out of trafficking coke, in a box or in a cell." I felt strangely at peace. I still had the Barry Seal contract hanging around my neck and it was only a matter of time until I either performed or was performed upon. Of course, Cumbamba, who figured the contract should have been his anyway, would probably inherit it now.

So this was it. I slowly opened the door of the Jag and stepped out.

The command rang through the bullhorn: "Put your hands on the hood of the car."

The next thing I knew I was spun around and slammed against the car. I was vaguely aware of a voice shouting, "You're under arrest for violation of U.S. narcotics laws," and they read me my rights.

There were forty guns pointed at me, a combined task force of local and federal lawmen, as I obediently, gratefully, placed my hands on the hood of the Jag.

I was surprised when they asked for permission to search my car. Apparently they didn't have a search warrant for it. I agreed. "Be my guest. But be careful. There is a loaded Walter TPH .22 in the glove compartment. The gun is legal."

Oh, shit! I suddenly thought. There was $20,000 cash stuffed in with the gun. I watched as the gun was removed. No mention of the money was made by the searching officer, though he had to have seen it. He merely took out the gun and shut the glove compartment. I knew right then that he would go back later for the cash and I'd seen the last of my $20,000.

Then it hit me how badly I had screwed up. For three days there had been $275,000 hidden under my bed, waiting to go down to my Panamanian account. Had I become careless, or did I subconsciously want to be taken down? The money house, that's where my cash should have been, was maybe a half-hour's drive away. As I was thinking these things, I was handcuffed, the bracelets snapped unnecessarily tight, and spun around to face forty guns: pistols, shotguns, and automatic assault weapons. And yet I was calm, even serene inside.

The arresting officers in their blue jackets swarmed around me and I could see the names of their agencies stenciled in white on the backs: FBI, DEA, Customs, Broward County Sheriff's Department; they were all there.

Traffic on busy Griffin Road was now backed up in both directions by the police cars with flashing blue lights. The cops were having a ball.

I was roughly wrestled into the back of an unmarked two-door Thunderbird, a DEA car, and was told once more that I was under arrest for violation of U.S. narcotics laws. The agent beside the driver turned in his seat and read me my rights again as the T-Bird moved out. As if I hadn't understood them the first time.

Meantime, the rest of the task force descended on my home. Cristina told me later that eight or ten cars pulled into the driveway, sirens wailing, lights flashing. At least thirty agents in blue surrounded my house waving guns. They started screaming at the workers. "Everybody freeze! Drop! Hit the ground!" The terrified workmen fell face down on the ground.

The DEA guys banged on the door until Cristina came out to face what looked like an army of cops. They handed her the search warrant and said, "We have the right to search your house."

"Go search," she replied.

Arturo, unable to speak English, recognized only that they were being invaded by cops. One of the DEA agents grabbed him and demanded to see his papers. Arturo was shaking. With Luis, my adopted seventeen-year-old son, as translator, Arturo admitted that he was illegal and had no papers. The agent grabbed Arturo by the neck and threw him against a wall. With that, Luis, a skinny kid, climbed onto the back of the burly agent, yelling, "What do you think you're doing to my uncle?" Another agent managed to restrain Luis, pulling him off the DEA agent.

It was about a half-hour's drive to the DEA office in Fort Lauderdale. I was led across the sidewalk into the field office, pushed down on a bench in front of a desk, and told to sit there. They started going through my pockets, dumping everything on the desk.

The handcuffs were biting deeply into my wrists, straining my shoulder blades. I tried to keep the pain to myself. I wasn't about to give them the satisfaction. They noticed my discomfort and started to look for the key to the handcuffs, but no one could find it. These were special cuffs, they told me, with a round key. For an hour and a half they made me sit there, no circulation in my fingers, just a throbbing pain from my shoulders, down my back and arms, to my wrists.

At last, with my hands turning white from lack of circulation, the DEA agent with the key showed up and uncuffed me. All that time nobody talked directly to me, just among themselves, as though I was some kind of an animal they had found.

Back at my house the search continued, and a photographer was taking pictures of everything. Although I didn't realize it at the time, I was being held by the DEA in Fort Lauderdale in expectation that they would find a big load of dope at my house. They found the money I had hidden under my bed, but nothing else incriminating.

The task force took their time and went through the whole place thoroughly, with the workers lying all over the driveway under the cops' guns and Cristina's relatives scared to death and sitting quietly on a bench outside.

They took all the papers they could find and all of Cristina's jewelry. But they couldn't find a trace of drugs. They even brought in two dogs to go through the place, end to end, sniffing for dope, and of course there was nothing but the money.

Even if I'd hidden the money more cleverly, the dogs would have found it. Dope money always has the smell of coke on it. The street dealers handle money with coke on their hands. If we left the money we collected in a closed box for two or three days and then opened it up, it always had the pungent smell of coke.

The thirty agents searching the house were impressed with my collection of hunting rifles and ammunition. The handguns I had were registered. They took down the serial numbers, and the firearms were eventually put in the hands of one of my lawyers. But the gun find still gave them something to boast about.

After about five hours the task force finally left my place with a trembling, weeping Arturo, his wife, Estela, and Cristina's maid in custody.

All of them spent the next fifteen days in jail until their papers could be straightened out or they were deported. Melba suffered a stroke shortly after the terrifying ordeal and could hardly speak a word for the next three months. Old Lee, her ex-cop husband, had fared the best, watching stoically as the house was pulled apart.

While the search of my place was going on, I was having big problems in the Fort Lauderdale DEA office.

"Hey, any of you guys read Spanish?" one of the agents called out. He was going through my wallet. I felt sick to my stomach as he fingered the bits of paper tucked in there. What the hell had happened to the careful, meticulous Max who had brought fifty-six tons of Colombian snow into the United States without ever so much as one mistake?

The DEA agent was studying the slip of paper Rafa had given me with all his notes on how I could best find, identify, and kill Barry Seal. Here was this stuff written in clear Spanish, no code words. It made me a conspirator to murder if they killed Seal, which I knew they would.

"No Spanish, you guys?" the agent asked. "Too bad. I'll just put it in with the other personal items."

After more talk among themselves the DEA agents led me into a small room. "Strip! And bend over the table!" one of them shouted. I hesitated and was roughly shoved against the table. "Get 'em off!" another agent bellowed. Slowly I did as commanded. An agent with a sadistic smile on his face whacked me in the bare butt and I leaned over the table.

"Okay, reach back and spread 'em," the little pervert yelled.

I reached behind and spread my cheeks. "Seen enough?" I sneered, after I'd been kept in that awkward position for a full minute.

"All right, get your clothes on," another agent ordered.

I wasted no time getting dressed again, and was led back into the other room, pushed into a sitting position on the bench, and handcuffed with my hands in front of me. I was attached to a chain, hooked to the floor next to the bench. Like a slave.

I sat there, just waiting. I didn't talk to them and they didn't talk to me. Finally after an hour's standoff I said, "I want to make a phone call. I want to call my lawyer."

One of the agents growled out, "When you get to where you're going you can make a phone call."

"Where am I going?" I asked.

"You'll find out when you get there."

It was another half hour or so before they said, "Let's go." They unhooked me from the shackle on the floor and handcuffed me behind my back again. Outside, they shoved me into a police car.

They never told me the specific charges against me or where the charges originated. Just "narcotics violations." By law, they are supposed to tell you what you are charged with, give you a complaint or warrant or something. There was nothing.

We drove for a while and finally pulled into the North Dade county lockup. Three DEA agents hauled me out of the car and dumped me inside. "Enjoy yourself," the sadist said, and they were off.

Once again I was strip-searched, photographed, and fingerprinted. Only then did they allow me to call Martin Senior, my lawyer.

"Marty, they nailed me," I said. "I'm in North Dade. Get down here now."

I was put in a large cage with two tables, four seats at each table, all welded-construction, institution-type furniture. Within the cage were eight small cells with a shower in the middle. I found myself in with seven other hoods. No sheets, no pillowcase, no towels. And no dinner. It had already been served.

Marty Senior got there about an hour and a half after I called him and I was allowed to go into a small conference room with him. Marty knew how to reach out for specialists when needed, like the immigration attorney who had thwarted the DEA on the cartel's behalf.

"Marty, I don't know what this is about, nobody's telling me shit. My wife doesn't know where I am. Do me a favor, get hold of her, let her know where I am. Make the arrangements that have to be made. Get the bail set. You know what you have to do."

"I know what I have to do, but I'm not a criminal lawyer. I'll get hold of Billy Clay and get it all set up."

Clay was a top criminal lawyer I had taken the trouble to become acquainted with in case of just such a situation as this. No charges had been brought that Marty Senior could address, so we could do nothing but wait until a court appearance was called.

"Do me a favor before you leave," I asked Marty. "Get me some cigarettes. There's a machine outside."

Marty bought a couple of packs of cigarettes and handed them through the bars to me. He also dropped some money off with the guard in case I wanted to buy more. I didn't know how long I would be in there before bail could be posted. I just hoped I could get before a judge the next day. Meantime, I was spending my first time in jail ever, and it was a weird feeling.

They called lockdown at ten o'clock and one of the guys in the cage with me told me to get in my cell. I stepped into it and the electronically operated door closed with the loudest clang I'd ever heard. I lay down on the thin mattress. I was so exhausted and traumatized I just passed out. Gone.

I woke up the next morning still feeling like hell.

I hung in all day Thursday, just hoping I'd get before a magistrate and have my bail set. On Friday morning Marty showed up at the jail with the sickening news that I would not be arraigned until Monday. I wasn't allowed to wash up, trim my beard, or receive a change of clothes in those four days; nor was I permitted a visit or phone call from my wife.

It was a time for deep reflection on my life and my future. How had I come to this, I asked myself, looking around the jail. I thought of the first time I had seen Cristina, at the club in the Sheraton Hotel in Puerto Rico. I couldn't blame myself for pursuing such a gorgeous woman. It was like karma, fate, hers and mine were intertwined. I was destined to live through all that had happened. But how different life would have been if I had gone somewhere else that night. It wasn't her fault I had become a trafficker, but it was impossible not to have been exposed to the temptations of coke dealing once I married this Colombian girl and was brought into contact with her friends and family. Marriage to Cristina had brought me up to the open, beckoning door of big-money dope dealing. But I could not deny that it was my own greed and lust that swept me over the threshold into the glittering and deadly world I had inhabited for the past five years.

Over that long, lonely, and deeply dismaying weekend I thought about this a great deal. That "What am I doing here, for God's sake?" rumination never left me.

Finally, on Monday, they took me to the Fort Lauderdale Federal Courthouse. Marty Senior had tried to get Billy Clay to represent me at the criminal hearing, but he was on his honeymoon in Spain. Billy's associate Steve Haguel was there to represent me.

Dirty and stinking, I was led into the courtroom, still wearing the clothes in which I'd been arrested. Cristina was sitting in the front row, and by her side were Melba and a friend. We smiled at each other, sadly, and then the proceedings began.

Judge Nimkoff started off by addressing the schoolmarm-severe assistant U.S. attorney. "What are the charges here?" he asked her.

"We can't state the charges. The defendant was arrested under a sealed California indictment, Your Honor. The charges can't be revealed."

The magistrate frowned and leaned across the bench. He was clearly angry. "You mean you have arrested this man without advising him of the charges against him?"

"Your Honor, there are other people named in the indictment who have not yet been arrested, so we have not been authorized to unseal it."

Judge Nimkoff stared at her unbelievingly. "Either you are going to unseal the indictment, tell this man what the charges are against him, or I'm going to turn him loose now. How can you hold a man without charges?"

"There are other people in the indictment," the U.S. attorney repeated. "They will find out that they are being charged and try to avoid arrest if we unseal it."

Nimkoff's tone was scathing. "Excuse me, Counselor, but aren't you aware of the law in this country? A man is entitled to know what he is charged with. It's not my fault that you arrested this man before you arrested the others. He is entitled to know the charges, and I repeat: either you state the charges or I release him."

Nonplussed, the U.S. attorney turned to the California DEA agent at the table with her. He was six foot three and sported a chrome-plated .45, which he had shoved in my face during the arrest on Wednesday. After an urgent whispered conference, she reluctantly produced a stack of papers. She handed a copy of the indictment to the judge and another copy to my lawyer. We studied the charges for fifteen minutes.

I realized immediately that Morgan Hettrick, his name disguised with a code number, was behind the charges. He had turned witness. Two counts of conspiracy to import cocaine and four counts of possession of cocaine in California, dating back to 1981, were cited. All of these counts rested solely on the word of Morgan Hettrick. Also on the indictment were Rafael Cardona Salazar, George Bergin, and three Colombians we used in California, Julio Silva, Rodrigo Silva, and Claudia Martinez.

I deduced that with DeLorean winning his case against the government, seriously embarrassing the prosecutor, Hettrick's only chance to receive favorable treatment was to help make more cases for the U.S. Attorney's office, and he had fingered me.

Now all that was left was to determine bail.

"Does the defendant plead guilty or not guilty?" the magistrate asked my lawyer.

"Not guilty, Your Honor," I replied heartily.

As Steve asked the magistrate to set bail, the U.S. attorney jumped to her feet. "Your Honor," she cried, "this man is worth fifty million dollars. It is guaranteed that he will run. He speaks Spanish!"

Nimkoff stared at her in disgust. "A lot of people speak Spanish. *I* speak Spanish. Are you going to hold that against me?" He gave her a fierce look.

"No, Your Honor." Her voice faltered, then, with renewed resolve, she said, "The Government requests that this defendant be held without bail."

Nimkoff flashed an "Are you crazy?" look at her. "You know better. Everybody is entitled to bail."

The disgruntled U.S. attorney responded, "Your Honor, the Government seeks two million dollars bail."

Now Steve jumped in. "Your Honor, this man is married, he has children. He has spent his entire life on the East Coast of the United States between New York and Florida. He is an honest man who wants to clear his name. He will not jump bail."

"Your Honor!" the U.S. attorney shouted. "This man had twenty-five loaded guns in his house. He carried a loaded handgun in the glove compartment of his car. Two hundred and seventy-five thousand dollars cash was found hidden under his bed. He is a major drug dealer. We request that an extremely high bail be set."

I noticed that the $20,000 that had been in the glove compartment of my car was not mentioned. So it had disappeared during my arrest, just as I'd figured.

"Your Honor," Steve said, "those guns were registered legally. The rifles were strictly for hunting and target shooting."

After further vigorous protests by the U.S. attorney, Nimkoff made his decision. "Bail is set at $550,000 property bail."

This meant that nobody could come down to the courthouse with $550,000 in cash and spring me. The bail had to be in the form of titles to legitimately purchased property, acceptable to the judge. I immediately started calculating how to do it. My lawyers should be able to assemble title to my Miami Lakes property and land owned by friends, in two days at the most.

While we were still standing before the magistrate, I whispered to Steve, "Do me a favor. Tell this guy that I've been four days without my blood pressure medication; I'm starting to feel dizzy, I can't see straight. These people refuse to let me see a doctor or have medication sent in."

Eloquently, Steve told the magistrate my problem.

Nimkoff turned to the U.S. attorney. "Where are you holding this man?"

"At North Dade, Your Honor."

"Before tonight you are moving him to MCC Miami," he commanded. "And I want him to see a doctor."

As I was led out of the courtroom I waved to Cristina and asked Steve to explain to her where I would be held.

I was taken to Miami in a sheriff's van and processed into the Metropolitan Correctional Center. That afternoon I called Cristina to tell her what the visiting hours were and asked her to come see me the next day. I also told her it shouldn't take long to make the bail. She was totally traumatized by what had happened, but my assurances that I would be back with her soon made her feel better.

But the next day, before my lawyers could get the property bail assembled, Steve was notified that no sooner had Magistrate Nimkoff walked out of his courtroom than the U.S. attorney's office in Florida called their counterpart office in Southern California and before the day was over an ex parte hearing had been called before a Los Angeles federal judge. This is a hearing, like a grand jury proceeding, where neither the target defendant nor counsel representing him is present. The California judge had overruled Nimkoff, a mere magistrate, and increased my bail to $2 million property bail. Now I really was in trouble.

It is interesting to note here that Magistrate Nimkoff, disgusted by the heavy-handed, not to mention unconstitutional, measures employed by the Florida prosecutors, resigned in protest and nearly caused a scandal in Florida legal circles.

For six weeks Steve Haguel and Billy Clay, back from his honeymoon, were able to delay my extradition to California through special hearings. Cristina could come see me every day. There was no immediate money problem; we still had some money in our bank accounts, and Rafa's people, I thought, following the code of drug dealers' ethics, would make sure the family wanted for nothing. I had sent word to Rafa, in Colombia, that he was also on the indictment. Months later I learned that Rafa had known about the indictment for some time but had never thought to warn me. His frequent freebasing sessions had eroded his mind and played havoc with his reasoning processes.

I had been in MCC Miami a week when the next scheduled flight from Colombia to Lakeland with five hundred kilos came around. My cut on these flights was $650,000 each; without me the operation would have to be discontinued. Jimmy Cooley, despite being a fugitive, was now supervising the air missions and training new pilots. Mickey Munday, as always, was in charge of ground operations. Even in jail I was still the link between the U.S. air operations and the Colombians.

I called collect from the jail's public phone to one of my Colombian friends in Miami and asked him to patch me through to Roberto, my contact to the Barranquilla cartel, which was headed by Julian Sanabria Molina. Sanabria, to whom I'd given $1 million for Jorge and thus killed an arms deal a year before, was now totally independent of the Medellín traffickers. Besides being a major cocaine supplier, he was the biggest contractor in Barranquilla, building high-rise office buildings, hotels, and condominiums. Roberto was Sanabria's cousin. I was now in the precarious position of having to put the two sides of the Barranquilla-Florida operation together so they could operate without me in the future. I had no other choice. This load had to go through; I needed the money for legal expenses.

When I got through to Roberto, I told him to expect a call from Jon Roberts, who would make the flight arrangements from Barranquilla to Lakeland, and the delivery from Lakeland to Sanabria's Miami connection.

It was no secret that every call made out of the MCC was monitored. There was a sign over the phone advertising the fact. But the rapid-fire, highly specialized Spanish I threw at Roberto would have been unintelligible to any jail employee given the task of making sense out of our conversation. Having prepared Roberto to receive instructions from Jon Roberts, I put a call through to Jon.

After an exchange of pleasantries I said, "I expect to see you soon." Hardly the truth, but I didn't want Jon to think I wouldn't be around to protect my interests.

"That's good to hear," he said jovially. "Anything I can do to help until then, pal?"

"Call Roberto, he's got some information for you." I gave him the number in the code I always used for telephone numbers, adding one digit to each of the last three numbers, and wished him luck. "Remember me" were my last words to him.

Time went slowly in MCC Miami, relieved only by Cristina's regular visits in the afternoons. I called Roberto and learned that the last flight from Barranquilla had come through without a problem. When Cristina came to see me I asked her if Jon Roberts had sent her any of the money he now owed me.

"No," she replied, "and I can't locate him. He doesn't return my phone calls."

"Okay, forget it." I had been double-crossed by Roberts, but there wasn't anything I could do about it where I was sitting. Money has a way of bringing out a person's true colors. Jon was in control now; Rafa was in Colombia and I was in jail. In Jon's entire life, he had never held as much loot in his two hands as when he received the transportation money for the load from Sanabria. I wondered if he kept the pilots' share too.

Well, what goes around comes around, I thought. Fate has a way of settling debts. And Jon Roberts was gambling with fate.

I nailed him later.

CHAPTER EIGHTEEN

*

Caged

I was in MCC Miami but my arraignment would take place in California, where the indictment originated. Before I was taken out of Florida I was acutely aware of one big festering problem that had to be dealt with.

While I was in the Miami Correctional Center another of Rafa's Colombians was brought in, busted for possession with intent to sell. It happened every day. The Colombian told me that a hit squad was coming up from Colombia to finish Barry Seal. I knew it was a mistake. In race-conscious Baton Rouge, the Colombians would stick out like raisins in white rice. There was no doubt in my mind that Cumbamba would be involved in the hit and that he would nail Seal. But he was too stupid—all chin, no brain—to know that the law would nail him back. He was a dead man going in, but the cartel would win big. Even if Jorge Ochoa lost his legal battle and was extradited to the States from Spain instead of being deported to Colombia, there would be no witness to testify against him. Except, I realized, me.

The hit order had been given by Fabio Ochoa and Pablo Escobar personally. They had no other Americans that they trusted besides me, so, in desperation, they had to use their own people. And that piece of paper with Rafa's notes on Seal haunted me. The minute Seal went down I would be the fall guy, charged with conspiracy to commit murder. I got on the phone and sent a strong message down to Rafa in Colombia: "Leave Barry Seal alone! The piece of paper you wrote was on me when I was arrested. If anything happens to Seal, I get nailed."

A month or so went by before I got word back from Rafa. The message basically was, "Go fuck yourself, Seal's going down."

I immediately got hold of Bill Clay, my criminal lawyer in Miami, and told him the whole story.

"You're in too deep here, Max. You had better tell somebody what's about to happen," he counseled.

"Call Dick Gregorie, the U.S. Attorney in Miami," I instructed Clay.

Clay immediately called Gregorie and filled him in. Gregorie did what he had to do. He called Barry Seal's attorney, and Seal was notified. But Seal refused to go into the witness protection program.

At least my actions removed me from the conspiracy, and eliminated any involvement in his demise. But it ate at me that the Colombians would let me stand for a murder rap and essentially throw my life away. It was one of the things that eventually led me to turn against them.

Shortly after this they moved me from MCC Miami—the Miami Country Club, as they called it—to Terminal Island Prison in California. That was one incredible trip, nine days in hell.

The bus came rolling in at about four in the morning, a big school bus run by the federal marshals. The prisoners being transported were chained at the waist, ankles, and wrists and told to board the bus; altogether there were about fifty of us. Two U.S. marshals stayed with the bus. The marshal with the sawed-off shotgun climbed into the small cage in the back of the bus, the cage with the shooting ports; the marshal who was driving climbed into the cage in front, protected from the prisoners.

The first leg of the trip was from Miami to Tallahassee, an all-day journey. We were not allowed to carry cigarettes or any possessions; they were shipped separately.

At about nine o'clock they broke out breakfast, which was a box lunch, and I encountered government bologna for the first time. Mystery meat. You can't really call it food; my dog would bite me if I ever served it to him. It was a rough, depressing ride, only stopping for pee breaks. The marshals let us out all at once to relieve ourselves in the bushes by the side of the road. It was humiliating and they knew it.

At around one we had lunch, and it was exactly the same thing as breakfast, a box lunch featuring the mystery meat again—this time with stale bread.

I looked out through the heavy wire mesh at the passing drivers and envied them. My bail was now set at $2 million, but I was still hopeful that Rafa, my wife, and my attorneys were hard at work trying to raise the bond. They would have to prove it was clean money, not drug money, but we had done that kind of thing many times before. I felt that in a short time I would be back out there with those drivers, in my Jag.

But what I didn't know was that while I was on my way to California, the feds were hard at work trying to bury me in the judicial system.

After twelve hours on the bus, we arrived in Tallahassee. It was already night. In Tallahassee I learned that every time a prisoner gets to a new joint he is given the full treatment: photographs, fingerprints, and strip search—every cavity checked for drugs. After we were processed, we were fed, assigned to cells, and told to go to sleep.

The next morning we were rousted out of bed, put in irons, and hustled to the waiting school bus. They drove us to the Tallahassee airport and up to a parked Convair CV 520. I shuddered when I saw it. The Convair was a two-engine propeller plane dating from the 1950s. Most of them had been decommissioned by 1960. I wouldn't have taken that wreck on a drug run from Miami to Fort Lauderdale, much less cross-country. By now we were sixty prisoners, about ten more than had left Miami.

We took off from Tallahassee and after the first stop an hour later, I knew I was on the milk run. We stopped to drop off a few prisoners and pick up some additional ones who were destined for somewhere else.

The guards stayed behind closed doors in the front and the rear of the plane; we couldn't see them, but they could see us. With our handcuffs tied to the waist chains we couldn't lift our hands more than a few inches. When we had to go to the bathroom they didn't take the chains off, so we had a real wrestling match with ourselves in the toilet. And some of the guys had diarrhea and weren't lucky enough to reach the toilet in time, or somebody was using it; it wasn't long before the plane smelled vile.

In all, we made four stops before we hit our destination that day, the Federal Penitentiary in Talladega, Alabama. We went through the usual process, and I was dumped into solitary, which was standard procedure for anyone they didn't want talking.

I spent four days in that cell, a six-by-eight-foot cube, with a bunk, a toilet, and a sink. It was there that I started to get the feeling that I had irretrievably lost my freedom. I had only one small window to look out of, and I clung to the sight of that small patch of grass. By sheer will, I overcame the feeling of desperation. It was all part of the routine to break my spirit and get me to cooperate. I kept trying to convince myself that by the time I got to California, my wife and Rafa would have posted my bail, and I'd walk out into the California sunshine. These guards weren't going to break me. Two million was a lot of bail, but it could be raised and I could be free.

Early on the fifth morning, a guard banged on my cell door. "Let's go, you're moving," he said.

They chained me up and I joined the rest of the waiting prisoners.

They took us back to the same airport and loaded us into the same plane. I looked out the window and saw the bastards fueling the plane with us chained in our damned seats. Why had they waited to pump the fuel until after we got on board the plane? All I could think of was fire, and us trying to run, burning, in irons.

The milk run took off again. We did the same thing as before, stopping in four or five locations to take on and drop off prisoners. That night we were taken to El Reno Federal Prison in Oklahoma. The stink of human waste and death permeated the place. Rats and cockroaches ran wild.

The next morning I was back on the Convair. Seven hours and four stops later, we landed in Arizona; that night we wound up in MCC Tucson, where I spent two nights. It was the same drill as before: strip search, fingerprints, and into solitary.

The next morning, Saturday, they picked up four of us in a van and told us we were going to Terminal Island, California. One of the marshals told us that he was Wild Bill Hickok and that we had to behave ourselves. Dressed in black, with cowboy boots, a ten-gallon hat, and a quick-draw rig to hold his piece, he did look like Wild Bill Hickok. This was one sick cop, but at least he broke the monotony of the trip and added a little humor. With the two marshals in the front of the van and us in the cage behind, we took off on a fourteen-hour drive to California. I sat in the cage and stared at the three other bozos with me. It wasn't long before I was dying for a cigarette. In those days I was smoking three packs a day, but no matter; I wasn't going to get one.

We hit Terminal Island on Saturday night. The prison is on San Pedro Island off Los Angeles. It had been a naval disciplinary barracks and prison during World War II, run by the Marine Corps. On the other side of the island was a Coast Guard station.

It was a big place, and slated to be my home for a lot longer than I had any idea at the time. The North Yard was the original prison, old-style cells with bars. The North Yard was for people awaiting trial, the South Yard for people serving sentences, but when the South got too full they shipped the prisoners over to the North. The prison could hold about two hundred prisoners on each side. It was old, cold, and damp. Six guntowers ringed the prison, and the cold black Pacific Ocean waited for any fool who dared take that route.

After a strip search, fingerprinting, and photo session, the four of us were stuck in the hole, the disciplinary cell, and we weren't released for two days. It was degrading and humiliating, designed to squash your soul.

Now all I could think about was getting out, and I wondered constantly about what they were doing. Had they raised the bond for me? What was the government up to? One way or another, I was going to get out. I was going to walk out that door, whether somebody opened it or blew it open.

I struggled to think clearly.

On Monday they took me out of the hole and assigned me to a cell. My roommate was an arsonist.

On Tuesday I met Tom Johnston, my California lawyer, for the first time, and what a surprise I got. He explained things to me. "Max, bad news. I'm afraid the Assistant U.S. Attorney has increased the charges against you. They got you now on a CCE—continuing criminal enterprise charge."

"Which means I'm now facing life with no chance of parole."

"If they get a conviction."

"Maybe I should cooperate. I got a weird feeling my Colombians might stiff me, leave me to twist in the wind."

"Not yet. It's too early to be talking about a deal with the government. Let's just let it lie and see what happens next. We haven't even seen their case."

"How the hell can they just change the charges? I wasn't even there to defend myself, make any kind of plea! How can they do that, just raise the charges?"

"They did it, Max. The grand jury just rubber-stamped it for them. I hear that the picture they painted of you to the judge would make Al Capone look like a choirboy. Let's just see what kind of case they really have. There was no dope, the cash seized is not enough to convict. We'll wait."

Depressed as hell, I returned to my cell and to Charlie Real, my new cellmate and teacher. I was to have many cellmates over the next year, and they all wanted to teach me their trade. Jail is, at the very least, a college for criminals.

I noticed Charlie stealing Coffee-mate one day and gave him a questioning look. Back in the cell he explained. "Max, this Coffee-mate"—he was holding the package in the air—"is highly flammable. Watch." Charlie poured the crystals onto a lighted match he was holding extended from his body and *whoosh!* the crystals ignited so fast he had to drop the match and the package.

"Now, Max, this is what we do with it." He reached under his bed and pulled out a tennis ball. "Know what this is, Max?"

"Tennis ball."

"Firebomb," he said, as he shoved it under my nose for closer inspection. "I've filled this ball with match-stick heads and Coffee-mate. We put a little fuse in here, right here in this little hole I cut out, and bango, we got a firebomb."

"What the hell do you use that for in here?" I asked.

"I sell them to the other cons; if somebody wants to firebomb a cell, he just walks past and tosses it in like an incendiary grenade. Primitive, but it does the job!"

"I'm sure it does," I mumbled to myself.

Jail was not like you see it on television. The basic rule was, if you don't fuck with them, they won't fuck with you. Everybody had to get along with everybody else. They were all there, the bikers, the Aryan Brotherhood, the Black Muslims, the Mexican Mafia, the Italian Mafia. Each group had its own little gang, its clique; and I was with the Colombians, the drug dealers. I was accepted by them as one of their own.

It was in fact Julio Silva, one of my co-defendants and a man I had known in California, who acted as my contact. He had been told I was coming to Terminal Island and was waiting for me. When I was released from solitary into the prison population, I got everything I needed from Julio: cigarettes, soap, razor, magazines. Anything I needed, he got.

In prison, I was learning, whatever rank you held on the outside was the same rank you'd hold on the inside. But it was still only a small step up from being an animal, and I was starting to wonder what was in store for me.

We could make collect calls to anywhere inside the country, but all calls were recorded. I talked to Cristina every day in Miami, sometimes two or three times a day, so I knew everything that was going on at home. Messages were easily passed through to Colombia and back to me.

The cartel knew about the bail being raised to $2 million, and they hedged. That was my first indication that I was in deep trouble. The message I received back from Colombia was: "Do a little time until we can get the bail reduced, and we'll see what happens."

We'll see what happens! That's just great, I said to myself. I was covering their asses, and they should cover mine.

There was more grief. Rafa was supposed to be giving Cristina a certain amount of money every month to take care of her expenses and the kids.

They were coming up short; sometimes they didn't give her any cash at all, and Cristina had to chase them for the dough. Often she had to go to weird locations to pick up the money. There was a total lack of respect for me; they were treating me like they hardly knew me.

I had had an arrangement with Rafa, and therefore with the cartel: if I ever got in trouble, they would look after things for me while I was in the slammer, and that included my bail.

I was sick about the $275,000 I had left under my bed. It was a major blunder, a blunder I had to squeeze out of my mind or it would drive me crazy. Had I subconsciously left it around? Certainly there had been plenty of chances to stash it.

Finally, I contacted the cartel directly. I got messages through to Fabio Ochoa and Pablo Escobar to lay out the money for me, pay my bail, get me the hell out of the stinking prison. I even promised to make it up to them, pay them back with hard work.

And word came back: "Can't do it."

There were additional problems. The government was getting much tougher in checking out bail bonds put up for narcotics violators, making sure the money was clean. But we had managed to get around that before. In fact, just before I was busted, Rafa had laid a million dollars cash on the line to get two Colombians out of jail who had gone down in a lab raid in Miami. He paid up, and the Colombians hit the road back to Colombia. So I had no reason to disbelieve Rafa when he said he would post my bond.

But nothing was happening. Time was grinding away and prison life was rough and boring. I was spending a little time with my lawyers on almost a daily basis, trying for a bail reduction hearing and discussing my case, but it wasn't enough. I needed something else to occupy my time.

Then one day Julio told me that Osvaldo Blanco, Griselda's son, was waiting to come out of solitary and join the general population. He was known to the authorities under an alias. Julio and I were waiting when he came out, and once I had personally identified him I wasted no time letting the government know who they had.

Since Griselda had put out a contract on both Rafa and me, Julio, on my behalf, had some of the prison's most hardened "soul brothers" talk to Osvaldo and he was effectively neutralized. Before I left Terminal Island all three of Griselda's older sons were inside; they will be in prison for the remainder of this century. I have no idea what happened to Michael Corleone Sepulveda, Griselda's youngest son.

Everybody worked in prison, unless he was medically unfit. So I went over to the education office and got a job as a teacher. I was one of the few literates in the place; the illiteracy rate in prisons is phenomenal. Anyone with a college degree or some type of education is at a premium. I taught English to the Mexicans, because I was bilingual, and I taught basic mathematics, like adding and subtracting, multiplying and dividing. I did this for five or six months, and then that started to get boring too.

There were other ways to entertain oneself. Basically, a prisoner could get whatever he wanted, including sex. There were plenty of gays floating around the joint, if that was your preference. And if you wanted a woman, there were a couple of female guards who sold their services. One of them, a pretty black woman, was available for $200 a pop. The arrangements for a rendezvous would be made in advance, and a Western Union money order sent to the guard from outside the joint. Once the money arrived, she would take the con to an authorized area that was off-limits to prisoners and drop her drawers for him for a fast screw or give him a quick blow job. I never partook of these services.

Sometimes the prisoners would use their attorneys to get laid. Attorneys' visits took place in a conference room, which was a private, closed-door session. The attorneys were allowed to bring in a legal assistant or secretary. Instead, they'd bring in a hooker. While the lawyer occupied himself with his briefs or whatever, the hooker took care of the prisoner.

I didn't go for any of that, but since no conjugal visits were allowed in the federal prison system, it was tough going. We were allowed "contact visits"; that is, you could hug and kiss your wife when she arrived and when she left. We met in a large room, like a cafeteria, with tables and chairs and vending machines.

A couple hundred people at a time used this room and some of them just didn't care. Many acted like animals, trying to get laid while kids ran around and men tried to talk with their wives. Some women would kneel under the table or straddle a prisoner's lap, grinding away. Others just put their head in their man's lap. Or a prisoner would stand up and turn his back while the woman sat in front of him, working him over. I hated having Cristina visit me there and see this.

Drugs were purchased from the guards or inmates in the same way sex could be procured. Send them a Western Union money order through a contact on the outside and either the guard would deliver it or it would be passed from inmate to inmate. Anything you wanted: marijuana, crack, coke, heroin, speed—you name it, they had it.

It was only during my Terminal Island sojourn that I came into personal contact with the effects of drugs on the greater population of the United States. I had never actually known street-level dealers or addicts. It seemed as though three-quarters of the prisoners were in there for drug-related offenses. I began to understand for the first time the irreparable harm that cocaine trafficking was doing in America, and as the narcotics horror stories were played out before me every day a sense of remorse began creeping over me. I didn't use drugs, but I had helped make them a part of American life.

In November 1985 I got some really bad news. Cumbamba had gone out to my house to give my wife some money. He delivered the money with this remark: "We understand that your husband might be thinking of doing something that he shouldn't. Tell him if he does, you're dead, the kids are dead, your entire family is dead."

When Cristina told me this I went off the deep end. Threaten my family? Never! Nobody threatens my family!

If they weren't going to protect my family, I'd find someone who could. It was after this threat that I started to think seriously about cooperating with the government.

The final blow was struck in March 1986, when Cristina heard from Rafa. He called her from Colombia and threatened her directly. "You must be careful, and you must tell my compadre to be careful," he told her. "He must not utter a word to the authorities or I will kill you and your whole family down here in Colombia. Do you understand me?"

"Yes," she answered, trembling.

"That's good, because there can be no misunderstanding here. The lives of you, your children, and your entire family depend on it."

I called Tom Johnston, my lawyer, and said, "Let's make a deal with the feds."

"You sure, Max?" he asked. "I don't like it. I recommend against it. I think the government is going to screw you."

"Tom, please, just go ahead and do it. Make the best deal you can, and keep in close touch."

"You got it. I'll call them today."

The negotiations started. They were complicated, and would take a long time, but the die was cast.

Shortly after this decision, Pablo Escobar decided it was time to do something. He had heard rumors of how angry I was. Escobar sent a list of properties he owned that he had authorized to be used for my bail. The list contained addresses of the properties and the dummy Panamanian corporations that held title to the properties. Hardly the sort of assets that would meet the goverment's simon-pure criteria.

But in any case, it was too late. I had made my decision and given my word to the government. Besides, I suspected that the cartel only wanted to bail me out in order to get rid of me. It was the easy way to silence me. They would get me released, kill me, and make sure the body was found so that they could get their bond money back. They had done it before.

I felt an enormous weight lift from my shoulders. I knew the negotiations with the government would be long and hard, but I felt elated, happy, free. And I began to cope a little bit better with my prison environment.

Drugs had brought me to prison, and I soon saw that drugs were a major part of prison life. They were everywhere; there was no end to the ingenuity in meeting the demand. Balloons were a common trick. A prisoner's wife or girlfriend would hide a small balloon in her mouth and when they kissed she would pass it to him. The prisoner would swallow the balloon and later retrieve it when he passed it.

The Frisbee trick was always good. A boat would speed by the South Yard of Terminal Island, passing as close to shore as possible, and a Frisbee would be sailed over the barbed-wire fence and into the yard. The prisoners would rush to the Frisbee and pull out the drugs tucked up inside the rim. By the time the guards got there the Frisbee would look normal. They banned Frisbees forever as recreational equipment when they found one hung up in the fence with an ounce of coke taped inside the lip. In the MCC in Tucson, they would shoot the dope over the fence with a bow and arrow.

Drugs are going to get into the prisons; there is no way in the world that anyone is going to stop it. But I learned that the prime source is the guards: they're the ones who bring it in, sell it, and get rich.

My little group on Terminal Island was growing every day. When I arrived, there were about forty Colombians out of a prison population of seven or eight hundred people. When I left, a year later, there were two hundred Colombians inside.

After six months in prison, negotiations with the Feds were almost complete, and I was ready to live up to my agreement. Both the government and I knew that I was potentially the best witness they had ever had.

Finally, we reached an agreement. I pled guilty and signed the agreement under seal, which meant the contents were not to be disclosed, ever. Things were looking good, until my cover was blown by an assistant U.S. attorney by the name of Ralph Hoeffer, may he rot in hell.

After I made my deal with the government, Julio Silva, my co-defendant, was still to be disposed of as far as the courts were concerned. For some reason, Hoeffer decided on his own that he would dispose of the case quickly. He wrote a letter to Silva's attorney telling him that Mermelstein had pled guilty and had decided to cooperate with the government, and that it would behoove Mr. Silva to do the same. I had no knowledge of this letter, and neither did anyone else.

The next time I met Silva in the yard and he flashed Hoeffer's letter at me. "What's this shit? What's going on?"

"Julio, you know me, I'd never hurt you."

"I know, but what are you doing?"

"I'm talking to them. I haven't made any deal yet," I lied. "They made me an offer. I want to see what they are going to say to me."

He bought it. He knew that if I did talk I would not hurt him; my word was my word.

I walked back to my unit, almost running. I was trembling with rage, sheer unadulterated rage. I could've torn Hoeffer's heart out with my bare hands.

I immediately called Tom Johnston, my attorney, but he wasn't in. Next I tried calling Assistant U.S. Attorney Jim Walsh, who was in charge of the criminal division; he wasn't around either. So I placed a call to U.S. Attorney Dick Gregorie in Miami.

It was the first time I had ever spoken to him; my attorneys had negotiated with him on my behalf. I introduced myself on the telephone; he knew who I was.

"What's the problem?" Gregorie asked.

I explained the problem to him in detail. When I was done, he let out a blood-chilling yell of disbelief. "I can't believe it. Okay, it will be taken care of, I promise you."

Dick Gregorie called Washington, and Washington jumped all over Jim Walsh in California. Walsh had to take the heat; he was the U.S. attorney responsible for the narcotics unit in California, and Hoeffer worked for Walsh.

Hoeffer wound up leaving the Justice Department and Walsh was showered with the toughest reprimands. In the long run it hurt me, because Walsh wound up hating my guts for a long time. Anyway, we are friends today, and Walsh is a good prosecutor, even though he lost the DeLorean case. He's a good prosecutor and a hard man—hard as nails.

The next dumb thing that happened was the feds wanted to move me out of Terminal Island. "No, no, not yet," I pleaded to the U.S. Attorney's office. "The minute you move me, the Colombians will know I've flipped. My wife and family are still in Miami, sitting ducks. My wife knows nothing about these negotiations." Until the deal went into effect, there was no reason for anyone to know.

"It's time to call her," they said. "Get her out here and tell her what's happening."

I called Cristina and told her to come out that weekend, that we had to sit down and talk.

I settled down to wait for her. The one condition I had put on my sealed agreement was that my wife must also agree. The signed agreement would be held in abeyance until she gave her consent to enter Witsec, the witness protection program, with our children.

But jailhouse life went on. During this time I was offered a phenomenal deal. A fellow inmate came to me and told me he had a contact on the outside with a black guy named White, who had done time on Terminal Island. White had asked the inmate to find a good coke connection, somebody who was willing to buy gold at a reduced rate and pay for it in cocaine at wholesale value. White needed a big-time supplier, not a street dealer.

"How much gold do they have?" I asked.

"Around ten thousand ounces," he answered.

"Where'd they get it?"

"Stolen in South Africa, and they're bringing it into the U.S."

"What form is the gold in?" I asked.

"Krugerrands and gold bars."

"Is it in the U.S. now?"

"There's three thousand ounces in the country. The rest will be here shortly."

"What's the price of the gold?"

"One hundred dollars an ounce, against rock-bottom wholesale on the coke, say twenty grand a kilo, for ninety-nine percent pure powder."

"Why me? Why'd you come to me with this deal?"

"We got word that you are connected, and this will involve some real weight. We're talking about ten million dollars' worth."

"That's five hundred kilos."

"That's right. Can you deliver?"

"Yeah, let's go with it. Give me about a week with my people," I said.

"You got it! I'll tell White we got a deal."

I immediately got hold of Tom Johnston, my attorney, and told him what I had been offered. "Tom, get this to the FBI, or find out which government agency it is that does this stuff."

Tom went to the U.S. Attorney's office, and they sent him to a special division of the FBI that handled business like this. I found out later that it should have been Customs that handled it, but they didn't. It proved to me again that the government is big and clumsy and often doesn't know who handles what.

So it was turned over to the FBI and I gave them chapter and verse, exact details, of what was going on. They licked their chops and told me, "Keep negotiating. We'll set 'em up for a sting and nail their asses."

I did what the FBI told me to do. I played White along, kept negotiating with his inside contact, and finally a time and place were set, the code names were set, and my representative was to meet with White to pick up three thousand ounces of gold. I informed the FBI in plenty of time, two weeks ahead. "The deal is on," I told them. "Three thousand ounces of gold at one hundred dollars an ounce, for one hundred and fifty kilos of coke." I gave them the code names, the time, the location, everything they needed for the sting.

Later, I got the bad news. White was there, as promised, waiting on the goddamn corner with three thousand ounces of gold. The FBI never showed. And they never said why. I had to do some fast talking on that one to keep any kind of credibility in the joint and stay alive.

Cristina arrived on Friday. Arrangements had been made with the U.S. Attorney's office that when she arrived we would not meet on Terminal Island but at the Federal Courthouse in Los Angeles, in a conference room with Assistant U.S. Attorney Walsh and my attorney present, so that the Witsec program could be explained.

I explained in Spanish, "Cristina, I have made a decision that affects us both. I am facing a charge of life in prison with no chance of parole. That means if they convict me, I will spend the rest of my life in jail."

She started to cry. I went over it all again. "There is a chance I could beat the charges, but it's a big chance to take. And now that the government believes I am a drug dealer, they will hound me to my grave. I have no choice but to cooperate with them, and I am going to do just that. I am going to cooperate."

Cristina sobbed uncontrollably. I held her, holding back my own tears. The thing I wanted most in the world I had right there in my arms, my wife, my family, and I was going to do whatever it took to be with them. I was as angry at Rafa and the cartel as I had ever been in my life. They had taken away my freedom and my self-respect.

Gradually her tears subsided. I knew what was racing through her head: our little family was as good as dead, and all Cristina's relatives in Colombia were dead. She knew the cartel's retribution could be swift and decisive.

"Max, *te amo*. I love you. I will do as you wish, and the children will do as you wish. I thought this might happen, and I have been to see a priest and I asked him about it."

"What did he say?"

"He said that if this was the course that was chosen, it should be done with a full heart, that much wrong has been done and we must try to make it right. I agree with him. Those people, Rafa and Cumbamba, they are evil, Max. They are on the side of the devil and they make devils out of people, this I know."

I held her and said nothing. Walsh and Johnston rose from the table and walked away, leaving us to ourselves.

Cristina sniffled and reached in her purse for a Kleenex. She whispered to me, "Max, you must promise me one thing now."

"Anything."

"Promise me you will come to the church, the Catholic church will save you. If we get through this safely, you will join the church, promise me."

"I promise," I said, wiping away her tears with my thumb. I caressed her beautiful face. "I promise."

"And my family, Max? What about my family in Colombia?"

"We've thought about that. They will be looked after. Just listen now to what these men have to say."

Walsh and a U.S. marshal explained what life inside the Witsec program would be like, and I translated for her. I could imagine what she was thinking. Rafa and Cumbamba had scared her beyond fear. She knew that these men were entirely capable of killing her and the family and never thinking about it again. And if I were to jump bail she knew we would have to run off with the children somewhere and live like fugitives hidden in the mountains of Colombia, always in fear of being extradited to the U.S. She was a terrific woman and she loved me. I knew it now more than I ever knew it. She loved me totally, with her whole being, and I was proud and grateful.

When they were done, she turned to me and said, "Max, I am not sure about the family, I am still scared for them. They could kill my brother, my sister . . ."

"No, Cristina, all the arrangements have been made. Everyone who wants to come into the program will be taken care of. We will bring up the ones from Colombia who want the same protection. We'll do it before anyone knows anything. Everybody will be safe."

I held Cristina's hand as I explained things to her. I didn't tell her that when I had made this a condition of the deal, that the entire family had to be protected, the government people had gone nuts. They climbed the walls. They complained bitterly. But as I explained to them, Colombian criminals are not like the Mafia, who hold the family sacrosanct. Colombian criminals look at a man's family as his weakness. They threaten the family first. They warn you, once, maybe twice, then they kill your family, one by one, or all at the same time, and they do it as easily as snuffing out a candle.

"Max, has someone threatened Cristina?" Tom Johnston asked when he saw how upset she was. I told him what Rafa had said to Cristina on the telephone.

Jim Walsh listened; he stared at me for a second and said quietly, "That little prick isn't going to do anything to anyone. Your wife's going into the program today, Max. And you aren't going back to the general population at Terminal Island, not with all those Colombians there."

My wife went back to Miami and was picked up by the marshals. Then all the family members who were in the U.S. were picked up, and arrangements made to get the rest of the family up from Colombia. Thirty-one people were contacted and given the opportunity to go into Witsec. Sixteen chose to go. The DEA was asked to provide protection until the family was assembled by the marshals, but they refused to fill the request. No reason was ever given. My wife stayed at our home in Miami, unprotected, until the family came up from Colombia. The family was finally united and everyone disappeared at once.

The witness protection program had never taken in sixteen people before to protect one witness. But they did it, and they did it fast. The government, through the marshals, acted exactly as they said they would; they kept their word.

And as long as Cristina and I knew that the family was safe, then we did what we had to do.

I was put in the hole in Terminal Island, to keep people from being suspicious that I had flipped. They had written an "incident report" on me. The report said that I had had a fistfight with a marshal in the courthouse, and that I was doing time in solitary as punishment.

I had lots of time in the hole to think about my deal. It was not a great deal, but it was a start and, if I worked hard, I thought I could better it. The secret agreement stipulated that the feds would drop their recommendation of a life sentence on the continuing criminal enterprise charge; they would ask for ten years on the CCE. That meant ten years minimum, mandatory. The judge had to give me at least ten years under the law, but beyond that it was left to the judge's discretion; I could get up to sixty years. It depended on what the judge thought of the quality of my cooperation and my efforts to help the government. In other words, I had no guarantees.

My greatest disappointment was when Luis, my adopted son, came to visit me. He was twenty-one at the time.

"I do not agree with what you are doing," he said. "Mother has told me everything, and I have to tell you that I am against such a thing. You cannot inform on these people."

"My life is at stake here, and 'these people' threatened to kill you as well as her," I snapped back.

"That was only if you talked!"

"I have no choice. They have done nothing that they said they would. They have not honored our agreement."

"I cannot agree," Luis said angrily.

"It's not up to you to agree. It's my life. You do what you have to do, I'll do what I have to do."

"As you like," he said, and walked away. It was the last time I ever saw him. We talked over patched-in telephone circuits on occasion but our relationship was shattered by my decision, and it broke my wife's heart. Nevertheless, she stuck with me.

I stayed in solitary until my family was picked up and put in Witsec. Then I disappeared off Terminal Island and into Witsec.

But I was still in jail.

• • •

Later, I heard that the Krugerrand deal finally went down just as my prison contact had wanted it to go down. White eventually found another supplier and traded the gold for cocaine. I was told he used the proceeds from the sale of the dope to buy guns for guerrillas in South Africa, and those guns were used to start the bloodbath down there.

Part Five

* *
* *

TURNING
WITNESS

CHAPTER NINETEEN

*

Gang Bangs

I am considered the most valuable witness that the government has ever turned against the cartel. When I first started to talk in 1986, the government really didn't have any grasp of the enormity of the cocaine cartels in Colombia. The Medellín cartel was fully established and rolling. Its cash flow, its net profits, rivaled the profits of General Motors. The government was treating each case as an individual isolated case and no one had yet put together the cases to discover that it was a massive conspiracy called "the cartel." It's hard to believe that no prosecutor had assembled and united the cases, but if you know how the government works, like a lumbering uncoordinated giant, particularly the law enforcement agencies, then it isn't so hard to believe.

Hardly anyone had heard of the drug "cartel" in 1986. In ten short years, the bosses had grown from little more than Colombian peasants to appear on *Forbes'* list of the richest men in the world. I was amazed at how little the government knew.

Part of the problem is that the federal agencies are all jealous of each other, and therefore play their cards close to their vests. They simply do not want to share information; it is too hard to come by, and sometimes too dangerous to give out to other agencies, because there can be damaging leaks or internal corruption. The net result is the federal agencies' motto: "Nobody talks to nobody."

Another problem is the Colombians themselves. They are unique, like no group that U.S. law enforcement has ever seen. They move like nomads through a desert, changing addresses at least once a month. Their names alone are daunting; they read like gobbledygook to most agency personnel who do not speak Spanish, and most of them don't.

Colombian criminals never buy a home, they only rent, so they can be gone in a flash. They are masters at false papers, and can give themselves new identities every week if they wish. Even their cars are in the names of nonexistent people. They have no ties to material possessions; they deal only in cash. And they have plenty of it, so they can leave behind whatever they want. Just walk away. If they believe their house is under surveillance, they simply never go back there again. They leave their clothes in the closet and food in the fridge. Surveillance has to be different on Colombians than it is for any other group.

I told the cops who talked to me to throw their manuals out the window; the old rules don't work on Colombian criminals.

And if Colombians get caught, they don't care. They know they'll be bailed out. Then they either flee or they get instant new identities and go back into business the next day. They have no problems kissing the bail bond goodbye. In a month they can make it up by selling dope. And the very worst thing they face is deportation. Big deal. Send them back to Colombia, and given time they'll make their way to Mexico and slip back into the U.S. over the Texas border, with new papers. Most of the time the cops don't understand that the goon they've just caught has been caught half a dozen times before.

And finally, the Colombians hold the sword of Damocles over the heads of their own people. The Colombian kingpins threaten to kill the families of the people who work for them if they ever inform or turn against them. And they do it, often. They will burst into a house in Colombia and kill everyone in sight and everything—the dog, the cat, even the goldfish. If there is anything left breathing in the house, they will kill it. I know this firsthand.

That was one of the reasons the cartel put an instant $1 million bounty on my head, dead or alive. I had too high a position within the cartel, I was well-known, and they did not want me to become the inspiration for everyone else to defect.

I had a lot of information to give, and I had a ball with the cops when I started to tell them what I knew. They had a ball, too, when I gave them the information. They wound up calling the debriefing sessions "gang bangs."

I kept a careful log of these sessions. They were intense and productive—for the cops.

Even though they tried to keep my identity secret, word spread in law enforcement circles like jungle drums, and anyone who had a case where he thought I might be of help was immediately on the road to wherever I was, to talk to me. I had total immunity, so I could speak freely about what I knew, and I did. I held nothing back.

At first they had trouble believing me.

I was in a session that included about twenty people. Al Singleton, a homicide sergeant in Miami's Metro-Dade and a member of Centac 26, a combined task force of DEA and Metro-Dade cops, was there. When he gave me that haven't-I-seen-you-before look, I reminded him where it had been. He had arrested Elbia Sepulveda at the Miami airport after Diego's funeral. She was accompanying her brother's body back to Colombia. She was also carrying $30,000 in drug cash to launder back home as well as my name and address on a piece of paper. Singleton had no charges against me that day when he came to my house to ask about Elbia. But, he said, he had always figured I was somehow connected to the Colombians.

He turned out to be a good guy, a hell of a cop, and a dedicated one. Singleton loved solving murders, and there was almost one a day being committed in Miami in the late seventies and early eighties. He listened in fascination as I told of the van ride in 1978 when Rafa shot Chino. I gave him all the details of that awful night.

When I was done Singleton bolted from the room to make some calls. When he came back, he said, "He's right. That's case 335213, Antonio Arles Vargas, discovered murdered Christmas Day in a field. Cause of death was multiple gunshot wounds to the head and torso from a .38-caliber weapon. His a/k/a was Chino. That's him, all right!"

A silence fell over the room. It was almost as if the people interrogating me were imagining the nightmare that had happened in the van that night in 1978, eight years before. I knew that they would talk about it among themselves, and that it would irrefutably establish my credibility. And it did.

For a solid year I was a one-man band, providing witness against the cartel and many of its players. I talked to the DEA, the FBI, Customs, Metro-Dade Police and Internal Affairs, scores of federal prosecutors, and the State Department.

I told them the details of the cartel routes into the United States, I helped them solve unsolved murders. I told them about Griselda Blanco's operation and about the death of Marta Ochoa Saldarriaga at Griselda's hands. I spoke of my own gang, which was under an investigation code-named "Operation Beacon." I helped to bring it down. I told them of the Cali connection and how the Cali cartel and the Medellín cartel were structured. I told them of dirty Bahamians such as Cordell Thompson of the Ministry of Tourism. I told them of the Barranquilla operation and Jon Roberts.

In May 1986 I told U.S. Attorney Lee Stapleton and Gary Wallace of Alcohol, Tobacco and Firearms about my deal to buy arms from a dirty Metro-Dade cop and where they could find the "order list." And I talked to Dennis Todaro of Metro-Dade Internal Affairs about the same thing.

My information was all gratefully accepted, and most of it was acted upon and eventually led to busts. But it was my debriefing on June 9, 1986, that stopped them dead in their tracks.

I was inside a windowless "submarine," a bunkerlike steel-and-concrete building. The U.S. Marshals Service keeps these structures around the country for protected witnesses and others who need special security, such as defectors. The submarine was somewhere in South Florida; I had a bedroom, a bathroom, and a TV set, no windows.

I was being debriefed by Dick Gregorie, the Miami U.S. attorney, and Al Winters, the Louisiana U.S. attorney. Lynn Wheeler and Carol Cooper were also in the room; they were both with the DEA.

Barry Seal had been murdered in Baton Rouge on February 19, 1986, by a Colombian hit squad. It had gone down just as I said it would.

Cumbamba got the job after the cops busted me. The cartel had hired private detectives to find Barry Seal. Federal judge Frank Polozola had sentenced Seal to probation for narcotics violations, but forced him to live in a Baton Rouge Salvation Army halfway house from six at night to at least six in the morning. Judge Polozola had announced in open court the address of the halfway house and even stripped Seal of the bodyguards he had hired to see him in and out of his exposed quarters. The judge ruled that armed bodyguards constituted constructive possession of a firearm; the bodyguards were under Seal's direct control, and so, strictly speaking, he could instruct them to kill. All this occurred despite the pleas of federal prosecutors, who desperately wanted to keep Seal alive. He was to be their prime witness in the trial of Jorge Ochoa, who they fully expected to be extradited to the United States from Spain.

The judge might as well have pulled the trigger himself. Polozola had been told how vicious these Colombian assassins were, and he didn't listen. He said he was going to bury Barry Seal away in jail; instead, he buried him six feet under the good Louisiana earth.

With the time of Barry Seal's nightly return to the halfway house a matter of public record, Cumbamba, Quintero Cruz, and Bernardo Vasquez merely drove into Baton Rouge just after dark on that February night and waited until Seal appeared at six o'clock in his Cadillac. As Seal parked the car the Colombian hit team, who were hiding in the shadows, opened up with a silenced Mac-10.

Three bullets hit Seal in the left side of the head, two of them entering right behind his ear. A fourth bullet traced a ridge of his scalp, a fifth and sixth blew through his chest. Every bullet passed through his body clean. When it was over, Seal lay on the bloody front seat of the car, his hands gripping his ears as though he was trying to deafen the horror of what was happening to him.

The three Colombians, so obvious as they mingled with the population of Louisiana, were apprehended within twenty-four hours of the shooting. It had to happen that way.

As Winters was describing the actual killing and the murder weapon to me I experienced a vivid flashback.

Joan Campenella was a big, near six-footer of a woman, heavy, round faced, with red hair that fell to her shoulders. She was the realtor who found the houses for us to rent. Since we rented separate $1,000-a-month houses in which to stash our coke and cash, usually at the rate of two a month, her commissions (one month's rent) with me ran two grand a month. We'd keep a house for, at the most, three months and then abandoned it, forfeiting the deposit.

Joan was a real piece of work. She always wore long pants and carried a .38 revolver in an ankle holster. She also packed a .22 Derringer in her purse. Her redneck husband, Joe, was an auto mechanic and gun nut who was particularly enamored of machine guns. Although we never told her what line of work we were in, she must have guessed because she told me after renting me the second or third house that if I wanted to buy specialized weaponry she and Joe had access to almost anything I could name.

When Rafa was putting the finishing touches on his hacienda south of Medellín he asked me to find him a suitable weapon to mount on the water tower overlooking his private airstrip. I asked Joan what she might have available. Two weeks later on the down leg of a coke flight I sent Rafa a Mauser 7.62-mm-caliber heavy machine gun with half a dozen 250-round belts of ammunition. When the war between Griselda's shooters and Rafa's pistolocos broke out over the death of Marta Ochoa, I supplied Jaime Bravo with a KG-9 and silencer provided by Joan. Unfortunately he only enjoyed the weapon for two weeks before being busted by the cops for possession of two keys of coke and the hand-held fully automatic machine gun.

Then, during the course of turning over a couple of new stash houses to me, Joan came up with a prize. She proudly showed me a new Mac-

10 with a silencer her husband Joe had specially modified for this weapon. In gun shops the Mac-10s were sold without the selector switch which allows the gun to shoot one round at a time or fire on full automatic. Only the semi-automatic model can be sold legitimately. The model Joan showed me had the selector switch in place and thus the awesome capability of pouring out thirty rounds a second from an extended magazine.

The weapon came in what she called a "CIA attaché case" and could be fired from within the case with a trigger in the handle. The crowning achievement was the fact that Joe had drilled out the serial numbers. Filing them off does not truly obliterate them; there is a chemical that can re-create the numbers. But the way Joe had done it, there was absolutely no way to trace the weapon through its serial numbers.

I asked her how much she wanted for it. Five thousand, she replied. I suggested she show it to Rafa and I would tell him I recommended the buy.

One afternoon in 1984 Rafa arrived at the house I had rented in the Golden Beach area of Miami. He was carrying the black CIA attaché case. We went back to the swimming pool and Rafa proudly took out the Mac-10. "Let's try it out," he said. "You're a gun expert."

"Not here at my home."

"Why not? Nobody will hear with the silencer on it." He was like a kid with the greatest toy he'd ever been given.

"Okay," I agreed. "But I don't want lead sprayed all over the neighborhood. I'll figure something out."

I led the way into a wood-paneled chauffeur's apartment at the back of the concrete-block garage, and found a big Styrofoam cooler, which I filled with water and stuffed with six telephone books. When they had absorbed the water and were soggy I gestured at the box.

"Okay, go to it, but for God's sake, not on full automatic. One shot at a time." I made sure Rafa had flipped the selector switch to "semi" and then stepped back.

Rafa must have fired a dozen shots; some hit the Styrofoam bullet absorber I had rigged, but a number of them smacked into the wall. With a big grin on his face he packed his new toy back in its case and snapped it shut.

I interrupted Al Winters as he was giving me the details of Barry Seal's murder. "Did the Mac-10 have a silencer that was covered with black, armor-flex insulating tape held in place by duct tape, and were the serial numbers drilled out?"

"Yes," Winters answered, holding his breath.

"The serial numbers were drilled out, not just filed out, right?"

"Right!"

"I know that gun!" I exclaimed. "It was fired at my house, and I can tell in what wall you can find the bullets."

You could actually feel the energy fill the air in the room. Everybody looked at each other. Then they moved. They rushed to get a subpoena to tear up the wall in the expensive home some unsuspecting family was renting or had purchased in Golden Beach. They called Alcohol, Tobacco and Firearms experts to go with them.

Gary Wallace, the ATF agent, dug the bullets out of the wall of the chauffeur's apartment in the garage. They were exactly where I told them they would be, and they never would have been found without me. The bullets tied everything together.

The ballistics tests on the bullets matched the ones on the slugs that had killed Barry Seal.

They returned the next day and I continued to talk while they sat in total silence. I explained how I had been ordered to kill Seal by Fabio Ochoa and Pablo Escobar. I thought they were going to hug me and do cartwheels when I was finished.

The U.S. attorneys knew exactly what they had. They had the Medellín cartel tied directly to a murder rap. They could try the Ochoas, Pablo Escobar, Rodriguez Gacha, and Rafael Cardona on a murder charge— if they could extradite them.

CHAPTER TWENTY

*

Operation Beacon

I was in the special security section of Terminal Island on June 10, 1986, when I was debriefed on my own gang, the Cooley-Munday group, which was code-named "Operation Beacon." I talked to Ron Shure, Assistant U.S. Attorney, Pete Girard from Customs, and Bill Temple and John Donovan of the FBI. It was a combined FBI-Customs investigation.

They were at a deadlock when they talked to me, and were ready to drop the case. They had no information; their source had dried up. They didn't know where the dope was going and who was really behind the ring. I filled them in and gave them exact details and they went back on the operation.

What no one knew was that before we launched Operation Beacon, I had sent a message out to Jimmy Cooley and Mickey Munday: "Don't go back into business, stop everything. Don't be stupid, stop now!" But the smell of big money was too much for them. They started moving loads again, and they cut their own throats. I did what I had to do, and now they were going to do what they thought they had to do.

I gave the Feds the exact location of the airstrip in Lakeland, Florida. It was an airport condo, with five-acre tracts running along the runway. Mickey and Jimmy owned the property, and they sold five-acre lots to people who wanted to have their own runway in their backyard and park their plane next to their house. The lots were all purchased by friends of theirs.

I also gave the government the addresses of all the warehouses that were used to stash the cocaine, and the marinas where the boats were loaded onto trailers so they could be hauled away with the dope hidden inside.

Mickey and Jimmy had continued to use all the same locations we had used together. They were careless and lazy. Sometimes all that money can lull you into a sense of security, and that leads to a sure fall.

The surveillance and investigation lasted until September 21, 1986, when they finally busted them. It was a well-coordinated and executed bust. I got a full report after it went down. The agents waited until the Piper Navajo carrying the dope landed at Lakeland. The Navajo was immediately "jumped on" by a Blackhawk helicopter that disgorged ten Customs officers armed with machine guns. Ten more agents stormed the property from the ground. The agents hit both the plane and the "ranch."

I had warned them that Mickey would fight and that they should be extra careful. I gave them a full profile on him, but they ignored my advice.

Mickey, as predicted, fought back. He tipped over a fifty-five-gallon drum of aviation fuel and shot at the fuel with a flare gun. Mickey had put those drums there precisely for this use, in case he was ever busted. The flare ricocheted off the drum, spiraling harmlessly onto the grass.

"Come any closer and I'll blow it up!" Mickey screamed, as he frantically reloaded the flare gun and aimed it this time at the plane's fuel tanks.

"Drop the gun!" the agents responded, their machine guns leveled at him, ready to fire.

Mickey dropped the gun and ran for the woods. He had always told me that the cops, particularly the feds, would never shoot a "fleeing felon" unless their lives were endangered. I guess this was where he decided to prove his theory.

He was right. They didn't shoot, and Mickey disappeared into the woods. He got away; he's still a fugitive. But the cops grabbed the rest of them.

They arrested ten people, including Jimmy Cooley and Jon Roberts, the same Jon Roberts who had helped me with the Barry Seal contract, and who ripped me off for $650,000 on the Barranquilla deal. He didn't really beat me; I would have had to turn the money over to the government, so I guess you could say Jon Roberts beat the U.S. government out of the money.

The federal agents nailed five of the ten people in Mickey's radio scanning room. They also raided a high-rise condominium at 19390 Collins Avenue, overlooking Haulover Cut, and arrested one of Mickey's people who was acting as a lookout.

In total they confiscated 1,106 pounds of cocaine and $1 million in cash inside the ranch house on the airstrip. Later, they found $500,000 of Mickey's "mad money" in the trunk of his car outside his house in North Miami.

They also seized twenty-eight boats and four more planes that were stored in hangars 42–A&B at the Fort Lauderdale Executive Airport. And they picked up $100,000 in cash at Jimmy Cooley's Cooper City home.

Operation Beacon was the combined effort of the FBI and Customs, but it was the FBI that I got in a fight with over Jon Roberts. Roberts promised to cooperate if they released him on bail.

I told the lead agent, "Don't be nuts. Roberts is only conning you. You let him go and he'll split. He'll run like a rabbit."

"No," the FBI man said, "don't *you* be stupid. He'll work with us and lead us to more busts."

"Sure, sure he will, he'll lead you right down the garden path is where he'll lead you. For Chrissake, he's rich, why would he help you? He's facing a murder rap."

"What the hell are you talking about, Max?"

"There are conspiracy to commit murder charges pending against him in Louisiana. And he told me he contracted for somebody to kill a guy in Illinois a number of years ago, and there is an agency investigating that right now."

"Sure, Max. Maybe you just have it in for him because of reasons of your own."

And the FBI, being what they are, thickheaded mostly, did not believe me: they let him out on bail. That's when I finally agreed with what so many people, including law enforcement people, had told me: FBI stands for "Famous But Ignorant."

Immediately upon his release on bail Jon Roberts hit the road, and has not been seen again. By the authorities, that is.

I saw him in Boston a little while later. I was being transported by the marshals and we were walking through Logan Airport, and there he was, Jon Roberts, in the flesh. But he didn't see me. He was walking out of the airport. I didn't say anything to the marshal who was my escort, although it's their job to pick up fugitives. I knew there was a warrant out on Roberts, but I also knew my safety came first for them. With me in tow they wouldn't have done anything.

I heard later, through the grapevine, that Jimmy Cooley opted to do the right thing and cooperate. He, like me, is now in the witness protection program, in jail somewhere and helping the feds.

Good luck, Jimmy.

CHAPTER TWENTY-ONE

*

The Extraditables

The bedside clock told me it was 5:00 A.M. when I woke up in my cubicle in the Miami "submarine." There were no windows in the place; a TV set was my only window on the world. There was no point in trying to sleep any longer. My motor was running at full throttle.

This might well be the most important day of my life. Through an incredible chain of circumstances, I was now the most valuable asset to the careers of these prosecutors who had once wanted to put me away for life. It was my chance to win the final points that would get me out of the mire.

With the assassination of Barry Seal, I had clearly succeeded to his slot as the government's most important witness against the cartel. In fact I was far more valuable than Seal had ever been. I could provide the evidence to indict the cartel on charges of conspiracy to murder, in addition to drug trafficking.

In just a few hours, the marshals would be delivering me in a closed van to the U.S. District Court in the Southern District of Florida.

It was August 1, 1986, and I was to appear before the grand jury. My testimony in all likelihood would lead to an extradition order that might someday bring them all to the bar of U.S. justice.

The government was turning itself inside out to speed these proceedings along. They were concerned that Colombia might cancel the extradition treaty with the U.S. that was in effect at this time. Jorge Ochoa was in a Cartagena prison, tenuously held on illegal bull-importation charges, and the U.S. government was waiting to grab him.

How ironic, I thought as I prowled around my top-security room in the government safe house, that when it appeared that Jorge would be extradited from Spain to the U.S., the cartel's most pressing priority had been to kill Barry Seal. Now that Seal was dead, and Jorge, at least temporarily, had defeated the U.S. efforts to extradite him, the frantic meetings of the cartel death squad were focused on me.

This was my chance to perform a great service to the government that could win me my freedom to rejoin my wife and children. I had an early breakfast and meditated on the briefing Dick Gregorie had given me in preparation for this day: "Just tell the truth, no embellishments, no explanations, no excuses. Tell them what you did, and what you were ready to do," Dick counseled.

No promises were made, but I knew this was my chance, not only to do what was right but what would help me, help the drug prosecutors, and help the country rid itself of the drug scourge which I had helped bring on.

At nine thirty I was escorted by two marshals into the small conference room outside the grand jury chamber. I waited nervously to testify. I lit up one cigarette after another and gulped down the paper cups of coffee a marshal kept bringing in to me as I waited to make my appearance. I had to do well!

Promptly at 10:00 A.M.—by then I had been awake and revved up for five hours—I was called into the grand jury chamber. The marshals could not go into the room. As I was led inside I realized that, for the first time, I was out of sight of the Marshals Service.

The chamber was a small bare room, wood paneled, with a couple of windows high up on one wall letting in some natural light. I don't know what I expected to find when I was put in front of the grand jury. It sounded pretty impressive, but I was reassured to see a group of thoroughly ordinary men and women.

The jurors sat slouched on chairs in front of me, looking uninterested in the proceedings. The intimidation I felt started to drift away like smoke. I had expected to find twenty-four men and women, lean and mean, knowledgeable and irate, ready to pounce on me with questions I would rather not have to answer.

To my left, at a small table, sat a black woman, the foreperson of the jury, and beside her the court reporter, a gaunt, birdlike woman of indeterminate age, hunched over her shorthand machine. To my right, standing at a lectern, was Dick Gregorie. The foreperson stood up and swore me in. Then Gregorie opened the proceedings.

"Mr. Mermelstein," he began, "this grand jury is investigating violations of federal law, in particular, violations of Title 18, United States Code, Section 1962, which is what we call the RICO Statute. It is investigating . . . the Medellín cartel, the Medellín organization and their pattern of racketeering and importing cocaine."

I heard a sound and Gregorie looked up from his notes on the lectern. "There is a knock at the door," he announced. A juror walked over and opened it. A tall, skinny, raw-boned, middle-aged fellow, obviously a late juror, straggled in sheepishly. Once again I knew a sense of relief that I was appearing before ordinary Americans. Gregorie waited until the tardy juror was seated, and then went on.

"The matters in the racketeering activities, importing cocaine, conspiracy to commit murder, interstate transportation in aid of racketeering, and possible other violations of federal laws—" He stopped without completing his sentence and fixed me with a stare. "You, sir, are not a target in these violations. In fact, you have been told whatever testimony you give cannot be used against you in later prosecutions, is that correct?"

I looked into those intense eyes below the balding head; with his trimmed beard he looked like a professor. I nodded. "That is correct."

"However," he continued sternly, "if there is information that is totally unrelated to this case that could be used to prosecute you on another matter, that *can* be used against you. Do you understand?"

I nodded. I had no intention of confessing under immunity to a few crimes that hadn't caught up to me yet in hopes of gaining immunity from future prosecution if they should be found out. It was a game criminals tried to play when testifying under immunity, but I wasn't here to play games. I was here to score points for sentencing leniency.

Gregorie held up the California indictment against me and had me confirm that I had pled guilty to four counts of narcotics violations and that I could be sentenced up to sixty years in jail. I also confirmed that the government would recommend only a ten-year sentence at the time of sentencing, but that the judge could still give me sixty years. Then Gregorie took me through my criminal past, going back to moving the few keys of coke that Rafael Cardona supplied to me and all the way up to the cartel's instructions to murder Barry Seal.

Having firmly established the cartel's responsibility for the murder of Barry Seal, I told the jurors about Jon Roberts and Reed Barton and then further tied Fabio Ochoa into the murder conspiracy. I described meeting with Fabio's messenger outside the Chinese restaurant, and admitted taking the cardboard box containing $100,000: expense money for the Barry Seal hit. I then brought out that Carlos Arango—Cumbamba, "The Chin"—really wanted to carry out the hit on Seal.

And of course, as it happened, he did execute the contract after my arrest.

It was a long day of testifying but, at the end, there was no doubt that the grand jury was ready to hand down a murder indictment against the cartel.

The drama, the force of my testimony, was driven home when at the end of the day a juror asked, "Did you really think when you saw Rafael Cardona kill Chino that he owned you from then on?"

"Yes," I replied.

Another juror wanted to have his say. "And why didn't you kill him?" The juror's eyes flashed, his face grimaced. He probably would have killed Rafa, he was the type. "They were going to kill you later. Look what you are in for, thirty years in prison. You should have went ahead and shot that man. Run the truck into the canal and—"

Dick Gregorie tried to cut off any further exchanges. "I think that the record is clear, we can't suggest that anyone violate the law—that might be going a little far."

But one juror had to get it off his chest. "Get rid of those drug peddlers!" he snarled.

I was glad that day was over, even though all I had to look forward to was the high-security cubicle and the TV set. Back in the conference room, Dick Gregorie congratulated me on my testimony. I could only hope I was making up for my past and earning another chance to live a normal life with my family.

Back in prison I received word that on August 16 the grand jury ratified the indictment against the cartel based to a large extent on my testimony.

The drug prosecutors were confident that extradition warrants would soon follow in Colombia. And then came the shocking though certainly not surprising news. Once again, Jorge Ochoa had bought his way out of detention. Three days before the indictment was handed down, Judge Fabio Pastrana Hoyos, a young customs judge in Cartagena, despite strict instructions from the outgoing minister of justice, paroled Jorge Ochoa on $11,500 bond, telling him to check in every two weeks. Pastrana was fired on August 21 and Jorge Ochoa never bothered to report to any judge.

Now there was nothing more for me to do but wait for the next opportunity to be of service to the government while I awaited my sentencing somewhere down the line. I prayed that the DEA, FBI, and the various prosecutors would take into account my cooperation with them in their efforts to lop off the tentacles of the Colombian cartel that reached into all areas of the United States. Month followed lonely, despondent month and soon it was late fall. In Colombia, as I knew would be the case, the extradition treaty with the United States was canceled. It would now be impossible to extradite the drug lords. I could hear the collective sigh of relief within the cartel hierarchy all the way up in my prison cell. But I knew that someday the drug lords would have to settle their account with society.

With fifteen members of Cristina's family spread throughout the country in Witsec, I tried to keep in touch with all of them from the prison in which I was incarcerated. Some of the inmates called it the Rat Trap. There were other names for the prisons that held those of us who were cooperating with the government; sometimes we even called ourselves rats.

I was able to get my calls patched through to the family members in the program. I called Cristina every day. In early November 1986 she told me she was seriously worried about her brother Arturo. Although at the time we didn't know where Witsec had placed him, we later found out it was in an apartment in Memphis, Tennessee. He and his wife and their eight-year-old boy spoke no English and the people with whom they came in contact spoke no Spanish. They were virtually in solitary confinement together.

Jack Donnelly, the marshal overseeing Arturo's case, said he was too sickly to work as a welder, which was his trade. Neither Arturo nor his wife could get a driver's license since the tests were given in English. As a result, Arturo, totally demoralized, had not much else to do but brood over all the things that had happened to him in his unsuccessful life.

His woes had all started with Rafa making him help us clean up the van after Chino's blood, bone, and brains had been splattered over the back seat. That had been a traumatic experience for all of us but especially for Arturo, basically a quiet man who never wanted to be involved in drugs and violence.

Then Rafa had taken Arturo back to Colombia with him as a hostage so that Cristina and I would not talk about the murder. Other unfortunate circumstances had plagued the life of this poor born loser of a brother-in-law of mine. His rough treatment at my home after I was arrested and the subsequent imprisonment and deportation he suffered constantly preyed on his mind.

"They have dumped him in a city he can't understand," Cristina told me. "He needs psychiatric help. He can't cope with his life."

On Monday, November 10, I was patched through to Arturo and talked to him for almost an hour. He was in a thoroughly morose mood and recited to me everything that had happened to him. On Tuesday I called an official in the Marshals Service and asked for help in getting psychiatric counseling for Arturo. The service referred me back to Donnelly, in charge of the case.

The same day Cristina had a call placed to Jack Donnelly and pleaded with him to get a Spanish-speaking psychiatrist to help her brother. Donnelly said he would try, but he was going on vacation Thursday, the thirteenth, and if he couldn't do anything by then he would take care of the situation when he came back.

On Thursday, Cristina again had a call placed to Donnelly. "I'm going on vacation this afternoon," he said. "If Arturo gets a psychiatrist this afternoon I'll escort the doctor to his apartment. Otherwise it will have to wait until I get back."

It was impossible to find a Spanish-speaking psychiatrist on such short notice but I managed to get through to Arturo on Thursday afternoon and told him to be strong, that things would be better soon and when the marshal returned from vacation a special doctor would counsel him.

On Friday, November 14, the day before his forty-ninth birthday, Arturo hanged himself in a closet of the apartment Witsec had provided for him. He had fed a rope over the hanger rail and looped it around his neck. Then, determined to die, he had knelt on the floor of the closet and hauled on the rope with both hands, pulling himself off the floor by the neck, strangling himself and collapsing, dead, back into the kneeling position in which he was found.

It was a family tragedy compounded by the fact that nobody knew where the other members were, although they could talk to each other through the Marshals Service communications center.

The Witsec administration refused to allow the family to go to the funeral service for Arturo. I wasn't surprised that I was not given leave to go, but I tried to reason with the service on behalf of the rest of the family. "They all agree on one thing," I told the marshals. "If they are not permitted to go to Arturo's funeral they will sign themselves out of Witsec altogether, take their chances on the cartel's vengeance, and attend the services."

The Marshals Service polled the family members on this point and found out that I had not exaggerated their feelings. One way or the other they would attend Arturo's funeral. Each family member reiterated that he or she would risk Rafa's wrath over my flip-flop rather than miss the funeral. The marshals finally capitulated, and perhaps the most secure funeral rites ever held were those for Arturo Jaramillo, on November 18, 1986, at St. Michael's Church in Flushing, New York, the same church in which my daughter, Ana, was baptized in 1979.

From all over the country the marshals brought in the fourteen remaining members of the family. They were flown into New York and then picked up in armored cars and taken to the church, which had been cleared of all other people except for the priest who would conduct the service. From all corners of the church armed marshals peered out, alert for the expected Colombian death squad to charge in, spraying machine gun bullets. During the funeral service, other marshals cleared every soul out of the cemetery and posted security guards. The family, in bulletproof cars, followed the hearse to the cemetery gates and drove past machine gun- and shotgun-toting marshals to the interment site where Arturo was finally buried.

This was the first, and to this day the last, occasion when the family was all together in one spot. No sooner had the casket been lowered than everyone was whisked away to different airports for different destinations. But the Marshals Service had come through.

CHAPTER TWENTY-TWO

*

Murder Trial

I was helping the government and they were helping me. The government kept postponing my sentencing so that I could build up points for my sentencing hearing.

Now I had another chance. I was to be the key witness at the trial of Cumbamba and the two other Colombian shooters who had murdered Barry Seal.

Dick Gregorie and Al Winters, Assistant U.S. Attorney in Baton Rouge, had built up a brilliant strategy for me that I would use over and over again in court, with devastating results against the Colombian criminals. The strategy that Gregorie had developed was simple and difficult at the same time.

"Max," he explained, "you are going to tell the truth. And I don't just mean the truth, I mean the absolute, rock-bottom, 'oh my God!' truth. You have total immunity here, so you don't have to worry about anything you say being used against you."

"I intend to tell the truth."

"I know you do, Max, but it has to be soul-baring absolute truth. You are going to be up against the best criminal defense lawyers in America. The Colombians can afford the best. You hide anything and their lawyers will pick up the lie. They'll follow it like a blood spoor and tear your heart out; you will be discredited on the spot. That will be their strategy, to discredit you, but we can reverse it."

"How, exactly?"

"You answer every question honestly and calmly; you never let them bait you. If the defense says, 'You yourself had the contract to kill Seal, so how can you stand here in front of us decent people accusing someone else?' you simply answer, 'Yes, I did.' Never defend what you did, just state it. The jury will know you are telling the truth. If you don't elaborate, don't try to cover your tail, the more the defense attacks, the more the jury will believe you are telling the truth. The defense will dig their own grave with their own shovel trying to destroy your credibility. Just remember, juries understand far more than attorneys ever give them credit for."

Al Winters prepared me for the trial. We spent the first week together going over the facts of my life of crime. I had to be precise.

Al had been a prosecutor for fifteen years, and was a living legend in New Orleans. He had actually tried Barry Seal years before and convicted him on a "multi-kilo" charge. Winters was a careful man. After I had told him of my trips to Baton Rouge, he sent a small army of investigators to verify what I had told him. He even checked the long-distance calls from the public phone I had used in a mall to call Colombia. And sure enough, the calls were recorded: dates, times, everything exactly as I had said.

The second and third weeks he cross-examined me, tough and hard, exactly as he expected the defense attorney to do.

All was in readiness: I was about to become a witness at my first trial. But it still took a while. I began by waiting, waiting, waiting. I waited to get called out to Baton Rouge for the trial. Then there was a change of venue to Lake Charles, Louisiana, the same place where Jimmy Cooley had hid out after the Tampa bust.

This was a major trial, with a circus atmosphere. They picked the jury in a rodeo arena in Lake Charles. So many potential jurors were called that the arena was the only place that was big enough to hold them all.

Premila Burns of Baton Rouge was the prosecutor. She was obsessed with this case: it was the biggest trial of her career, and she wanted a conviction. In her twelve years as a prosecutor, she had lost only three jury trials out of one hundred.

I also wanted a conviction. If this trial went the way I wanted it to go, and if my next case ended in a conviction, then I was going to go before the judge for my sentencing.

Finally, the day of the trial was confirmed, the jury was selected, and I made the trip to Lake Charles, a trip I'll never forget.

I was moved from the federal holding facility, which I can't mention, to Lake Charles by private plane. It was a Cessna 414, owned and operated by the Marshals Service. In the plane were the pilot, co-pilot, and my personal escort—four U.S. marshals armed with side arms, shotguns, and automatic weapons. These men were with me not to keep me from escaping, but to keep me from getting killed.

The flight was eleven grueling hours. We did not land at Lake Charles. We landed in Texas in the dead of night, where we were met by a caravan of bulletproof cars. There were twenty marshals surrounding the airstrip. Everyone was armed with side arms and automatic weapons. I was hustled into a car and we set off on a six-hour ride in convoy, five bulletproof cars driving through the black Texas night.

We approached the courthouse and stopped. I got out of the car and noticed we were surrounded by men in black jumpsuits and black hats, carrying side arms and MP-5 submachine guns with laser sights that emitted little red beams of light. Lay the red spot on a target, squeeze the trigger, and it's blown away. The men in black were everywhere. On the rooftops, in the streets, in the doorway of the courthouse, and in the halls inside. They kept moving around; they would appear, disappear, and reappear.

"What's going on here?" I asked one of the marshals.

"Those are our Black Ninjas. SOGs, Special Operations Group, anti-terrorist trained. They pick up anything we might miss. They're here in case any of your Colombian pals decide to show their ugly faces. They know what to do."

The U.S. marshals were to be with me on many future operations, and as far as I am concerned they are the best. I would see them in action many times. You don't hear much about what they do, because they don't make mistakes.

I had been on the road eighteen hours when we slipped in the back door of the Lake Charles courthouse. The marshals had prepared a holding cell for me right inside the courthouse; there was a toilet and a cot, no shower. I dropped onto the cot, exhausted, and slept. The next day the marshals rigged a shower head to a rubber hose and, escorted by four armed marshals, I walked to the boiler room in the basement, stripped, and took a shower.

I had a day to rest and then we were on. At six in the morning on April 29, 1987, the marshals took me to the judge's chambers. The reason they came so early was that they needed the holding cells for Cumbamba and his crew.

Though it was a state trial, it was held in the Lake Charles Federal Building. The three members of the Colombian hit squad—Cumbamba, Quintero Cruz, and Vasquez—were brought in to face first-degree murder charges for the death of Barry Seal. The state was seeking the death penalty, the electric chair.

The courtroom was open to the public. Everyone who entered was put through a magnetometer search. The Black Ninjas were posted outside and inside the building. The marshals protecting me had side arms, shotguns, and automatic weapons. Inside the courtroom the last row was made up of marshals with their backs to the wall. This gave them a view of everyone in the room. I was seated in the stand with two marshals behind me, also facing the crowd.

They gave me careful instructions in case of trouble. I was told "Follow the lead marshal, who is standing on your right; do exactly what he says, go where he goes, do what he does, don't worry about anything else, don't stop to see what's going on. The other marshals know what they have to do if there's trouble, and they will do it. The lead marshal's job is to protect you, and that's all he is going to do. Your safety is all he is thinking about, so if there is trouble, do what he says."

The judge was a Cajun, Judge Quientaly. He sat behind a desk draped with red, white, and blue ribbons. There were seven defense lawyers, led by Richard Sharpstein, a top criminal lawyer from Miami. The jury consisted of ten women and two men; when they took their places at 9:00 A.M., the trial began.

I took a long, deep breath and Premila Burns got right into it. She quickly established that I was indicted on six felony violations in California, to which I had pled guilty and made a deal to become a government witness.

Richard Sharpstein immediately hit her with a series of verbal jabs. He objected to almost everything Burns asked me as leading, prejudicial, and influencing the witness. In almost every case the judge overruled him. It was distracting and annoying. I'm sure the jury must have felt the same; ultimately I think these constant interruptions went against him and his client.

Then Burns asked me, "Could you tell the jury what amount of cocaine you were responsible for importing between 1981 and June of 1985, when you were arrested?"

"It would be just shy of fifty-six tons, 111,000 pounds."

I knew those were astounding numbers to the jury. I wanted to look at them and see their reaction, but I kept my gaze on Prem Burns. I talked in as calm a voice as I could, delivering my responses in a monotone.

Burns: "Did this cocaine originate from any particular country?"

"Yes, it did; from Colombia."

Burns: "During this time who did you work with, if anyone, in Colombia?"

"During that time I worked with Rafael Cardona and the Medellín cartel."

Burns: "Would you explain what a cartel is?"

"A group of people who join forces for their common interests and benefit."

Burns then took off on establishing my background, that I spoke Spanish and had been to Colombia. She asked me how I had met Rafa.

I knew that this was the easy part. Burns was taking me through my extensive background, slowly, precisely, to establish that I was an expert and that I was a top player inside the cartel. I was one of the bad guys, so I knew all about them.

Burns finished her preliminaries at noon and we took a lunch break. After lunch it started to get interesting.

Burns: "Have you ever previously seen either Exhibit 14 or 15?" She handed me a Mac-10 and a silencer.

I immediately cocked and cleared the piece. I always did that with any gun I handled to make sure it was empty. I looked down the short barrel to make sure it wasn't loaded. I heard the gasp of the jury as I pulled the slide back. Finished with my examination, I held Exhibits 14 and 15 in my hands. I spoke without emotion. The gun spoke for itself.

"Yes, I have."

Burns: "Would you tell the jury the circumstances under which you first saw them?"

"April or May of 1984, they were brought to my residence."

Burns: "By whom were they brought?"

"By Rafael Cardona."

Burns: "And why did he have that weapon with him?"

"He wanted to show it to me."

Burns: "Was anything done with that weapon when it got to your residence?"

"He showed it to me, and told me he wanted to test-fire it at the pool."

Burns: "What was your response?"

"I told him I wouldn't let him test-fire it by the pool."

Burns: "Did he fire it in your home?"

"Yes, he did. We had a small apartment behind the garage. We went in there to test-fire it."

Burns: "How was it test-fired?"

"In the garage I picked up a Styrofoam cooler and half a dozen phone books. I filled up the cooler halfway with water, soaked the phone books, and told him he could fire into the phone books."

Burns: "Did he do so?"

"He put a clip in the weapon, cocked it, and fired it into the phone books."

Burns: "And did any of the bullets that were fired from that weapon go any other place, other than that cooler?"

"A number of the bullets went into the wall behind the cooler."

Burns continued, establishing that those same bullets, retrieved from the wall, matched the murder weapon. As I spoke to her, explaining what had happened in the garage, I saw again those exploding phone books, the bullets tearing the pages, the shredded paper fluttering in the air like torn leaves. The Mac-10 fired .45-caliber rounds. It was a devastating, deadly weapon. And I imagined those same rounds cutting and tearing into the body of Barry Seal. I silently thanked God that it wasn't me.

I then described the case that the Mac-10 was carried in. "It was a black attaché case that was set up on the inside with wooden blocks to hold the gun itself in position, and a hole drilled through the side of the case so the muzzle would fit right into the hole. The outside of that hole was covered by a business card. A trigger mechanism was installed in the case so that the gun could be fired from outside the case; and there were elastic bands and compartments to hold the silencer and extra clips."

Burns: "After the weapon was test-fired in your home in the spring of 1984, did you ever see it again?"

"On numerous occasions, yes."

Burns: "In whose possession would that weapon be?"

"Either with Rafael Cardona when he was alone, or when Cumbamba was with him, Cumbamba would usually carry the case."

Burns: "Is this 'Cumbamba' the same person you previously identified today?"

"Yes, it is."

Eventually, Burns got to the all-important meeting I had with Cumbamba in my shoe store, "Papuchi."

Burns: "After Rafael Cardona Salazar left with Bam-Bam, was anybody left remaining in that room with you?"

"Yes, Cumbamba was there."

Burns: "Did Cumbamba discuss the contract on Barry Seal's life at this time? Did he inquire about the contract?"

"Yes, he did."

Burns: "And what did he ask you?"

"He said, how come a contract was given out and he wasn't being involved with it. He was upset."

Burns: "Did he ask you the price of the contract?"

"Yes, he did."

Burns: "Did he inquire as to any other details of the contract?"

"Just how much it was and why I was having so much trouble in accomplishing it."

Burns: "What reason did you give him for not having killed Seal?"

"I told him that Seal lived in a secluded area, that his house was one way in, one way out, just one road. The road ends in a dead end and that there was no way. It couldn't be done unless everybody in the house was taken out and I wasn't about to do that."

Burns: "And did he say anything about taking out other people who might be in the house such as the wife and the kids?"

Sharpstein leaped to his feet, as he did many times throughout my testimony. "Leading the witness!" he yelled.

Judge Quientaly told Burns to rephrase the question.

Burns: "What was said about the area that the house was located in?"

"That being in a secluded area and the fact that the family lived there didn't bother him at all. He would just go in there and take everybody out."

Burns: "How many times did Cumbamba tell you that he wanted in on this contract?"

"Several times."

Burns: "What did you tell him about getting permission to take over the contract?"

"I told him I had no authority to allow him anywhere near the area or do anything about it. The contract was given by Fabio Ochoa, Pablo Escobar, and Rafa. They were the only ones who could make any decision as to any changes. He told me he would talk to them."

Burns: "Do you see that person in the courtroom today, who made these statements to you?"

"Yes, I do." I looked directly at Cumbamba, who was fixing me with a steely-eyed death-stare and smiling grimly.

Burns: "Would you identify him for the record?"

"Cumbamba. In the light blue sweater and the glasses."

The questioning by Burns continued in this vein for a little while longer, then it was the defense's turn.

Richard Sharpstein hammered away at me, and I just told the truth: that I was a major dope dealer and heavily involved with the cartel. He dug a huge hole for himself with his own shovel, just as Winters said he would.

Sharpstein: "Mr. Mermelstein, you helped dispose of a dead body, did you not?"

"Yes, sir."

Sharpstein: "Personally carried the body out and disposed of it. There were a lot of other crimes that you committed, Mr. Mermelstein, that you have been given blanket vindication and exoneration for; is that correct?"

"No, sir."

"Well, you don't think that anyone is going to prosecute you now, do you?"

"I hope they don't."

Sharpstein went through my whole life of crime; he almost did a better job than Premila Burns, the prosecutor.

Sharpstein: "How much money did you arrange to have taken out of the country?"

"Approximately three hundred million dollars." Again I heard the jury gasp. Even Sharpstein looked shocked.

Sharpstein: "You yourself were personally involved in arranging for three hundred million illegal dollars to be taken out of this country?"

"That's correct."

Sharpstein: "Excuse me for one second, Your Honor." Sharpstein walked over for a glass of water and to compose himself.

Then Sharpstein clearly established the fact that I had the original contract to kill Barry Seal.

Sharpstein: "And there was nothing unusual, nor did you balk at this offer that they made to you?"

"Which offer are you referring to, sir?"

Sharpstein: "To kill Barry Seal!"

"I accepted it, sir."

Sharpstein: "If you would have found Barry Seal standing in his driveway, when you came up here—I forget the date—you would have killed him, wouldn't you?"

"I had no weapons with me, sir."

Sharpstein: "You would have had someone kill him, correct?"

"Probably, sir."

I kept my voice smooth and even, not reacting to his constant attacks. I was so cool that at one point Sharpstein asked me if I had taken Valium before I entered the courtroom.

"No, sir," I replied, calmly.

Then Sharpstein went for broke. He described the meeting where Cumbamba asked me about the contract to kill Seal, where Cumbamba said he wanted to take it over.

Sharpstein paraphrased me, and almost tried to make a joke of the meeting.

Sharpstein: "You told the police that you had met with my client one time alone, at a shoe store called 'Papuchi,' and my client had said, 'Hey, I'm going to take over the contract' or 'I'm going to talk to Rafael,' right?"

"That's what he told me, yes, sir."

Sharpstein: "There is nobody to witness or corroborate that, is there?"

"No, sir."

Sharpstein: "So, Mr. Mermelstein, it's your word that this particular meeting occurred; isn't it?"

"Yes, sir, it did occur."

Sharpstein: "So says Max Mermelstein, correct?"

"That's correct, sir."

Sharpstein: "Just like everything else you told us here today is the truth?"

"Yes, sir."

With that, and after almost four hours of questioning, Richard Sharpstein finished.

Burns rose from her seat for redirect examination. She started where Sharpstein had started and, like an expert with a machete, she hacked away any ambiguities or misconceptions.

Burns: "Who was the last person you saw in physical possession of the Mac-10 and the silencer, state Exhibits 14 and 15?"

"Rafael Cardona and Cumbamba."

Burns: "And the date you last saw Exhibits 14 and 15 in the possession of either of these two?"

"A few days before I was arrested."

My testimony went on for six hours, and when it was over, I went into the judge's chambers and slumped into a chair; I was limp. But I felt good; it was Sharpstein's mind against mine, and I felt I had done well.

In the middle of that night I was spirited out of Lake Charles. The caravan of bulletproof cars was re-formed, and we made the drive back to the Texas airfield.

I heard later that Premila Burns had actually handed the Mac-10 and the silencer to the jury. She wanted them to handle the gun: the touch of the cold metal made death real.

She had plenty of other circumstantial evidence, and it took five weeks to try the case. Burns put 118 witnesses on the stand. The defense called none.

Sharpstein did everything he could to discredit my testimony. How could the jury believe a known criminal like me? But Burns, in her closing arguments, countered masterfully, telling the jurors, "If you try the devil, you take your witnesses from hell."

It took the jury thirty minutes to decide in favor of life imprisonment for Cumbamba. "The Chin" faced the verdict without a trace of emotion crossing his face.

CHAPTER TWENTY-THREE

*

Operation Goldmine

In May 1987, a month after the Barry Seal murder trial ended in Cumbamba's conviction and life sentence, I was introduced to the "Goldmine" case. The government already had the case under way. They had made the arrests; the defendants were big-time money launderers, and heavily involved in the sale of cocaine. The charge was "conspiracy to launder money." The feds had seized a bunch of records, but they didn't know what the hell they had. Nobody could interpret the records.

I was in the Miami debriefing facility when Dick Gregorie and Rodney Clark, who was with the IRS Criminal Division, walked in. Rodney threw down the records they had seized and said, "Take a look at these. What do you think?"

I studied them for a minute or two and said, "These are drug records."

"What kind?" Gregorie asked.

"Distribution and money—two separate sets."

"Can you interpret them?" Rodney asked.

"Of course. They are basically the same records as I kept; same codes."

"Will you testify as an expert witness?" Gregorie asked.

"Can you establish me as an expert witness in the federal court system?"

"You're an expert, aren't you, Max?"

I laughed. "Sorry to say that I am."

"Well, if you're an expert, and act like one on the stand, I'll establish you as an expert."

"How?" Rodney asked. "How are you going to do that?"

"The same way that Max won the Barry Seal trial for us. We'll just have him tell the truth, the whole truth, and nothing but the truth, right, Max?" Dick laughed. "Kill 'em with veracity."

I knew exactly what he was talking about. It was the same song as in the Seal trial but different words. The defense couldn't really attack me, because the only way they could attack was to use my criminal record, and by attacking my criminal record, all it did was make me more credible as a witness. It was a real Catch-22.

The trial began in Miami on May 29, 1987, in front of Judge William H. Hoeveler.

The principal defendant was Luis Javier Castano-Ochoa. He was part of the Ochoa clan, and a big shooter, a major figure in the cartel hierarchy, and an elected official in Colombia, equivalent to a congressman. Although there was no way of proving possession of cocaine against Castano-Ochoa, the prosecution felt that with my help they could win a money-laundering case against him, based on a record book found in his Miami residence. If the jury could be convinced that these were records of cocaine money-laundering accounts, he would be convicted and another main cartel tentacle in the U.S. severed. Castano-Ochoa was represented by Neal Sonnett, one of Florida's most successful defense attorneys. The prosecution was up against a cunning adversary.

Dick Gregorie led off. His first job was to establish me as an expert witness on the cartel.

At a sidebar conference with the judge, Gregorie said, "If I am going to show the man as an expert, I've got to show to what degree he's an expert, Judge. This is a business; it's like any other business. If we were discussing ITT or AT&T, if I brought in the president, I'd have him explain how big a company he worked for."

Gregorie started in with me and was relentless in drawing out the facts.

Gregorie: "Did you keep records? Give the jury an idea of what kind of records you kept."

"Yes; the records were kept flight by flight, records of how much I received, where it went, who it was delivered to, how much was collected . . ."

Gregorie: "Did you use the actual names, like 'This load belongs to Pablo Correa'?"

"No, we used nicknames."

Gregorie then handed me the detailed records that they had grabbed when Castano-Ochoa was arrested. He established that I knew that these were drug records, and that I could read them and break the code.

Gregorie: "You see in the left-hand corner is written MCIA?"

"Yes."

Gregorie: "Are you familiar with that symbol? If so, what does it stand for?"

"Yes, it is the symbol of the Medellín cartel. The symbol designates that it is the Medellín cartel cocaine. C-i-a means 'company' in Spanish."

The prosecutors had blown up single pages of the record book and they asked me to interpret the code. I stood and walked to the page that was resting on an easel. They handed me a pointer, and like a teacher in school I told the jury what was on those pages. The jurors had never in all their lives seen numbers like this. It was more money than most Fortune 500 companies handled.

Gregorie: "Can you explain what is on this particular record?"

"Basically, what I see is that the cartel shipped a total of 1,623 kilos of cocaine in this load. The breakdown of how much was to be received for it is: 785 at $24,000 a key, 312 at $21,000 a key, 526 at $20,000 a key.

"Next, we have to add transportation charges, which are: thirty-seven kilos at $7,000 a key, seven kilos at $7,000 a key, and a flat transportation fee of $250,000 on the rest.

"The total revenue expected by the cartel would be $36,469,000. Now there was a payment made toward this account of $9,674,575, made by GLL, which would be the abbreviation for Guillermo.

"GC would be Tinkle, who paid $4,356,300, and CP would be Compadre, who paid $2,000,000. This means that they paid a total of $16,030,875 for their coke, and that left a balance of $20,438,125 still owed to MCIA, the cartel."

Gregorie: "Were you able to determine from these documents what the total amount of cocaine was, and the value?"

"On these pages the total amount of cocaine is spelled out as 2,957 kilos. That was the weight of cocaine actually received and distributed in the United States, and the amount of money received I have calculated roughly as $55 to $56 million for this load."

I went on like this for hours, through the several pages that the prosecution had blown up. I explained how the Cali cartel code was different, and what all the various initials meant. There was no question in my mind that when I sat back down in the witness chair, the jury believed that I knew those codes backward and forward.

Later, during a recess, Dick Gregorie told me of his private conversation in the judge's chambers with Neal Sonnett, the defense attorney. Sonnett wanted to get a look at my grand jury testimony, which the judge finally agreed to, but it didn't help him. The plight he faced in this situation started to dawn on him.

In chambers, Neal Sonnett said to the judge, "For me to cross-examine

Max Mermelstein on the depth of his involvement in drugs simply allows me to dig the hole a little deeper. I establish the credentials and the credibility that the government would like me to establish for them."

But full realization of his dilemma didn't stop the defense attorney from plowing ahead anyway. He did what he was trained in law school to do. He attacked my credibility and so built the government's case.

Sonnett: "Is it fair to say that between 1981 and 1985 your criminal activities were extensive and varied?"

"Yes, sir."

Sonnett: "Would it be fair to say that you were, in effect, *a one-man crime wave* by the time you got arrested in 1985?"

Gregorie objected but it was halfhearted, merely pro forma. He let Sonnett continue establishing me as an expert.

Sonnett: "You were involved in deliveries of cocaine, were you not?"

"Yes, sir."

Sonnett: "You were involved in a conspiracy to import marijuana?"

"Yes, sir."

Sonnett: "You were involved in money laundering for drug dealers, were you not?"

"Yes, sir."

Sonnett: "And collecting money for drug dealers?"

"Yes, sir."

Sonnett: "In smuggling of aliens?"

"Yes, sir."

Sonnett: "You were involved in the creation and sale of false documents, travel documents, and passports."

"Yes, sir."

Sonnett: "You were involved in at least one conspiracy to commit murder."

"Yes, sir."

Sonnett: "And accessory to commit murder."

"Yes, sir."

Sonnett: "You were involved in the delivery of weapons, were you not?"

"Yes, sir."

The defense attorney continued on and on in this fashion, while I quietly and calmly answered his questions. There were times when he got sincerely angry. Sonnett had firmly established that I was familiar with the cartel hierarchy.

Sonnett: "We have discussed the leaders of the cartel; is there anyone we have left out?"

"I don't know what you mean 'left out.' In what respect?"

Sonnett: "As a leader of the cartel, as one of the top folks, one of the world's biggest drug dealers?"

"I don't know what you are trying to get at with the word 'leader.' "

Sonnett: "You don't have to know what I am getting at with the word 'leader.' " He was shouting now.

Dick Gregorie leaped to his feet and outshouted Sonnett. "Objection, Your Honor. He is arguing with the witness."

The Judge: "Sustained. What is your next question, Mr. Sonnett?"

And so it went, until the defense attorney finished and I stepped down.

The government won the case; all the defendants were convicted and given maximum sentences. The government had confiscated $22 million, and had landed a "big fish" in Luis Javier Castano-Ochoa, who got sixteen years. Javier was a cousin of the Ochoas and the right-hand man to Pablo Correa. This was one more score the cartel would add to the day of reckoning it sorely longed to settle with me. My mere death would not come close to assuaging the hatred and fear in which I was held by them.

I shuddered at the thought of what would have happened to Barry Seal if Cumbamba had had the wit to kidnap him instead of just blowing him away in a parking lot. Torture has been developed to an exquisite art by the Latinos in general and the Colombians in particular.

Part Six

* *
*

DELIVERANCE

CHAPTER TWENTY-FOUR

*

Judged

I was sentenced on Friday, June 26, 1987, exactly two years and twenty-one days after I had been arrested. And that's how long it had been since I had made love to Cristina, my beautiful Cristina.

I was being sentenced by Judge James M. Ideman, one of the toughest judges on the bench in California. As I walked into the courtroom, I whispered to Tom Johnston, my lawyer, "Tom, we're walking out of here with time served. I just know it!"

"Max, you're a born optimist. Anything less than the recommended ten years will be a miracle."

Both Tom and I knew that even the ten years was not etched in stone. It was only what the U.S. attorneys were recommending. I was open to a potential sixty-year sentence. It was totally at the discretion of the judge.

But I had lived up to my agreement, and more. My grand jury testimony had led to an extradition affidavit against the most-wanted leaders of the cartel.

In "Operation Beacon" my information had busted my old gang.

The killers of Barry Seal were given life in prison largely because of my testimony.

"Operation Goldmine" had concluded only a few weeks before this hearing. The government had confiscated over $22 million in cash and put a major money-laundering ring away for a long time.

I was also cooperating on half a dozen other cases and even some undercover operations I had initiated myself.

I had written Judge Ideman an impassioned letter seeking leniency. Twenty-seven top law enforcement officials also wrote to the judge, asking for consideration on my behalf.

Halfway through the proceedings, I was ushered into Judge Ideman's chambers along with Bob Levinson, an FBI agent, and Steve Grilli, a DEA agent from Miami. Steve and I were working on several cases. Steve explained in great detail what we were working on together, and what was planned for me.

"Your Honor," Steve said, "Max can be of much more use to the government on the street than he ever could be in jail."

The judge listened intently as Steve spoke. He was well aware of the result of my efforts for the government to date. Judge Ideman had a great intuitive quality, maybe it came from years of listening to stories of human frailties on the bench. I believed he could tell what I was thinking just by looking at me.

I hoped he understood that I had come full circle from my days of drug dealing. Two years confined with prisoners who had suffered the ravages of drugs had implanted in me a deep feeling of remorse for my part in contributing to this plague. I sincerely felt that my redemption was an accomplished fact. Nevertheless, it was difficult for me to speak to others about remorse and redemption.

I thought I could see in the judge's face that he knew what was going through my mind.

Steve Grilli continued, "Also, he is safer on the street. We both know, Judge, that one of the easiest ways to have a person killed is to kill him in jail." He went on in this vein for almost half an hour. He was eloquent in his pleadings for me, giving the judge a full litany of my history as a witness.

Then Judge Ideman excused us and we went back into the courtroom. Once more the court was called to order and Judge Ideman reappeared and took his seat. He accepted the arguments of Grilli and the letters of the law enforcement officers and attorneys.

Even Jim Walsh, the Assistant U.S. Attorney from California who had actually indicted me and was vehemently against anything less than ten years, backed off when the judge said in his summation, "Mr. Walsh, I can't see giving Mr. Mermelstein ten years, when there are other people in this case who I've given less than ten years to, and who have not cooperated. The degree of Mr. Mermelstein's cooperation is extensive, and you are standing there and insisting on a ten-year sentence."

Walsh answered, "Maybe you are right, Your Honor. Maybe something less than ten years is indicated."

The judge spoke a while longer until, at last, the fateful moment: "Based on everything put before me, and my own analysis of the circumstances," he said, "I am sentencing Mr. Mermelstein to time served. He will remain on lifetime special parole and report monthly to his parole officer. It is so ordered." And with that he tapped his gavel, stood, and left the courtroom.

My knees felt like jelly and my breath was short. Tom Johnston gave me a hug and said quietly, "Max, you're free, you are a free man. You can do as you wish, there are no other constraints that the judge has requested. You can do anything you want from here on out."

"You mean I don't have to cooperate with the government anymore?" I asked.

"Not if you don't want to. But with a million dollars on your head, you will probably want to stay in the witness protection program."

I was too happy to think. "I'll worry about all that later," I said. "First I need to get used to being a free man."

Judge Ideman had shown faith in me by doing what he did. I decided right there that I would never let this man down.

I could have walked out of the courtroom then and there, a free man. But I was in the witness program and so were fourteen members of my family. The cartel's threat loomed over my head. I was still in other people's hands.

I went downstairs with the Miami marshals and back into the submarine. I figured that I would be meeting with my family the next day.

But I was wrong.

I spent that Friday night in a submarine in Los Angeles, then on Saturday I was shipped to the federal prison in Otisville, New York. I couldn't believe it. When I got there they started processing me back in. I heard that degrading command, "Okay, strip."

"What the hell are you people doing? I'm free!"

"We have no place to put you. It's Saturday, and we have orders from Washington," the marshal said.

"I don't give a damn. You can't put me back in jail. I'm a free man."

Two of the corrections officers started to go through my bags and I said, "Touch that bag and you are going up on charges. You don't have a search warrant."

They looked at me like I was nuts. "What are you talking about?" they asked.

"I'm a free man. The judge sentenced me to time served, and I've already done my time. Ask him!" I said, pointing to the marshal.

"Hey, I got my orders from Washington. You have to stay here until we can process you out and do the paperwork."

"That's crap! I'm a free man. This is all because someone in Washington doesn't want to authorize some overtime and expense money for a marshal to sit with me in a goddamn hotel room."

The two corrections officers looked at me and shrugged. "Look, man, we got nothing to do with this. We got no special place to put you. You gotta go in the lockup."

I wound up in the slammer, back in the general population. Off and on, I had been to Otisville for a total of maybe six months. I knew a lot of the people there and had made some good friends. I said good-bye to them. I also kept a close watch on my back. There were a number of Colombians there. From that day forward I would never know when the cartel had me in its sights. To get it in prison, when I was a free man, would have been a tragic irony.

Monday morning was no better. I was climbing the walls. Nobody knew anything, nobody had any of the paperwork, the unit manager showed up and he didn't know anything either.

I got to a telephone and called Tom Johnston. "Tom, I'm desperate. I've gotta get out of here. I want you to get me a writ of habeas corpus and if you don't hear from me by twelve o'clock your time, I want that writ of habeas corpus in front of Judge Ideman by one."

I finally got both the unit manager and the case manager in the joint and said, "You are holding me illegally. This is illegal imprisonment." They knew I was right, because they got right on the phone and called Washington and the marshals came to get me about half an hour later, around twelve noon. As I left I yelled at them over my shoulder, "The judge said 'time served,' not time served *plus three days!*"

I was taken to a safe house and given some money. They made arrangements to get me on a plane. Finally, I would see my family.

I had spoken to Cristina every day and written letters two or three times a week. And on occasion, she had come to visit me in prison. But now I was going to see her without walls and bars surrounding us.

I didn't know where I was going, in what town of what state Witsec had installed my family, until the last moment. The marshal took me to the airport, handed me an address along with my ticket, and said, "There will be a marshal waiting at the other end who will drive you to your new home. Good luck in your new life, Max." He shook my hand and walked away.

I was on my own, at least for a little while. All during my life in prison I had no idea where my wife was living. I had sent her letters through the Marshals Service, and they forwarded them to her; all my calls were patched through the marshals' switchboard. And Cristina was sworn to secrecy; she could never tell me where she was living. Now, at long last, I was going to see how she was living, with my own eyes.

The marshal who met me at the airport drove me for almost an hour, to a sprawling suburb of a medium-size city. He pulled up in front of a wood frame house in a nice enough section of town. Nothing like our seven-acre ranch in Fort Lauderdale, of course, but it looked comfortable. At least it was where my family lived, and that made it home. I pulled my one suitcase out of the trunk of the car, waved good-bye to the marshal, and started toward the house.

Cristina stood waiting for me at the front door as I walked up the little sidewalk. Halfway there, I dropped the small piece of luggage I was carrying and ran the rest of the way. I kissed her and crushed her gently in my arms, raising her feet off the floor. She was wearing a flowing white dress and I imagined her as a bride, my bride. She had done it, stuck with me and waited for me. As I held her in my arms, I knew I had everything I wanted. A wife whom I loved and who loved me, and my little family.

All that was missing was Luis, who no longer considered himself part of the family. He had done what he vowed to do when he came to visit me in prison: he refused to go into the Witsec program. Neither Cristina nor I mentioned his name at this, our first meeting.

Ana, now eight years old, tugged at my hands and looked up at me. My beautiful baby girl who spent the first few weeks of her life in a cardboard box in an attic in Brooklyn had sprouted up. I had not seen her in over two years. I reached down and picked her up, holding both her and Cristina in my arms.

Inside the house Consuelo was waiting, a young woman, reserved in her greeting, but once I embraced her, she put her head on my chest and cried. Then Cristina cried; then we all cried.

My little family and I sat around and soon we were chatting and they were telling me all the things in their life, little things, everyday things, but I couldn't get enough of it, enough of the details. I had to excuse myself and go into the bathroom, where I cried, cried for joy. "Time served"! It was still hard for me to believe I was free. I wiped away the tears and then carried out the first of my two promises to Cristina.

I cut my graying beard as close as I could with a pair of scissors and then shaved off the stubble. For the first time since almost a year before my arrest, I was clean-shaven. Even the moustache I had worn for years went down the sink in a glob of shaving cream. I studied my face in the mirror for a moment. I liked my new face; I had nothing to hide.

Cristina and the two girls stared in surprise as I returned to the living room and then with pleased shrieks they embraced me, touching my face and kissing me.

Cristina had prepared a wonderful dinner of Colombian food, which tasted even greater after prison food. When dinner was over we watched a little TV and eventually the girls went up to bed.

In our room I held Cristina in my arms and whispered, "I haven't forgotten my other promise. Will I have to go through instructions?"

"No, *cariño*. I have it all arranged with a very wonderful Colombian priest. You will see."

I started to speak again and she put her finger on my lips to silence me. Then we made love the way God meant it to be.

A few weeks later I was converted—in a hotel room. Cristina's Colombian priest understood our circumstances and solemnly received me into the Holy Roman Church. He blessed water drawn from a faucet into a vessel that he had carried with him for the occasion, and daubed it on my forehead.

I left the hotel room a full-fledged Catholic and attended mass with Cristina faithfully from that time on. Even when I was transported alone to be an expert witness at the trials of drug dealers, I tried to arrange to go to mass or at least watch a mass celebrated on television.

The words "time served" and the sound of Judge Ideman's gavel have never left me. There is no question in my mind that my sentence was a miracle, a miracle that I now have to live up to.

CHAPTER TWENTY-FIVE

*

Murder in Colombia

I lived in fear that the day would come when Rafa would kill me or I would have to kill him.

I had been free for just over a year, but I was still in the federal witness protection program when Jeff Leen, a reporter for the *Miami Herald*, made contact with me through the Marshals Service. Leen specialized in stories on drugs and Latinos. He wanted my story, or as much of it as I would tell, for a major article he was writing.

So I did a little reminiscing over the telephone and then forgot all about it until I read the article, published in the *Herald* on December 4, 1987. It is a shock to actually see in black and white the facts about yourself, the quotes attributed to you that you can't remember making, the image of yourself as seen through a journalist's eyes.

On Saturday, December 8, four days after the story about me hit the *Miami Herald*, I made a phone call to Frankie at Continental Arms. My gun collection had been turned over to the custody of my criminal lawyer, Bill Clay, by the government shortly after my arrest. When I was finally freed on parole I could not own firearms, so I had my rifles and handguns sent to my friends at Continental to be sold on consignment.

"Hey, Frankie," I said, "are you having any luck selling my guns?" I was sitting on a stool at the kitchen counter, talking on the wall phone. "You've had them a month now. I could sure use the money."

"We're doing the best we can," Frankie said. "We'll do better if we can find a single collector to take them all rather than trying to unload them one at a time." There was a pause, then he chortled. "That's quite a story about your ex-boss getting killed."

I literally fell off the stool and had to climb back up and grab the receiver, hanging by its cord. "What the hell are you talking about?" I shouted.

"Yeah. They gunned down Cardona in Medellín. It's in the paper today."

"Read it to me," I demanded.

Frankie found the newspaper and started reading the story to me.

" 'Unidentified gunmen driving a Renault entered Cardona's dealership near the industrial town of Endigado, a suburb of Medellín, about twelve miles away from Medellín. With a spray of automatic gunfire the assailants killed both Cardona and his twenty-eight-year-old secretary' "— my heart lurched—" 'Luz Estela Ospina.' "

Estela, Estelita. Little Stella.

A good kid. Maybe five foot one, nice figure, just a bit on the plump side. A natural blonde.

A sweet person. She had a son, who would be three or four years old. Everybody swore he was Rafa's kid. But he wasn't. Stella had been his secretary for a long time. She was a good person. She didn't deserve it. She was just in the wrong place at the wrong time.

"Frankie, read those last two paragraphs again."

Frankie went back over the two paragraphs my mind had skipped while thinking of Estelita.

" 'Cardona, thirty-five, well known by the nickname Rafa, was a principal member of the cartel. The DEA has been after him for a long time, said Jack Hook, agency spokesman.

" 'Cardona was wanted on charges of plotting to kill DEA informant Barry Seal, who was slain February 19, 1986, in Baton Rouge, Louisiana. Cardona was also charged with smuggling 1,650 pounds of cocaine.' "

"Okay, Frankie. Thanks. I'll call you back."

"What are you going to do?" he asked.

"I'm going to check and find out what happened."

I hung up and sat thinking about what I'd just heard.

What did I feel? Relief. Ecstatic relief. One of my biggest fears had just been eliminated. A ruthless man, a devil who would have spared no expense to kill me, was gone. Slowly, the stranglehold Rafa had always had over my life ebbed away. I was released.

Had I felt affection? Once I might have had affection for him, maybe, in the way a prisoner has affection for his keeper. But not at the end. He had threatened my family and turned me completely against him.

Hatred? No. Relief was what I felt more than anything else. And anger. It was all over too fast for him, too easy. He should have paid more dearly.

Who the hell was I going to call on a Saturday morning to find out more about what really happened? Then I remembered somewhere in a conversation a long time ago, Dick Gregorie had mentioned that he had a listed phone number.

Dick answered the phone and when I identified myself he immediately knew why I was calling. "Yes, it's true. I heard about it yesterday from the embassy in Bogotá. They're putting a complete report together, which I should get early next week. I don't suppose you are particularly cut up by it," he chuckled.

"I never felt so relieved in my life," I said. "Except," I added with a laugh, "when you people took me off the street."

"Say, Max." A serious note entered Dick's voice. "You still have a lot of Colombian connections who probably know more than we'll ever find out. I'll pass you all the information I get if you'll do the same."

"You bet your ass, Dick. I'll start reaching out for everything I can get right now."

Some people say I was directly responsible for Rafa's execution, that I might just as well have pulled the trigger myself as what I did do to him.

But I like to tell myself I'm not so sure. Rafa had a lot of enemies. The *Miami Herald* had told the story for the first time of how Rafa had murdered Antonio "Chino" Arles Vargas in the van that Christmas Eve. Chino had been popular with the Colombian underworld in both Miami and Medellín and now, at last, on December 4, 1987, everybody knew who had killed him and I'm sure it pissed them off.

In the *Herald* article I was quoted explaining the reason why Rafa's little daughter, Carolina, was going blind. Odila had told me many times how Rafa forced the girl to stay with him when he was freebasing day after day. Odila swore that the coke smoke was affecting Carolina's eyes, but Rafa wouldn't listen to her. By the time the news story was published the little girl could hardly see at all.

That *Herald* story, translated and read all over Colombia, would have been reason enough for Rafa to kill Odila. It could also have motivated Odila to have Rafa killed before he could do her in, and at the same time get revenge on him for his abuse of Carolina.

Odila had the money to hire the best assassins in the business, and the hit squad that wasted him was as professional as they get in Colombia. In all the years that I knew Odila and Rafa, she was stealing between two and three million dollars a year from him and salting it away. Plus, there was Rafa's emergency fund, the suitcase he always kept with two or three million in it. There were bank accounts in the kids' names and other stuff around. She was probably good for $25 million when he died.

And then there was the murder of Pablo Correa, the man who controlled the money laundering. Another Colombian connection of mine was present when Pablo blamed Rafa in public for the loss of a shipment worth several million dollars. Rafa remained unusually quiet during the tongue-lashing in front of a number of high-level dealers in Medellín. Pablo Correa stuck his finger in Rafa's skinny little chest and shouted, "You will pay for the loss!"

You didn't call Rafa down in front of people and you did not order him to pay something he didn't think he owed. Even the Ochoas, who were extremely powerful, were very careful of how they spoke to Rafa.

So it was inevitable that when Pablo Correa was gunned down in an ambush, Rafa was the chief suspect. Correa had many friends and family members who might have killed Rafa in retaliation.

But if not in fact, I'm guilty in my heart of Rafa's assassination. The December 4 *Miami Herald* story served as a reminder to the cartel that I was now the most powerful witness alive against them. I was an eye witness and I could put them all away for murder and for operating a continuing criminal enterprise, which meant life without chance of parole.

The code of the cartel decreed that anyone who guaranteed a fellow dealer was responsible for that person's future behavior, forever. Rafa had guaranteed me. Therefore my actions were his responsibility. When the death sentence was pronounced on me by the cartel and a price put on my head, Rafa Cardona was also named as a dead man.

Cristina was shocked when I told her the news, a happy shock like coming up with the winning ticket in a multimillion-dollar lottery. How much is it worth to get a dedicated killer off your ass? Together we started gathering all the facts we could get from Colombians in the know.

Autos Clásicos Las Vegas was more than a cover for Rafa's coke operation. He had a passion for antique automobiles. I'd always been on the lookout for classic cars I could buy for him and ship down to his dealership in Endigado, just outside Medellín. Rafa had a thing for Al Capone cars. He loved the old touring cars. The big Packards and the twelve-cylinder Lincolns were his favorites.

Late on Friday afternoon, December 7, Rafa was taking care of business as usual. As always at the end of the week, he was reviewing the efforts being made to locate and assassinate me. I was seldom out of his vengeful thoughts. In fact, I had become an obsession with Rafa. Just knowing that I was alive and free and happy with my family somewhere beyond his reach gnawed at his guts. I knew the cartel had made Rafa's survival contingent on my death. If I lived, Rafa had to die. The difference between his pursuit of Barry Seal and of me was that Seal's assassination was strictly a business matter. But Rafa hated me and considered me the Judas who had betrayed him.

Rafa was offering millions to any person or persons who could penetrate the security of the protected witness program and locate me.

The first floor of the dealership was a showroom where prospective customers could come in and look over the latest antiques Rafa had imported. Of course, basically these cars were rebuilt, the classic body put on top of a new engine and transmission, complete with air conditioning and other luxuries like tape decks and cellular phones.

The second floor was general office space and the third floor was all Rafa's, complete with kitchen and dining room. There probably aren't many CEOs with offices more luxurious than Rafa's.

It was about five o'clock on that Friday afternoon when a DAS (government secret police) squad variously estimated at from 15 to 30 men pulled up in front of Autos Clásicos Las Vegas and stormed into the building shouting, "Police! Don't move! Keep your hands up!"

Rafa had plenty of bodyguards around the building, but even the craziest pistolocos wouldn't shoot at police in their own country. So it was another police raid that Rafa would buy his way out of. The DAS squad knew the layout of the dealership and the schedule of the workers, most of whom had left.

While some of them ran up the stairs to the second and third floors, others disarmed the bodyguards. On the third floor they found Rafa and Estela with a couple of bodyguards. They were in the reception area trying to find out what was going on below.

"Police!" the cops shouted, and separated the bodyguards from Rafa and Estela. The shooters were afraid to draw their weapons on the police, particularly this many machine gun-carrying cops. They were forced back into the kitchen, leaving Rafa and Estela undefended.

"What is the *mordida?*" Rafa cried. How much? It was standard procedure to pay off DAS and the other branches of the national police when they mounted a raid.

His screams were heard all over the building when Rafa suddenly realized this was it. "You've got to arrest me! You've got to arrest me!" Four members of the DAS squad shoved Rafa and Estela into the large office with windows on three sides. Rafa was still shouting, "You can't just kill me! You've got to take me in!"

Before Estela could move away from Rafa, the cops opened up with their automatic weapons. Rafa was spun around first one way, then the other as the heavy-caliber bullets tore into him from all directions. Estela, though not the target, was hit several times as she fell to the floor. She was wearing a white blouse, white skirt, and white panties, all covered with spreading red splotches. The magazines of four machine guns were emptied into the office, leaving it and its occupants torn and shredded. The windows were blown out of their frames and the furniture and wood paneling were shot to splinters.

With military precision, the DAS squad moved through the building, blasting away with automatic fire. Out on the street, as a parting gesture, the government gunmen machine-gunned Rafa's red and white Nissan Samurai, ripping it apart. When the execution squad finally withdrew from the scene, more than fifty expended machine-gun magazines were left in the building and outside on the street.

Estela died on the way to the hospital in an ambulance. Rafa's body was so full of lead it must have weighed about twice his normal weight.

A friend in Medellín sent me a copy of the death certificate, which listed the principal cause of death as "traumatic shock resulting from multiple bullet penetrations."

A job of this magnitude performed by a hit squad of the Colombian national police cost the sponsors of the execution a minimum of $30,000 and more likely $40,000.

Rafa was aware that he was a candidate for a hit at any time, but he expected that it would come from a motorcycle assassin, the most popular form of killing in Colombia. For that, he was well prepared, with two and even three cars of shooters escorting him on the road. He kept two hand grenades under the seat of his car at all times. But why had he no contingency plan for a possible hit by the police?

To this day Odila is still wearing black. She's in widow's weeds, still in mourning, probably lamenting that there is no more money to steal. But it's possible she had him blown away.

It is typical of the Colombian sensibility that no mention was made in any official reports that Rafa was killed by a DAS hit squad.

The older I get the more I marvel at the justice handed down by the Higher Being. Rafa ruthlessly killed and just as ruthlessly was killed. The murders of Chino and Barry Seal, Arturo's suicide, and all the other deaths that could be laid at his feet were now in a sense avenged. Rodriguez Gacha, "The Mexican," died in a bloody raid of his home in December 1989. Drug traffickers live by fire, they can expect to die by fire. That is the price of dealing in death.

And what of the Ochoas—Fabio, Jorge, Juan David? What of Pablo Escobar? I believe there will be no more Paso Fino horses, no more bulls and exotic animals to enjoy. Their supposedly secret bank accounts are being discovered and seized. The cars, motorcycles, and airplanes are gone. It is only a matter of time until they themselves are tracked down in Panama, Colombia, or Peru and brought to justice. I will be waiting to testify. They are all young men still, in their thirties and forties. The mills of American justice grind slowly but inexorably. Life without parole in an American prison will give them a long time to consider the carnage they have wrought on the world.

I look forward to an opportunity to express my remorse for the enormity of what I myself did. Redemption was slow in coming but it arrived. It will be my testimony that helps seal the cartel's fate in a United States court of law.

And what of my own future? I and my family can only contemplate a life of concealment and altered identity, never being able to live totally freely in my country. As long as there is a single tentacle of the cartel reaching into America, my life, and the lives of my family, will be in jeopardy.

It is the price I must pay.

Index